An Inclusive Society

Strategies for tackling poverty

edited by
Carey Oppenheim

INSTITUTE FOR PUBLIC POLICY RESEARCH

30–32 Southampton Street, London WC2E 7RA
Tel: 0171 470 6100 Fax: 0171 470 6111
E-mail: ippr@easynet.co.uk
Web site: http://www.ippr.org.uk
Registered Charity No.800065

The Institute for Public Policy Research is an independent charity whose purpose is to contribute to public understanding of social, economic and political questions through research, discussion and publication. It was established in 1988 by leading figures in the academic, business and trade-union communities to provide an alternative to the free market think tanks.

IPPR's research agenda reflects the challenges facing Britain and Europe. Current programmes cover the areas of economic and industrial policy, Europe, governmental reform, human rights, defence, social policy, the environment and media issues.

Besides its programme of research and publication, IPPR also provides a forum for political and trade union leaders, academic experts and those from business, finance, government and the media, to meet and discuss issues of common concern.

Production & design by **EMPHASIS**
ISBN 1 86030 070 7
© IPPR 1998

CONTENTS

Acknowledgements

Most important, thanks to all the contributors to this book, academics, political advisors, MPs, those from the voluntary sector and policy researchers, who gave generously of their time and intellectual energy. Thanks also to all those who participated in the two day seminar on social exclusion at IPPR, many of their ideas have filtered into the book. We are very grateful to the Nuffield Foundation for their financial support and to Louie Burghes in particular. Special thanks are due to:Vickie Choitz , my intern from the US, who provided invaluable help with keeping this book on the road; to Jim McCormick and Gerry Holtham for their advice and support in getting the idea off the ground; to Judith Edwards and Stuart Scotten for their help in preparing for the seminar and helping it work so smoothly, to Fran Bennett and Gavin Kelly for their help with editing and support; to Jeffrey Weeks at South Bank University and to Helena Scott for all her work on the manuscript. Thanks of course to Bill, Maya and Naomi for all their support.

About the Contributors

Tony Atkinson is Warden of Nuffield College, Oxford and President of the Royal Economic Society. He was formerly a member of the Royal Commission on the Distribution of Income and Wealth, and of the Commission on Social Justice.

Fran Bennett is an independent researcher. She was formerly Director of the Child Poverty Action Group.

Dan Corry is a Special Advisor at the Department of Trade and Industry. Previously, he was Senior Economist at IPPR. He is writing in a personal capacity.

Katherine Duffy is Principle Lecturer the Business School, De Montford University and Director of Research for the Council of Europe Initiative in Human Dignity and Social Exclusion.

Howard Glennerster is Professor of Social Policy at the London school of Economics and Chairman at the Suntory and Toyota International Centres for Economics and Related Disciplines. He is author of the recent edition of *State of Welfare, Paying for welfare Towards 2000 and British Social Policy since 1945.*

Paul Gregg is Programme Director at the Centre for Economic Performance at the London School of Economics and a part-time advisor to the Chancellor of the Exchequer as a member of the council of Economic Advisors.

David Halpern is lecturer at the Faculty of Social and Political Sciences, University of Cambridge and a Director and co-founder of NEXUS, the Policy and Ideas network. He was previously a Prize Research Fellow at the Policy Studies Institute, London.

Gerald Holtham has been Director of IPPR since 1994. Previously he was chief economist for Lehman Brothers.

Gavin Kelly is a Researcher at the Political Economy Research Centre,

University of Sheffield, currently working on a Leverhulme project on corporate government.

Peter Kenway is director and co-founder of the New Policy Institute. He is an economist who previously worked for London Transport as a senior Manager.

Charles Leadbeater is a Senior Research Associate at the think tank Demos.

James McCormick has been Research Director of the Scottish Council Foundation, a network promoting independent thinking in public policy, since November 1997. Prior to that, he was a Research Fellow at IPPR, where he worked for the Commission on Social Justice and worked on Scottish devolution.

Eithne McLaughlin is Professor of Social Policy at Queen's University of Belfast, and was a member of the Commission on Social Justice and the Standing Advisory Commission on Human Rights.

Geoff Mulgan is Director of DEMOS and Special Advisor to the Prime Minister in Inequality and Social Exclusion. He is writing in a personal capacity.

Carey Oppenheim is Senior Research Fellow in Social Policy at the IPPR on secondment from South Bank University. She was research officer and acting deputy director at the Child Poverty Action group.

Jennifer Park is Research Assistant of the Department of Pharmacology, Faculty of Medicine, University of Leicester.

Chris Pond is Member of Parliament for Gravesham and former Director of the Low Pay Unit.

Peter Robinson is Senior Economist at the Institute for Public Policy Research. He is the editor of the IPPR journal *New Economy*. He is also a Research Associate at the Centre for Economic Performance at the London School of Economics.

Chris Trinder is Head of Research at the Association of University Teachers. Between 1990 and 1998 he was Chief Economist at the Chartered Institute of Public Finance and Accountancy. He has been a consultant to the OECD and ILO and lectured at Essex, York and London Universities.

Robert Walker is Director of the Social Security Unit at the Centre for Research in Social Policy, and Professor of Social Policy Research, Loughborough University.

Alison West is the Chief Executive of the Community Development Foundation, a Home-Office sponsored agency set up to strengthen communities and to advise others on ways of building up the capacity of local people to deal with the issues that affect their lives. She was as Head of Corporate Policy for the London Borough of Camden.

Robin Wilson is Director of the Belfast-based think tank Democratic Dialogue.

Introduction
Carey Oppenheim

The legacy of growing and deepening poverty over the last two decades poses a central challenge to government. It is a challenge of a special order for a government of the centre-left whose roots are embedded in a commitment to social justice. The material and social devastation which poverty brings to individuals and communities is not only in front of our very eyes, but has also been extensively documented and analysed. Less described are the plethora of imaginative locally rooted initiatives which attempt to tackle poverty on the doorstep. This government has bravely made a public commitment to address poverty and social exclusion. Both the 1998 Budget and the Green Paper on Welfare Reform set in train important measures to tackle poverty and the Green Paper develops a series of success measures with which to judge the government's progress. This follows close to two decades when in Orwellian style the word 'poverty' was expunged from all official documents. As a result of official silence and the bias of policy making we still know relatively little about how to address poverty and social exclusion – what works and what doesn't work at national, regional and local levels.

This book is an attempt to begin to redress the balance from a pre-occupation with the analysis of the causes and patterns of poverty to one which begins to set out the framework for possible solutions. It stems from a recognition that the marked changes in the socio-economic environment and the institutional and policy processes mean that old strategies have to be re-thought – the post-war world of stable economic growth is not the same as the world at the cusp of the new century. The book largely derives from a two day seminar on social exclusion held at IPPR in which academics from different disciplines, policy makers and practitioners from the public and private sectors participated. It is a collection of both chapters and comments. The inclusion of the comments attempts to convey the dialogue and the variety of voices which inform this debate, voices from different parts of the political spectrum and from inside and outside government. It represents the beginning of a debate rather than the last word on poverty and exclusion – there are notable omissions – particularly the dimensions of ethnicity and gender and a broader consideration of housing and public health. These will have to be part of our future work.

This introduction does not attempt to convey the full scope of the book, but to briefly explore some of the key controversies and themes which criss-cross through the chapters. The first, is one of definition – many of the chapters grapple with the differences between poverty, social exclusion and inequality. This reflects changes in the public debate as the European Commission, government and commentators have shifted their focus between these different conceptions (explored in depth in Katherine Duffy's chapter). For some an income definition of relative poverty provides the clearest target for government policy; it is this view which informs Tony Atkinson's case for government poverty targets and an official poverty report and Peter Robinson's equation of social inclusion with the reduction of income inequality. Others, notably Robert Walker and Jennifer Park, explore the multi-dimensional, dynamic and location of poverty and argue for conceptualising poverty as a series of trajectories or story-lines where labour market activity, income and expenditure, assets, human capital, dignity and autonomy combine over time to shape people's life-chances. If this approach were operationalised it would lead to a multi-dimensional set of indicators along the lines suggested by Catherine Howarth and Peter Kenway in their version of a poverty report.

Despite the strong political appeal of a clear focus on relative income poverty and the campaigning advantages of headline counts of poverty, the concern is that such an approach does not adequately capture the lived experience of poverty or social exclusion and therefore cannot provide a clear guide to policy intervention. By contrast a more complex view of poverty or social exclusion provides important clues to policy interventions which can be honed to prevent people moving into a downward spiral of poverty and social exclusion. However, whichever approach is preferred, the case for a regular official report on poverty or exclusion (see Chris Trinder's Chapter) which both analyses the inter-relationship between government policy and outside factors and forecasts future patterns is strong. As a government document it would carry both authority and weight, it has the potential to hold the government to account, what Gerald Holtham calls a 'self-embarrassment tool', and locates the discussion of poverty and exclusion at the centre of political arena.

A second theme is the insight offered by a lifetime/dynamic view of poverty and exclusion, highlighted in Paul Gregg's comment, which is crucial to both understanding the process of poverty and exclusion and evolving solutions to it. If there is something distinctive about social exclusion it must in part relate to the length of time that individuals or communities are in poverty. However, this approach does not let the government off lightly, the latest research from the Centre for Analysis of Social Exclusion shows that a dynamic view of poverty for example, one which tracks poverty over time, suggests that the 'poverty problem' appears to be 80-90% of the size captured by a snap-shot or cross-sectional approach (Hills, 1998).

A third theme is the role of employment in a strategy to tackle social exclusion. Peter Robinson is sceptical about how far increasing employment will reduce income inequality and the continuing pivotal role for tax and benefit policies to redistribute income. Clearly though, as Robinson concedes, employment has an important role in fostering social cohesion which is not captured exclusively by measures of income inequality. Dan Corry's contribution rightly argues that creating a competitive economy and the resulting employment is a key objective of social inclusion, one which is largely ignored by traditional accounts of poverty. But given the centrality of employment to the government's aims to both reduce life-time poverty and reduce the costs of social security, there remain important challenges: first is the relationship between policies which are geared to encouraging employment in the marginalised sector of the labour market and overall social security policy, in particular the future role of national insurance, highlighted in Eithne McLaughlin's contribution; second, the distribution of paid employment between households – the work rich and work poor; third, the role the state may still have in creating and fostering employment over and above encouraging employability. Andrea Westall points out, new jobs do not always filter down to highly deprived areas or multiply disadvantaged individuals. She argues for a pro-active policy to assist the creation of new enterprises and the generation of employment among existing small companies.

A fourth related strand is the role of the private sector. Largely neglected in the discussion of poverty and social exclusion, private sector solutions are distrusted by the left while the right see exclusion as irrelevant to the concerns of business. Gavin Kelly and James McCormick argue that 'ignoring the potential contribution of business makes little sense in a world in which many of the goods and services which are key to the question of exclusion are now supplied privately'. They suggest as does Dan Corry that the issues of social exclusion should pre-occupy the Department of Trade and Industry as much as the Department of Social Security. Different kinds of public-private partnerships which increase access to privately supplied goods and services for the socially excluded are examined. In doing so the authors explore the case for moving away from a traditional focus on redistribution through the tax and benefit system to one which unbundles the redistributive process using policies and regulation to address social exclusion at a number of different sites. While the tax benefit system will always be a primary site for redistribution, there remains an important role for company obligations in certain circumstances (for example, for the utilities to provide cross-subsidies for poorer consumers).

In their responses, Dan Corry and Fran Bennett argue that just because the kind or site of redistribution is different from the traditional one, the awkward political questions of gainers and losers do not disappear. While this is clearly so, there remain a number of important issues to explore. We know little about how the location of different froms of redistribution may affect the willingness of an individual to agree to different kinds of redistribution – does it matter whether it is a rise in income tax, or national insurance, or higher prices; how far does what the money is spent on affect the willingness to pay? Clearly kinds of redistribution can be more or less transparent with a variety of political risks attached. While less visible forms of redistribution may be politically attractive in the short term, they set in train the difficulty of broaching more explicit redistribution in the longer term. Thus, underlying the questions of forms of taxation and spending lie important democratic issues about the legitimacy of how we tax and spend.

A fifth theme, the involvement of public welfare state services in addressing poverty, is much more familiar territory. Education is the clarion call of much government policy and is seen as having an important long-term role in redressing what the Chancellor of the Exchequer has identified as primary poverty. Howard Glennerster takes a long hard look at the evidence on how far education can reduce widening income inequality and identifies several fruitful policy interventions: setting educational goals which measure the spread of performance and not just the average results, the importance of teaching basic mathematics skills (the evidence is that such skills are related to future earnings), and additional resources for improvements in teacher quality (one suggestion is to target maths specialists in Education Action Zones). In addition he discusses the thorny issue of the disinvestment of parental time in children and the impact of this on children's future life-chances. This is a particularly important in the context of the government's emphasis on welfare to work. A very different approach to the public sector is taken by Charles Leadbeater who explores the barriers to public sector innovation and change and develops the notion of civic entrepreneurship to equip the public sector to respond to the multi-dimensional challenge of social exclusion. Robin Wilson's piece echoes this theme identifying the crisis of centrally determined and top down welfare services, unable to cope with new kinds of risks, as the driving force for local solutions.

A sixth connecting current is the importance of the form, processes and practices of organisations involved in tackling social exclusion and how individuals and communities themselves participate in those different institutions. Alison West and James McCormick's Chapter makes an imaginative and practical case for a community response to social exclusion to both increase income within poor communities and build confidence. They point out how 'the process of getting involved in community based regeneration programmes strengthens networking and binds people together in common endeavour'. It is this fostering of social capital which has to underpin a more inclusive society. However, the Chapter raises tricky questions about the boundaries between and within local communities. How far can local responses buck national trends? What problems do divisions and differences within communities themselves pose? The latter point is picked up by Robin Wilson who writes within the context of Northern Ireland. For Wilson a key element of our response to social exclusion and the entrenchment of economic inactivity is the development of a local social economy which both legitimises informal economy and untapped social relationships.

The train of connections between the identification of a problem and policy and practice is examined towards the end of the book at European and national levels. Katherine Duffy shows how the scope for European initiatives is strongest in relation to the structural funds and remains highly restricted in relation to social protection. She criticises the increasing emphasis in European circles on employability and opportunities to work as the solution to social exclusion: 'the "downside" of this "opportunity" society is that an opportunity is not a right. There is a greater risk of poverty and social exclusion for those not able to grasp opportunities'. Hence, she argues, the need for a European strategy based on social rights. Despite her criticisms, Duffy highlights innovative forms of participation of both excluded people and Non Governmental Organisations and the ways in which imaginative lessons from individual programmes have influenced mainstream European programmes. Chris Pond MP's comment is more up-beat, emphasizing the scope for concerted European action on the social front given the shift to centre-left governments in a number of European countries. He returns to the earlier theme about the need to rethink traditional forms of redistribution, emphasizing the importance of tackling the root causes of poverty and inequality.

Finally, the concluding theme is the ways in which governments can intervene to address issues as broad and deep as social exclusion. At a national level the Social Exclusion Unit represents an innovative attempt to find interdepartmental solutions to problems which cross different areas. Geoff Mulgan and David Halpern highlight the considerable barriers posed by departmental and professional vested interests and the pre-occupation with outputs rather than outcomes. Both endorse the importance of local participation in the ownership and design of policies – the challenge is achieving, as Robin Wilson puts it, the 'real capacity for the mainstream official machine to learn and innovate from experience at its margin'.

These final chapters highlight a recurrent theme which extends beyond the immediate question of social exclusion – the role of government/state in achieving change. The government is attempting new forms of intervention – strategic commissioning, enabling, regulating, targeting by area in the form of zones or on particular groups of people, experimentation, its role as the site for the interchange of good practice as well as its role as provider. These new models of intervention signal in turn new roles for the private sector, for regions and the locality and for the public. The challenge is ensure that these diverse strategies do not fragment but are held together in a coherent framework. The book encompasses a vast array of policy ideas to address poverty and social exclusion. What underpins them all is the strong commitment to find imaginative and enduring solutions to the intensity and extent of poverty and social exclusion in the UK today.

References

Hills J (1998) 'Does Income Mobility Mean the We Do Not Need to Worry about Poverty?' in Atkinson A B and Hills J *Exclusion, Employment and Opportunity* Centre for Analysis of Social Exclusion, LSE.

I:Unravelling poverty and social exclusion

1. Poverty and Social Exclusion: An overview
Carey Oppenheim

Introduction

There is mounting evidence about the growth, extent and depth of poverty and social exclusion and yet strategies to tackle these trenchant problems are still in their infancy. The framework for policies has changed in important ways since the late seventies. New strategies have to take account of globalisation, changes in the labour market and family formation and a shift in how the individual sees his or her place in society with a greater role for autonomy, individuality, choice and risk. The development of new political institutions from European level to locality, the restructuring of the welfare state with much greater roles for the private and voluntary sectors, the extension of the market into new areas such as the utilities and public transport and the ambiguity of public support for traditional forms of income redistribution involve a re-thinking of the policy levers to address poverty and social exclusion.

This chapter explores why governments should address the questions of poverty and social exclusion; it identifies the possible goals for government policy, unpicking the differences between poverty and social exclusion; it explores how we view the 'problem' of social exclusion and goes on to briefly examine the empirical evidence for different aspects of poverty and social exclusion; finally it attempts to identify the broad parameters of strategies to address social exclusion.

Why governments should address poverty and social exclusion

There is of course a moral case, powerfully articulated by the Churches over the last two decades, that to live in an affluent and civilised society requires us to try to tackle the poverty and marginalisation of fellow citizens. The economic and social case was strongly articulated by the Commission on Social Justice (1994) and the Rowntree Report (1995) arguing that high levels of inequality and poverty damage the long-term health of the economy.[1] A strategy for enhancing economic growth and investment relies on reducing the levels of inequality and social exclusion. It is this yoking together of the economic and the social which has formed the kernel of one powerful critique of neo-liberalism. The Rowntree report (1995) emphasised the damage of growing divisions and poverty on the social fabric and the shared interest that we all have in social cohesion – the poverty of a minority rebounds on the more comfortable majority. The political case for tackling these issues is less often made, but equally important. The work of Putnam (1993) and others identifies the importance of high levels of social capital, trust and extensive horizontal networks of civic engagement in fostering healthy political institutions as well as economic prosperity. If refurbishing our democratic life is an important goal, redressing social exclusion will be one important element of such a strategy.

The former Conservative government eschewed any discussion of poverty. This government has nailed its colours to the mast and stressed the importance of tackling social exclusion by setting up the Social Exclusion Unit in the Cabinet Office.

Policy goals

Poverty, deprivation and social exclusion tend to be used inter-changeably. Here they are unraveled in order to clarify goals for government policy. The distinctions, outlined in Table 1.1, are over-simplified; many would quarrel with the definitions. However, they are, in a sense, ideal types attempting to capture the essence of different approaches to these issues. Poverty is defined as the lack of material resources, in particular income. In fact it is possible to stretch the concept of poverty to encompass deprivation and social exclusion as Townsend's (1979) work does. However, for Townsend the lack of an adequate income remains key – it is this which leads to material and social deprivation and in turn inability to participate in the norms and customs of a particular society. Policies are thus primarily focused on issues of distribution (income in particular). Deprivation is multi-faceted and attempts to capture the ways in which the lack of material and social resources overlap. Deprivation indicators are often used to look at the geography of poverty, where income data are harder to obtain, and in turn by government to allocate resources on an area basis. Policies are concerned with the distribution and access to a broader range of income, goods and services.

Table 1.1

Term	Definition	Solution
Poverty	lack of material resources, in particular income[a]	an adequate minimum income
Deprivation	lack of material standards(such as diet, clothing, housing) and services and amenities (recreational, educational, environmental, social)	an adequate minimum standard of living encompassing income services, amenities
Social Exclusion	"inability to participate effectively in economic, social, political and cultural life, alienation and distance from the mainstream society"[b]	social inclusion, common citizenship, identification, common membership
	"The process by which individuals and groups become isolated from major societal mechanisms, which produce or distribute social resources... "the condition of alienation from one or more of the main mechanisms: a. labour market, b. informal networks and c. the state"[c]	access to employment income and other social resources, family support, developing social capital, decentralisation, democratisation

Notes:

a. This can be an absolute or relative definition; income or expenditure may be used.

b. Duffy K (1995) Social Exclusion and Human Dignity in Europe: background report for the proposed initiative by the Council of Europe, Steering Committee on Social Policy, Council of Europe

c. Observatory on National Policies to Combat Social Exclusion, consolidated report, Greece, 1992 cited in Duffy K (1996), "Human Dignity and Social Exclusion: Developing a new Social Policy Agenda in Europe", Paper presented to Social Policy Association Conference, Sheffield Hallam, 18 July 1996.

Social exclusion differs from both of these; Room offers a helpful definition: 'Social exclusion is the process of being detached from the organisations and communities of which the society is composed and from the rights and obligations that they embody.'

Thus it is about the *processes* which lead people to being marginalised from the mainstream, what the European Commission has identified as the production and distribution of social resources: labour market, family and informal networks and the state. The relationship between poverty and social exclusion is not always clear. There are people who are on low incomes but are socially included (for example, the majority of students) and there may be people or groups – more rarely – who are not in poverty but are socially excluded for example on the grounds of ethnicity or mental illness or disability. However, the lack of material resources is likely to be a central element of social exclusion alongside other important factors. Policies are therefore concerned with a much wider range of tools, attempting to connect people back into the mainstream, giving them access to employment, income and other social resources, family support and social networks.

The advantages and disadvantages of these goals

In keeping with the Anglo-Saxon tradition we are more comfortable with the concept of poverty – material poverty has the advantage of being quantifiable with relatively easily identifiable policy tools to tackle it – for example access to employment, levels of social security benefits and a minimum wage. And yet poverty is multi-dimensional, a lived experience in which income is only one component, albeit a central one. Different aspects of poverty may be felt to different degrees – for example poor quality housing may be felt more keenly than other aspects of poverty, or high quality schooling or local services may compensate for being on a low income. This is important as it tells us something about priorities for policy. While deprivation captures the multi-dimensional nature of poverty it remains a static concept.

There seem to be a number of advantages in focusing on social exclusion. First, social exclusion is about processes rather than a static end-state. Mingione (1997) argues: 'In relation to social exclusion, we need to identify not only indicators of poverty but also the institutional processes that bring about exclusion'. This can be thought of quite concretely – take for example school exclusions – policy needs to look at the social and economic conditions of the children who are excluded, the quality of the relationships between teachers, parents and children and the institutional processes involved. Solving it is multi-faceted – poverty may be a central component, but it does not tell us the whole story. Second, social exclusion offers breadth, encompassing a range of factors that lead to social exclusion and therefore a richer set of goals. 'The idea of a combination of poverty and constraints on participation in citizenship is at the heart of the term social exclusion' (Mingione, 1997). Economic security is therefore not an end in itself but part of the achievement of a greater sense of well-being, active participation or common membership of our society. Third, social exclusion also allows us to capture some of the less tangible but crucial aspects of poverty such as loss of status, power, self-esteem and expectations. Finally, social exclusion is a 'relational' term – you are necessarily excluded from something; it therefore brings in the rest of society whether in the form of family, community or society itself. This is politically important as the role and responsibilities of the socially included have to be considered. This in turn indirectly touches on the question of inequality. The extent of inequality forms a crucial backdrop to social exclusion; if there is an ever-widening chasm between the affluent and the impoverished the sense of shared citizenship becomes harder to sustain (Miller, 1997). Thus while the reduction of inequality may not be a primary goal of policy it remains an important subsidiary one. It is beyond the scope of this chapter to discuss equality in any depth; however, the goal of greater equality needs to encompass three dimensions: lifetime equality, equality of respect and complex equality which ensures that power does not accrue to the same groups or individuals in all areas (see Franklin J (1997) for a thorough discussion).

While social inclusion policies offer a more all-embracing strategy the task of moving from the level of ideas to clearly defined policy goals is more difficult. What are the key elements of social exclusion, how should we judge whether people are more or less included and included into what and what role does poverty play?

Defining social exclusion

It is worth briefly outlining how we understand the 'problem' that is to be addressed. A first issue is whether we define social exclusion narrowly or broadly. A narrow definition might focus on a group which experiences persistent material hardship, multi-dimensional disadvantage and is located in particular places (Room, 1995). This has the advantage of setting more defined goals for policy. For example, drawing on the British Household Panel Survey, *Households Below Average Income (HBAI)* (DSS, 1997) shows that 6 per cent of the sample were in the bottom decile for five years continuously and 12 per cent were in the bottom three deciles in all five years. On the other hand, a larger group may be at risk of falling into this core group – *HBAI* (DSS, 1997) shows that 51 per cent of the sample were in the bottom three deciles for at least one year over a five year period. If policy is to be preventative then it needs to look beyond a very narrow group.

A second issue is how far social exclusion is equated with 'dependency'. Explaining why some people are on benefit for long periods of time is at the centre of dispute between those who see poverty or social exclusion as rooted in structural/economic explanations, and those who emphasise cultural reasons related to individual lifestyle. Each has different implications for the kinds of solutions that are sought. While the evidence to sustain a full-blown 'dependency' thesis is at best uncertain (Shaw *et al*, 1996, Bryson *et al*, 1997) we need to encompass the variety of factors which shape people's ability to escape disadvantage. These are not solely income based. Thus solutions need to pay attention to material, social and cultural dimensions and the interplay between them. For example, in some cases positive re-inforcement of a person's identity may increase their sense of agency and in turn allow them to view the risk of entering employment differently (Williams, 1996). Third, there is considerable movement at the bottom of the income distribution, but it is very often of the revolving door kind – from unemployment to low pay to unemployment again. Although people in poverty do move from the bottom rung of the ladder, a large proportion do not move up very far. However, it is not clear how to interpret the significance of the movement that there is, especially at the lower end – what is the difference in the quality of life between being in the bottom, second or third decile? While income obviously changes, it is important to know what other factors change such as access to education, new skills, new networks or improvements in housing and do these other factors shape whether people are likely to go back down the escalator to the very bottom again?

The evidence

While advocating the importance of social exclusion, our capacity to delineate who is socially excluded is more limited. Official sources of data are dominated by 'hard' measures of poverty rather than measures of social exclusion. Despite these limitations, income poverty statistics allow us, at the very least, to begin to identify the groups on which we should focus. HBAI (DSS, 1997) shows those who are at high risk of being in poverty (defined at 50 per cent of average income after housing costs). Lone parents, single pensioners, the unemployed, the economically inactive and children are all at a high risk (see Table 1.2). It is important to know more about the composition of those groups. We know that women are more likely to be concentrated in the bottom of the income distribution, particularly lone parents and pensioners.

Table 1.2
The risk of poverty by family status and socio-economic status in 1994/95

	% of each group with income below 50% of average income (after housing costs)
Pensioner couple	24
Pensioner single	32
Couple with children	22
Couple without children	10
Single with children	60
Single without children	22
Self-employed	22
Single/couple, all in FT work	2
One in FT work, one in PT work	3
One in FT work, one not working	17
One or more in PT work	33
Head/spouse aged 60+	29
Head/spouse uenmployed	74
Other	61
All family/economic types	23

Source: HBAI (DSS 1997), Tables F1 (AHC) and F2 (AHC)

Some ethnic minority groups are particularly at risk of poverty and other forms of disadvantage. The Fourth PSI Survey (Modood *et al*, 1997) documents the extent of multi-dimensional disadvantage that Pakistanis and Bangladeshis face in particular, and Caribbeans face to a slightly lesser degree. Table 1.3 shows the extent of income poverty faced by some ethnic minority groups – a staggering 80 per cent or so of the Pakistani and Bangladeshi populations were living in poverty. Modood (1997) also shows the concentration of high levels of unemployment among men under the age of 35 who have no qualifications: unemployment rates were 61 per cent for Caribbeans, 45 per cent for Pakistanis and Bangladeshis compared to 19 per cent of whites. These patterns of poverty and unemployment are in turn compounded by geographical concentration. At the same time, the PSI survey also shows the importance of educational qualifications in decreasing the likelihood of unemployment (though there are still marked differences between

Table 1.3
Households below average income by ethnic group

	Below half average	Between half and one and a half times average	Above one and a half times average
White	28	49	23
Caribbean	41	47	12
Indian	45	43	12
African Asian	39	46	15
Pakistani	82	17	1
Bangladeshi	84	15	2
Chinese	34	44	22

Source: Berthoud, R (1997) 'Income and Standards of Living' in Modood et al (1997), Ethnic Minorities in Britain, Diversity and Disadvantage, Policy Studies Institute.

groups).

Room (1995) has suggested three ways to pin down the concept of social exclusion, moving from a static to a dynamic analysis, from income/expenditure to multi-dimensional disadvantage, and from individual or household to the community which is located spatially. Again, HBAI (DSS, 1997), drawing on the British Household Panel Survey, provides a starting point by looking in more detail at the composition of those who are persistently on low income, (those in the bottom three income deciles for five years continuously). Table 1.4 shows the over-representation of pensioners, in particular single pensioners and lone parents in this group. It also shows the very high proportion of those of working age but without work in this group. The data also begin to capture the broad parameters of other dimensions of disadvantage – 63 per cent of this group have no educational qualifications and 56 per cent live in socially rented property. The overlap of economic and housing disadvantage is confirmed in other HBAI data which shows that close to two thirds of those in Local Authority/Housing Association accommodation are without any form of paid work (24 per cent are aged 60 or over, 39 per cent are unemployed or economically inactive). What the material does not show is where this group is likely to be living. However, the data clearly point to three broad priorities – access to paid work, increasing educational qualifications and changing the social mix of public housing.

Table 1.4

Characteristics of those in the bottom three deciles for five consecutive years between 1991 and 1995

	Persistently low income	Whole population
Family type		
Pensioner couple	16	10
Single pensioner	22	8
Couple with children	31	39
Couple without children	7	22
Single with children	19	7
Single without children	5	14
Household economic status		
Working age, fully employed	7	42
Working age, partially employed	16	30
Working age, workless	43	13
Pensioner household	35	16
Highest educational qualification		
Degree level	7	25
Below degree level	30	43
None	63	32
Tenure		
Owner occupied	36	70
Social rented	56	23
Private rented	8	7
Source: HBAI (1997) Table 7.7 adapted		

Material on poverty and place shows strong patterns of continuity in terms of area disadvantage (Hills, 1995). Table 1.5 drawn from Hills (1995) shows the ten local authority (LA) districts with the highest levels of deprivation. While the national unemployment rate was 9.3 per cent in 1991, unemployment in the most deprived LAs ranged from 22.5 per cent to 17.1 per cent; the national inactivity rate was 19.7 per cent but ranged from 32.3 per cent to 27.8 per cent in these LAs; nationally a third of households did not own a car while the poorest LAs showed a range from 65.6 per cent to 55.8 per cent. Between 1981 and 1991 there were two important changes, the increase in deprivation in Inner London Boroughs and widening polarisation at ward level. There was an increase in the concentration of poverty – in 1991 8.9 per cent of wards had concentrated poverty compared to 7.5 per cent in 1981 (Green, 1994).[2] These included Inner London, Merseyside, West Midlands, South Wales, the North East, Strathclyde and the coastline.

Table 1.5
Local Authority Districts: deprivation indicator league tables 1991 (GB)

Unemployment (%)		Inactivity Rate (%)		Households with no car (%)	
1 Hackney	22.5	1 Rhondda	32.3	1 Glasgow City	65.6
2 Knowsley	22.1	2 Easington	31.2	2 Hackney	61.7
3 Tower Hamlets	21.8	3 Merthyr Tydfil	30.4	3 Tower Hamlets	61.6
4 Liverpool	21.1	4 Afan	30.2	4 Islington	59.9
5 Newham	19.3	5 Rhymney Valley	29.3	5 Clydebank	58.7
6 Glasgow City	19.1	6 Blaenau Gwent	29.3	6 Southwark	58.0
7 Manchester	18.7	7 Cynon Valley	29.2	7 Westminster	57.7
8 Southwark	18.2	8 Knowsley	28.2	8 Liverpool	57.0
9 Haringey	17.7	9 Cumnock and DoonValley	28.0	9 Manchester	56.6
10 Lambeth	17.1	10 Glasgow City	55.8	10 Camden	27.8

Source: Green (1994), cited in Hills (1995), Inquiry into Income and Wealth (Vol 2), Joseph Rowntree Foundation.

It is this concentration of poverty in small areas that is identified in the work by Powers and Tunstall (1995) which focuses on the dramatic and increasing levels of unemployment and economic inactivity on 20 housing estates. Clearly Census data provide a vast and rich source of area based indicators of deprivation, the material cited here is simply a fleeting indication of the importance of locating poverty. Philo and McCormick (1995) identifiy common features of 'poor places': high levels of unemployment and non-employment, weak local economies because of lower purchasing power leading to an uncoupling of national and local trends, poorer services, as a result both of the decline in population and lower levels of bargaining power, loss of financial services, higher costs (particularly of food and transport in outer-estates) poorer health and the stigma of place. To this it is important to add lower levels of social capital.[3] However, despite the clear evidence that poverty clusters in places the causes of that poverty derive from many sources both *inside* and *outside* the locality. Policy thus has to cope with both levels, the ways in which national trends have particular expressions locally and how localities might carve out alternative or innovative strategies.

This has been a cursory look at three ways of approaching data on social exclusion. However, there are many things that the data do not tell us. First income, multi-dimensional disadvantage and small area analysis are not combined. (The Fourth PSI Survey on ethnic minorities is an exception combining some important elements of social exclusion.) Second, while material from *The 1990 Breadline Britain Survey* (Gordon *et al*, 1997) and recent work on childhood deprivation (Middleton *et al*, 1997) provide innovative material on different forms of participation, there remain aspects of social exclusion which are under-researched, such as participation in political and voluntary organisations, involvement in education (both formal qualifications or evening classes); access to financial services, the extent of networks of friendship and wider social networks, self-perceptions, sense of self-esteem or identity. We know quite a lot about some of these elements, particularly from small-scale qualitative research (Kempson, 1996), but this tends not to be related to larger data sets. Perhaps most importantly we don't know much about the dynamics and inter-relationships between different forms of exclusion and the ways in which they may reinforce each other.

Directions for policy

Despite the gaps in our knowledge, it is possible to map out broad directions for policy which are explored in depth in other Chapters. One useful way of envisaging a framework for social inclusion policy is to think about how to foster individual, family and community assets

(Room, 1995). These assets are financial (both income and capital) but they are also much broader, including employment, social and psychological skills, education, culture, shared resources and services. Assets represent past investment and the individual/family/community's ability to weather the storms of say unemployment, separation, illness or disability. This is a broader version of the Chancellor of the Exchequer Gordon Brown MP's emphasis on tackling *primary poverty*, which focuses on prevention and re-building people's endowments – in particular employment and skills (Brown, 1996).[4]

Table 1.6
Multiple deprivation among lone parents

Influences which **increase** multiple deprivation	Influences which **decrease** multiple deprivation
presence of more children	having any qualifications
having a child with a long-term or limiting illness	having grandparents available/co-resident
	having a paid job *
living in an urban area	living with a working partner *
being a smoker	having higher incomes *
living in socially-rented accommodation	having more savings

*very important influences

Source: Bryson A et al (1997), Making Work Pay, Lone mothers, employment and well-being, Policy Studies Institute.

An illustration of the need for a more rounded approach is provided by work undertaken by Bryson *et al* (1997) into lone parents. Using a multiple deprivation indicator (combining housing, diet, clothing, social participation, consumer durables, adult and child hardship, debts and health), they look at the factors which have an impact on hardship (see Table 1.6). They found that qualifications, access to support from grandparents, paid employment, higher incomes and savings were key factors which reduced multiple deprivation. In policy terms three issues stand out. First, the importance of employment over and above the rise in income represented by the earnings from such employment: the impact of employment is not reducible simply to a rise in income. Bryson *et al* (1997) suggest that earnings from employment allow access to fringe benefits and financial services which appear to alter consumption in a way which improves well-being. Second, they found that many things accounted for the variation in hardship besides income. Income seems to have a relatively weak effect on the hardship of lone parent families. Third, they found that support from grandparents was an important part of decreasing hardship, in particular allowing lone parents access to employment. This is a useful insight for the work on network poverty (Perri 6, 1997).[5] Overall this material indicates the variety of resources and strategies people use to exit from hardship.

Five broad areas for policies to address social exclusion are outlined briefly:

● *Access to employment* and the *quality* of employment are central aspects of social inclusion. Existing policies on welfare to work and the development of Intermediate Labour Markets under the Employment Zones are central elements of this strategy. But alongside these developments it is essential to explore other ways of creating employment whether through community enterprise, public/private sector partnerships or publicly funded part-time employment for the long term unemployed in the Local Authority or social sector (Holtham and Mayhew, 1996). Part of this strategy should also explore benefit reforms which legitimise small earnings both through benefit disregards and easing transitions between benefit and paid work. Wage subsidies will continue despite a minimum wage – there might be ways to link the receipt of such subsidies (for example in the case of lone parents) to access to training or education.

● *Education, qualifications and skills* – there is extensive evidence on the importance of educational qualifications in reducing unemployment and low wages. We also know that those with higher levels of education are more likely to be 'active' citizens and participate in a wider range of voluntary organisations and activities (Hall, 1997). Thus expanding access to education over people's lives might be one tool for fostering richer social networks.

● *Changing the public sector housing mix* – it essential to explore policies which tackle the segregation of public sector local authority and housing association property to further a greater social mix. At the same time policies need to be developed which address the multi-dimensional disadvantage faced on some estates bringing together a range of services from the public and private sectors.

● *Improved standards of living* – the impoverished cannot be active participating citizens. We need to explore a variety of tools to enhance the living standards of those who remain locked outside the labour market – these include increasing earnings disregards, improving benefit take-up, reducing costs, increasing benefit levels (in particular for the poorest pensioners) as well as access to better quality services.

● *Enhancement of social capital* – the extensiveness and quality of social networks is a central element of social inclusion; these networks are both important in labour market terms (connecting the unemployed to the employed) but also for those outside the labour market. Policies need to encourage the role of voluntary sector, extend volunteering (Macfarlane, 1997), in particular to poorer sections of the community and facilitate collective self-help initiatives (such as Local Exchange Trading Schemes, or Kids Clubs). Such initiatives need clear frameworks for funding and resources for those in poorer areas. There might be ways in which social security benefits could be used to provide incentives for participation. The New Deal represents an important shift from thinking about social security as income maintenance to a tool for enhancing employment. There might other kinds of activities (such as parental involvement in literacy or parenting classes) which social security policy might encourage in a non–punitive fashion.

The policy levers for combating social exclusion have changed in vital ways. While Lister is right to argue for 'reaffirming the importance of the welfare state as a force for inclusion in the face of exclusionary trends' (1997:102) the ways in which it does so is very different today from the late 1970s. There are some common features about the kinds of interventions that could be made. First, strategies have to be cross-departmental whether at national, regional or local level. For example, shifting child benefit expenditure for 16-19 year olds to an educational maintenance allowance for poorer school students might be a more effective strategy for tackling social exclusion for this age-group. Second, they have to scan the public/private continuum. On the public side the change in the role of the state in welfare provision (for example the development of quasi-markets and contracting out) means that the implementation of policies is much more fragmented – policies might address the components of contracts or incentive structures. Approaching social inclusion policies from the other end opens up the possibility of regulation in some areas such as the utilities or the provision of private pensions (McCormick, 1998) or offering incentives for private sector to take on certain obligations (the New Deal is one example of this). Third, given the fact that being in poverty for long periods increases social exclusion, policies should facilitate change, mobility and risk – one such policy would be to ease transitions between benefit and paid work (Walker and Wiseman, 1997, Oppenheim, 1998). Fourth, central and local dimensions have to be embraced, taking into account Regional Development Agencies and reforms to local government. And finally, policies need to see people as active participants, including them in the design and shape of local policies.

Imaginative policies on social inclusion have to take account of a transformed economy and a new relationship between the welfare state and society. Strategies have to identify smaller achievable goals while setting in train a more ambitious project.

References

Bryson A, Ford, R and White M (1997), *Making Work Pay, Lone mothers, Employment and Well Being*, PSI.

Brown G (1996), *New Labour and Equality*, The Second John Smith Memorial Lecture, 19 April 1996

Commission on Social Justice (1994), *Social Justice: strategies for national renewal*, Vintage.

DSS (1997), *Households below average income, a statistical analysis 1979-1994/95*, HMSO.

Gordon D *et al* (1995), *Breadline Britain in the 1990s*, Universty of Bristol.

Green A E (1994), *The Geography of Poverty and Wealth*, Evidence on the changing spatial distribution and segregation of poverty and wealth from the Census of population 1991 and 1981, Warwick, Institute of Employment Research.

Hall, P (1997), 'Social Capital, a fragile asset' in *The Wealth and Poverty of Networks: tackling social exclusion*, Demos Collection Issue 12.

Hills J (1995), *Inquiry into Income and Wealth*, Vol 1 and 2, Joseph Rowntree Foundation

Holtham G and Mayhew K (1996), *Tackling Long-Term Unemployment*, IPPR.

Kempson E (1996), *Life on a Low Income*, YPS for Joseph Rowntree Foundation.

Lister R (1997), 'Social Inclusion and Exclusion', in Kelly G, Kelly D and Gamble A, *Stakeholder capitalism*, Macmillian 1997.

Macfarlane R (1997), *Unshackling the poor*, A complementary approach to local economic develpoment. Joseph Rowntree Foundation.

McCormick J (1998), 'Pensions Policy' in *Welfare in Working Order*, IPPR

Middleton S, Ashworth K and Braithwaite I (1997), *Small Fortunes, Spending on children, childhood poverty and parental sacrifice*, Joseph Rowntree Foundation.

Miller D (1997), 'What kind of equality should the Left pursue'? in Franklin J, *Equality*, IPPR.

Mingione E (1997) 'Enterprise and Exclusion', in *The Wealth and Poverty of Networks: tackling social exclusion*, Demos Collection Issue 12

Modood T *et al* (1997), *Ethnic Minorities in Britain*, PSI.

Oppenheim C (1997), *The Post-Conservative Welfare State, Policies for the decade ahead*, PERC Policy Paper, Sheffield Universty.

Oppenheim C (1998), 'Welfare to Work, tax and benefit implications' in *Welfare in Working Order*, IPPR.

Perri 6 (1997), *Escaping Poverty: from safety nets to networks of opportunity*, Demos.

Philo C (1995), *Off the Map: The social geography of poverty in the UK*, CPAG.

Powers A and Tunstall J (1995), *Swimming against the tide: progress and polarisation on twenty unpopular council estates* 1980-1995, Joseph Rowntree Foundation.

Putnam R (1993), *Making Democracy Work: Civic Traditions in Modern Italy*, Princeton Universty Press.

Room G (1995), *Beyond the Threshold: The measurement and analysis of social exclusion*, The Policy Press.

Townsend P (1979), *Poverty in the UK*, Penguin.

Walker R and Wiseman M (1997), *An Earned Income Tax Credit, Possibilities and alternatives*, CRSP, Loughborough Universty.

Wann M (1995) *Building Social Capital: Self help in the twenty-first century Welfare State*, IPPR

White S (1997) 'What do egalitarians really want?' in Franklin J (ed) *Equality*, IPPR

Williams F and Pillinger J (1996), *New Thinking on Social Policy Research into Inequality: Social Exclusion and Poverty*, Centre for the Analysis of Social Policy, Bath Universty.

Endnotes

1. While this is a powerful argument, White (1997) has suggested that the link between economic efficiency and social justice is overstated – there will be needs that should be addressed on the grounds of social justice (such as the disabled) but which do not enhance economic growth.

2. Concentrated poverty was defined as wards which fell into the top tenth of wards nationally on three out of five indicators: unemployment rate, inactivity rate, socially rented housing, lack of car ownership and social class (Green, 1994, cited in Hills, 1995).

3. Many impoverished local areas have survived and flourished in the face of high levels of disadvantage (Campbell, 1992, Wann, 1994) however, they inevitably draw on lower levels of material/social resources.

4. While this new emphasis is largely right, it is important to note that re-building people's 'endowments' is expensive; there will always be a need for secondary redistribution for those who don't succeed in the market place whatever their assets and finally tackling primary poverty is a long term strategy – people need to be protected in the medium term (Oppenheim, 1997).

5. Perri 6 (1997) identifies the importance of different kinds of social networks at particular stages of the lifecycle – strong networks in childhood and old age and weak networks in adulthood to secure in employment. This is an over-simplification – for parents, in particular lone parents, it is the combination of strong and weak networks that is essential – in this case the strong networks offered by grandparents that give lone parents the freedom to develop their wider set of employment networks.

2. Unpicking poverty
by Robert Walker and Jennifer Park

Introduction

Not surprisingly 'New Labour, new poverty' was not a slogan used by Labour in the 1997 election campaign. Since coming to power, however, Labour ministers have been defining a new kind of poverty and proposing policies to combat it. New thinking about poverty is certainly required but it is doubtful whether Labour's new ideas go far enough or even in the appropriate direction.

It is instructive to unpack three assertions before attempting to unpick poverty. Take, first, the slogan. Spin-doctors would not want to associate Labour with poverty that is (almost) universally recognised to be a 'bad thing'.[1] Nobody wants to suffer poverty and it is widely recognised to impose social costs: crime, unpleasantness and high taxation. Second, in opposition, Labour charged that government could be held responsible for creating poverty but, since 1st May 1997, it has retreated from this position. Instead, poverty (new poverty?) is a matter of personal responsibility. Evidence is cited that poverty is self-induced or, at least, unnecessarily prolonged: the growth in claimant numbers since 1979; the drop in benefit claims when work obligations are enforced; the success of 'tell on a cheat' campaigns.

Such evidence is inevitably circumstantial. It neglects other things that have changed in the last nineteen years, notably the structure of the labour market and the benefit system itself. Hard evidence of a growing dependency culture is absent (Shaw et al, 1996; Walker, 1994, 1998a). Fraud can only explain a small portion of the benefits bill (Rowlingson et al 4, 1997). The conclusion, therefore, must be that Labour's new poverty is rooted in ideology rather than evidence. This does not mean that the approach is necessarily wrong. Politics is, after all, ideology put into practice. But policies test ideology against reality and mismatches court social disaster.

Third, it is asserted that social science has not served policy makers well, focusing more on issues of definition and measurement rather than on the causes and consequences of poverty. There has been advance: Rowntree's three studies (1901, 1922, Rowntree and Laver, 1951) spanning the first half of the century; Abel-Smith and Townsend's (1965) explicit recognition of the relative nature of poverty; Townsend's (1979) introduction of the broader concept of social deprivation; poverty measured in relation to collective views as to what is essential (Mack and Lansley 1985); perhaps, too, the adoption of the concept of exclusion with its emphasis on process and the capacity for society to exclude (Room,1995). But all these ideas were present in embryo in Rowntree's work. So, too, was the basic model of causation: some mix of structural and personal factors determining an individual's position vis-à-vis the labour market.

While the causes of poverty might exist as eternal verities, the precise motors of causality that applied in 1898 are unlikely to be relevant to the vastly different world of 1998. There has to be a new model of poverty to inform, and perhaps to correct, the policies born of Labour's new morality. This paper presents a first approximation of the kind of thinking that might produce such a model and explores some of the implications for policy.

The chapter divides into five. The multidimensional dynamics of poverty are first discussed before exploring the implications for understanding the nature of poverty and, then, its causes and consequences. Next, attention turns to the spatial processes that create 'poor places' before finally discussing the political imperative of poverty and policy implications of this new thinking about poverty.

Rethinking Poverty

The pyramid of poverty concepts (Figure 2.1) was used by Baulch (1996) to illuminate the 'fiercely contested intellectual terrain' that constitutes poverty research (see also Wilkes, 1997). One set of conflicts illustrated relates to the level that most accurately describes what poverty is and how it is experienced. Some analysts, particularly those engaged in global debates, focus solely on the apex of the pyramid – private individual consumption.[2] They argue that a lack of cash income is the root cause of poverty and advocate policies based on income enhancement. In contrast, others direct attention to the base of the pyramid, emphasising not just income and other cash like resources but also human capital and physical assets, stores and claims as well as dignity and autonomy. Policy responses to poverty defined in this fashion need to be more creative and comprehensive.

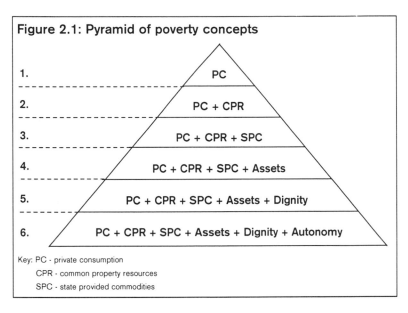

Figure 2.1: Pyramid of poverty concepts

1. PC
2. PC + CPR
3. PC + CPR + SPC
4. PC + CPR + SPC + Assets
5. PC + CPR + SPC + Assets + Dignity
6. PC + CPR + SPC + Assets + Dignity + Autonomy

Key: PC - private consumption
    CPR - common property resources
    SPC - state provided commodities

There seems little doubt that any comprehensive approach to understanding poverty has to take account of the complexity and multi-dimensionality of the phenomenon, to focus on the base rather than the apex of the pyramid. Each element in the base represents a component of poverty, or a dimension along which it can be assessed. Moreover, each element can be further expanded as illustrated in Figure 2.2. It is traditionally assumed that cumulating scores on each dimension provides a measure of the degree of poverty suffered, although it should be recognised that scores are not necessarily straightforwardly additive. It might be, for example, that a shortfall in cash assumes less importance in circumstances when people feel in control of their lives or are confident that the poverty will be short-lived.

This realisation also points to the possibility that varying scores on the different dimensions designate different kinds of poverty. The 'asset rich, income poor' status of some older owner-occupiers is already widely recognised. Likewise, the income poverty of certain women and children has been documented within ostensibly affluent households (Millar and Glendinning, 1992; Middleton et al, 1997). Such women may also suffer a loss of dignity and autonomy. Indeed some may even opt for another form of poverty: leaving home they forego common property income and assets preferring the autonomy offered by living in

Figure 2.2: Elucidating the elements of poverty

Labour market activity	Income[1]	Expenditure[1]	State transfers[2]	Assets	Shared property rights[3]	Human capital	Dignity	Autonomy
Employed - full time	Employment income	Spending	Social security payments	Savings	Within household	Qualifications	Social status	External locus of control
Employed part-time	Interest/ dividends		Social assistance payments	Investments	As assets	Experience	Social exclusion	Political exclusion
Self-employed	In kind		Concessions	Borrowings House(s)	Community Free/subsidised health care	Health status		
Outside labour force: carer				Consumer durables	Free/subsidised education			
sick				Vehicle(s)	Free/subsidised transport systems			
					Police			

1 Corresponds to private consumption in Baulch's pyramid.
2 Relates to cash transfers through the social security and social assistance systems, corresponding to a part of the state provided commodities (SPC) in Baulch's pyramid.
3 Corresponds to common property rights in Baulch's pyramid. In personal correspondence Baulch explains that in societies of the South this refers to resources such as land held in common. He was unsure what might be the counterpart in the North. A distinction is made here between resources shared within a household and commodies provided by the state that are free at the point of consumption.

refuges supported by social security (Leeming, Unell and Walker, 1994). In other circumstances, people may seek to avoid income poverty through coping strategies, such as crime and prostitution, that serve to exclude them from society's social and moral framework (Kempson, Bryson and Rowlingson, 1994).

An equally radical step in rethinking poverty is to take account of the dynamics and processes involved. People's scores on each dimension of poverty, that is the kind of poverty that they are suffering, is likely to influence both the chances of them remaining in poverty and the nature of the poverty that they may subsequently experience (Figure 2.3)[3]. So, for example, someone who is unemployed and living on income tested benefits but who has recent work experience, good qualifications and extensive social networks is likely rapidly to find work that pays above benefit levels (McKay et al, 1997; Walker and Shaw, 1998).

Figure 2.3: Dynamic explanations of the generation of poverty[1]

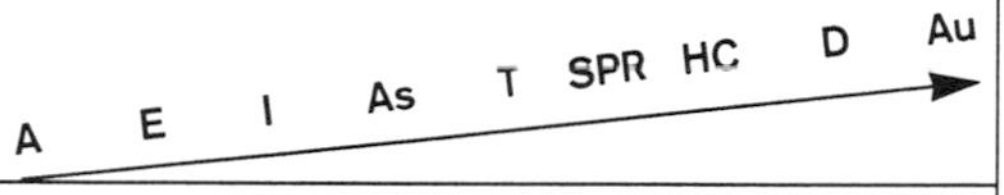

A E I As T SPR HC D Au →

Poverty Scores at Time T1	Poverty Scores at Time T2								
	A	E	I	As	T	SPR	HC	D	Au
Labour Market Activity (A)	⇒	⇒	⇒	⇒	⇒	→	→	→	→
Expenditure (E)	→	⇒	→	→	→	→	→	→	→
Income (I)	→	⇒	⇒	⇒	⇒	→	→	→	⇒
Assets (As)	→	→	⇒	⇒	→	→	→	→	→
Transfers (T)	→	→	→	→	⇒	→	→	⇒	⇒
Shared Property Rights (SPR)	→	→	→	→	→	⇒	→	⇒	⇒
Human Capital (HC)	→	→	⇒	→	→	→	⇒	→	→
Dignity (D)	→	→	→	→	→	→	→	⇒	→
Autonomy (Au)	→	→	→	→	→	→	→	→	⇒

1: This diagram shows that a person's score on each and every dimension of poverty in time T₁ is likely to help determine his or hers scores on these dimensions in subsequent time periods T₂....Tₙ. The following symbols indicate that:
⇒ Poverty on this dimension is likely to have a strong influence on the poverty in the next time period.
→ Poverty on this dimension is likely to have an influence on poverty in the next time period.

Their chances of experiencing further spells of poverty, though greater than someone who has never suffered poverty, are also comparatively low and fall quickly as their spell of comparative affluence lengthens. Alternatively someone in their late 50s, and who suffers chronic ill-health and has no fixed address is likely to remain trapped in poverty (Vincent, Deacon and Walker, 1995).

This dynamic perspective calls into question the traditional view of poverty as homogeneous and essentially static; the poor are contrasted with the non-poor as if they never exchanged places. Instead, poverty is differentiated and considered to be a recursive process: changes in one period help bring about changes in the next which in turn affect future experiences. The result is that people are recognised to follow trajectories through different kinds of poverty that may alternate with periods of relative affluence. Transitions or steps in these trajectories are mediated by the interaction of individual attributes and the opportunity sets determined by social institutions (Gershuny, 1998). Traditional poverty counts can be no more than 'stills' taken from the movie of life.

Descriptive Dynamics

So what changes if poverty is viewed as a movie instead of a series of stills? First, the size of the problem is increased. The poverty rate in Britain – measured as income of less than half the median – was 12.7 per cent in 1990/1 and 14.5 per cent in 1993/4, but over 36 per cent of people were poor in at least one year between those two dates (Jarvis and Jenkins, 1996). This suggests that the poor do indeed swap positions with the non-poor. Moreover, if poverty is measured over a shorter time period, the numbers suffering poverty escalate still further. When measured in this way, poverty is no longer the affliction of a small minority; it is the personal experience of many – perhaps even most – families.

The fact that longitudinal estimates of poverty are so much greater than cross-sectional ones provides a second insight. It reveals that, on average, spells of poverty are short. Had the longitudinal and cross-sectional estimates been the same, the conclusion would be that the same people were poor in each year. This would have meant that poverty is more or less permanent. In fact 'only' seven per cent of individuals were poor throughout the four year period, 1990/1-1993/4; that is one in five of all those who experienced any poverty. This provides good evidence that the poor in Britain generally do not constitute an economic underclass cut off from mainstream society. Eighty-one per cent of individuals who experienced poverty during the first part of the decade enjoyed at least a year when their incomes were above poverty levels (although, it has to be said that only a minority enjoyed great prosperity).

Table 2.1: Durations of poverty[1] in Britain, 1990/1-1993/4

Years	Number of years poor per cent	Per cent poor at least X years
One	13.2	36.2
Two	9.0	22.9
Three	6.9	13.9
Four	7.0	7.0
None	63.9	N/A

[1] Income in lowest quintile.
Source: Jarvis and Jenkins (1996, 1997)

Most poverty, then, is not permanent. Nevertheless, it is still important to ask how long poverty lasts. Unfortunately, there are as yet no unbiased estimates of the duration of income poverty for Britain. It is known that, in the early 1990s, 13 per cent of people were poor one year out of four and that 14 per cent were poor for three years *or more* (Table 2.1). The problem is to estimate the likely duration of spells of poverty that have not yet ended.

Some estimates of this kind are available for spells of benefit receipt. In the early 1990s the median length of time that unemployed claimants remained on income support was four months. For other groups, spells of benefit receipt were longer though probably not as long as media hype would suggest. On average lone parents stayed on benefit for 20 months and claimants with disabilities for two years. As might be expected, pensioners tended to claim income support for much longer: 70 per cent for over two years with many staying on benefit for the rest of their lives.

To escape from poverty is not necessarily a passport to prosperity. Moreover, the lightning of penury has a habit of striking more than once. Three out of ten of those who escape poverty (income in the lowest quintile) in one year are known to be poor again the next. Likewise, people who move off income related benefits are prone to return. A quarter of people moving off benefit after a spell of unemployment are back on benefit within a year (Shaw *et al*, 1996). Likewise, nearly four in ten lone mothers who move off income support are forced to reclaim within a similar period. In the USA, where it is possible to track people for 30 years, it is apparent that repeated spells of poverty are the norm rather than the exception (Walker, 1994; Ashworth, Hill and Walker, 1994).

Causes and Consequences

Returning to the analogy of film, dynamic analyses of poverty focus attention on the story-line of cause and effect which static studies do not. This is not only intellectually more satisfying, it can – as shown in the final section below – suggest points in the plot at which policy interventions may be appropriate.

More on income poverty

It is appropriate to dwell for a moment on some antecedents of spells of income poverty. Table 2.2 points to the importance of employment and family changes. Thirty per cent of individuals who began a spell of poverty in the early 1990s did so when someone in their household lost employment. About one in seven of those becoming poor lost an adult as the result of divorce, separation, death or some other reason. These same factors, together with the ending of entitlement to social insurance benefits, are important triggers of poverty in other advanced western countries (Walker, 1997; Duncan *et al*, 1993). However, it is also apparent from Table 2.2 that neither the loss of a job nor the departure of an adult from a household is either a necessary or a sufficient cause of poverty. About 73 per cent of individuals who either lost a job or lived in a household where someone else ceased employment escaped poverty, as did 75 per cent of those experiencing the loss of an adult. They must have been protected in some way from the worst consequences of events such as unemployment and relationship breakdown.

Table 2.2: Events coincident with the beginning of a spell of poverty[1] in Britain 1990/1-1993/4

Household event	Percentage of persons who become poor and experience event[2]	Percentage of persons experiencing event who become poor[3]
Loss of earner (s)	30	27
Increase in number of earners	14	14
Loss of adult (s)	14	25
Addition of adult (s)	7	10
Loss of child(ren)	8	14
Addition of child(ren)	6	16

[1] Defined as below 50 per cent of mean income in 1990/1.
[2] The top cell reads: 30 per cent of people who become poor live in households that have recently lost an earner
[3] The top cell reads: 27 per cent of persons living in households that suffer the loss of an earner subsequently become poor.

Calculated from Jarvis and Jenkins (1997).

The source of such protection may on occasion be found among the other potential components of well-being. For example, poverty may be avoided in the event of unemployment by the provision of social security benefits. This is certainly the norm in much of continental Europe although, in Britain, even before the introduction of jobseeker's allowance less than a fifth of unemployed people were protected by insurance benefits and needed to claim social assistance.

That said, a tenth of the people becoming unemployed during the recession of the early 1990s did not claim any unemployment-related benefit (Walker and Ashworth, 1998). A proportion of these will have failed to take up their benefit entitlement. Others will have enjoyed other forms of protection against income poverty: redundancy pay, savings and, perhaps most important, a working partner.

Figure 2.4: Downward poverty trajectory: health and work

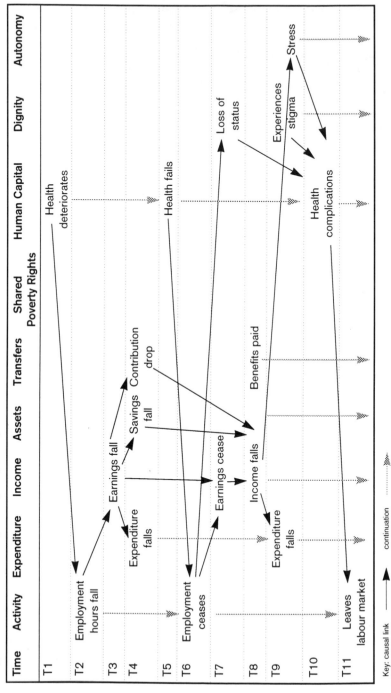

Key: causal link ——▶   continuation ········▶

Health and Unemployment

But while people may be protected from some forms of poverty by resources in other dimensions, the elements of poverty can interact in a destructive sense. The relationship between health and employment is a good example. People with a history of ill health face an enhanced risk of unemployment and people who are unemployed are less healthy than those in work. Poor employment records associated with ill-health probably deny people access to unemployment insurance and result in having few financial resources or assets to draw on in the event of unemployment. Trajectories followed by some people suffering ill-health have the characteristics of a downward spiral (Figure 2.4).

In the early 1990s 53 per cent of income support recipients reported a long-standing health problem. Some 30 per cent believed that their health restricted the kind of work that they could do. Objective evidence supports this contention: in 1995/6 a health problem reduced the chance of finding work by 22 per cent (McKay et al, 1997). What precise mechanisms were at work is less clear. Perhaps employers calculated that the ill-health or disability imposed an untenable limit on productivity. Perhaps claimants with a health problem unnecessarily reduced the jobs that they applied for. There was, though, no evidence that they were any less enthusiastic to find work than other claimants.

So people with a health problem are more likely than others to become unemployed and then less likely to find work again. But unemployment, even the fear of unemployment, itself undermines health (Ferrie et al, 1998). Uncertainty induced by organisational change can lead to significant increases in blood pressure and detrimental movements in body mass indices as well as deterioration in self-reported health status and a rise in the number of symptoms. It is at least possible, though as yet not researched, that morbidity induced by insecure employment itself causes people to leave the labour market on health grounds or to become unemployed.

Unemployment has a marked effect on mortality and morbidity, even after controlling for those who are out of the workforce due to ill-health: for men, aged 40-59, unemployment increases the risk of premature death by 50 per cent (Morris et al, 1994). Taking account of prior ill-health raises the differential in mortality to a massive 314 per cent. Adding in other factors, such as previous experience of unemployment, is likely to further increase the differential between workers and non-workers. Unemployment is also implicated in mental ill-health (Dennehy *et al*, 1997). The processes seem not only to involve the stresses caused by having to cope with a lower income but also loss of the non-financial benefits of work: status, purpose, social contacts and life structure (Smith, 1985). In such circumstances, when negative processes become mutually reinforcing, a person's downward trajectory can become vortex-like.

From income poverty to exclusion

Another downward trajectory finds people moving from income poverty to social exclusion, slipping from a point of keeping their heads above water, through 'sinking', to 'drowning' (Figure 2.5). This trajectory could be triggered in a family by unemployment and compounded by structural factors. The chances of finding work and hence escaping poverty might objectively be low: few qualifications, obsolete skills, slack labour demand. This in turn may undermine the morale and hope that is essential if people are to continue seeking work and trying to make ends meet. They may, as a consequence, have no choice but to employ socially unacceptable strategies and hence step outside society's norms.

Even before this point the family may have become detached from social institutions and the multi-faceted nature of social exclusion will have become evident. Preventative health care may have been neglected. The demands of mutual reciprocity may have limited visits to all but closest kin, and stress and depression may have added impetus to this social retreat. Lack of finance may have prevented children from engaging in the full range of intra-and extra-curriculum educational activities with significant implications for their educational and social development. Confronted by the asocial behaviour to which the family has succumbed, the reaction of external organisations may confound attempts by the family to fight their social exclusion. Creditors may seek to repossess goods and landlords threaten eviction. Potential employers may be put off by inadequate personal references and social welfare agencies may move to more coercive policies. The process of social exclusion will have become vary hard to reverse.

Figure 2.5: A trajectory from income poverty to social exclusion

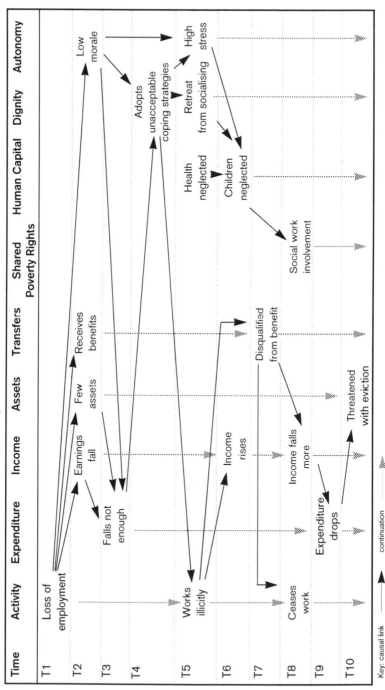

Key: causal link ——— continuation

Kempson *et al* (1994) found 12 out of 28 low income families following this kind of trajectory over a two year period with the direction influenced by three, sometimes inter-related, determinants: the level of resources, the management of resources and the steps taken to maximise resources. In fact, it is sometimes possible to reverse a downward trajectory even with a modest increase in resources: eight out of 28 people who appeared to be drowning managed to lift themselves off the bottom rung of the economic ladder.

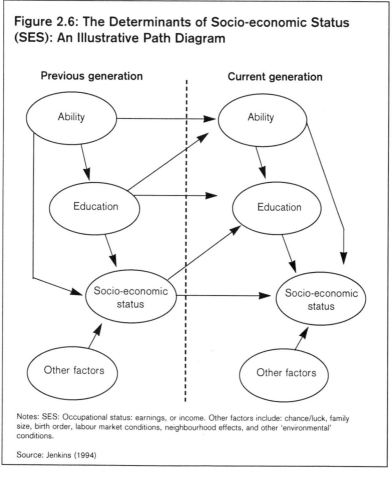

Figure 2.6: The Determinants of Socio-economic Status (SES): An Illustrative Path Diagram

Previous generation   Current generation

Ability → Ability

Education   Education

Socio-economic status   Socio-economic status

Other factors   Other factors

Notes: SES: Occupational status: earnings, or income. Other factors include: chance/luck, family size, birth order, labour market conditions, neighbourhood effects, and other 'environmental' conditions.

Source: Jenkins (1994)

From one generation to the next

There is evidence that some at least of these processes can work across generations. The most important links are between the financial components of parental poverty and the attainments of children in adulthood. Children's future employment, earnings and wages are related to the economic resources of their parents more than to anything else. Moreover, the effect is not linear: parents being poor matters a lot for their children. (Jenkins, 1994 and Corcoran and Burgess 1994).

But the detail of these processes is much less clear. Figure 2.6 summarises the links that have been explored and the simplicity of the diagram emphasises how much work still needs to be done. In the USA the strongest effect seems to be the direct one between the economic status of parent and child, whereas in Britain it may be that the direct effect is partially mediated through the education system.[4] However, there is little evidence that the non-financial components of poverty are important in themselves: neither the deviant values or cultural norms of parents or the latter's limited self-confidence or perceived lack of control seem to have much effect on the economic performance of their children. Rather the driving mechanisms seem to relate to the limited options open to parents and children (Ellwood, 1988). Even such dramatic social upheavals as parental divorce pale into comparative insignificance when account is taken of economic circumstances.

So, while the causal story certainly spans generations, the plot remains a mystery thriller for social science to unravel.

Spatial processes

Time is not just the medium in which poverty occurs it also shapes the experience. The same is true of space. Moreover, space and time intersect to further differentiate poverty.

This can be illustrated by reference to housing (Lee and Murie, 1997). Poor housing is both a consequence and a cause of poverty defined in its broadest sense (the base of Baulch's pyramid). Lack of employment and income restrict housing options: 'those with the least options in the market and bureaucratic allocations systems end up in the least desirable properties' (*Ibid* p51). The health and education of those in the worst properties are affected. So, too, is access to employment opportunities.

Take the case of council housing. Originally the tenure was attractive to the more aspiring affluent working classes. Estates had a good social mix. Subsequently as new building declined, council house sales were expanded, need exceeded supply and allocation policies limited intake to the most disadvantaged groups. Estates became the refuges of lone parents, pensioners and others receiving welfare benefits. Moreover, these changes happened faster than was envisaged because analysts focused on cross-sectional statistics that reflected the stock of residents rather than the flows of people to and from the local authority sector (Holmans, 1991). But there were two additional twists in this process of residualisation. First, since local authority housing is spatially concentrated, its evolution into a residual tenure resulted in the creation of residual areas, poor places. But secondly, working residents on local authority estates tended to hold jobs that were particularly at risk during the recessions of the 1980s and early 1990s. The demise of these jobs had the effect of further concentrating unemployment and income poverty on council estates.

In some cases the spatial concentration of worklessness and income poverty triggered a spiral of despair. The declining local economy further reduced jobs as shops and other commercial ventures ceased trading. Public services were placed under strain due to increased demand which in turn led to a decline in the social infrastructure. Pressure within families spilled over into tensions between neighbours and led to erosion of community ties. Crime increased and the fear of crime escalated.

Real though this experience is, there is a danger of it becoming a stereotype. Space, time and poverty do not always interact in the same way. Lee and Murray (1997) note that many council estates retain a social mix and also that the map of deprivation, both at national and local level, differs markedly from a map of tenure. The critical task is to determine which processes are operating where.

The political imperative: setting thresholds by listening rather than by design

The setting of poverty thresholds is a political rather than scientific matter.

Poverty has to be differentiated both in order to understand the experiences of people who suffer poverty and to evolve appropriate policy responses. But whether poverty exists as a 'concrete' entity beyond the experiences of poor people and outside the minds and hearts of those who are not currently poor is surely debatable.

Townsend (1979) would argue that it does and that the boundaries can be defined by the point on the income to needs dimension where a further fall begins to have a disproportionate effect on people's behaviour and social participation. However, the supporting evidence for this contention is weak. Moreover, such an approach cannot easily accommodate the dynamics discussed above.

Rather the various dimensions of poverty are probably better construed as *continua* which define people's experience. These can only be dichotomised into 'poor' and 'not-poor' on the basis of judgement. The weight given to scores on each dimension is also a matter of judgement. The reference point in such judgmental decisions has to be social unacceptability since it is this that distinguishes poverty from more neutral terms such as low income or living standard. There is an imperative to act inherent in poverty because its existence is socially unacceptable (Piachaud, 1987).

If this view is accepted, poverty thresholds become political tools used to engender support for policy change and to provide targets in policy implementation. Science can help to determine the processes involved and inform the method by which the poverty thresholds are fixed but not to determine their level.

Within this framework the appropriate tools are consensual ones: measures based on the views of citizens. These might derive from interview surveys in which people are explicitly asked what income is required to avoid poverty (Townsend *et al*, 1997) or to determine lists of socially perceived necessities (Gordon and Pantazis, 1997). Other researchers have encouraged lay people from diverse backgrounds to reach consensus about poverty thresholds through discussion, (Middleton *et al*, 1994; 1997).

These kinds of study indicate that most people readily accept that poverty is relative rather than absolute and explicitly take into account all the elements in the base of Baulch's pyramid. A large majority – 70 per cent in 1990 – also take the view that Government has done too little to help poor people (Townsend, 1997). Poverty thresholds are typically set some way above the levels supported by means-tested benefits. Moreover, sizeable numbers of people claim that they would be prepared to be worse off if that would lessen poverty: 75 per cent would support an increase in income tax of 1p in the £, 43 per cent an increase of 5p.

Policy implications

A number of immediate political and policy implications arise from unpicking poverty. Labour's legitimisation of the use of the term poverty is itself an important instrument for social change. Speaking its name creates an impetus for reform.

But if poverty is a vital rallying cry, as currently conceived it acts as an impediment to policy development. The reason is that poverty is usually undifferentiated and treated as essentially static. It embraces a vast range of conditions and circumstances that are different in kind, vary in their aetiology and probably have different personal and social consequences. Moreover, far from being permanent, most of the experiences that are labelled as poverty are short-lived, even if comparatively large numbers of people repeatedly move in and out of states of poverty.

It is only fairly recently that poverty has been differentiated in any way except degree. While distinctions between severe and less severe poverty – measured as income against needs – are undoubtedly important, they may be of less value than differences defined according to duration and periodicity.[5] A single short spell of poverty is inherently different from repeated ones and recurrent poverty is not the same phenomenon as when it is permanent. The policy lessons are comparatively straightforward. Transient spells of income poverty can be prevented relatively easily through social or personal insurance or saving. On the other hand, those suffering recurrent poverty may well have insufficient periods of comparative affluence in which to accumulate adequate bridging funding. In many such cases, the empirical evidence points to a need to invest in measures that enhance earning power (Walker, 1994). In instances of permanent poverty, multiple policy interventions may well be required.

However, even these refined distinctions give insufficient purchase on the nature of poverty to offer significant leverage for policy. The multifaceted nature of poverty creates a myriad of different conditions. One understandable response is for the policy maker to retreat from such complexity and to say that, since administrative responses have to be workable, they need to be simple even if that creates rough justice. In fact, this response can also result in inefficiency. Indeed the justification of the New Deal welfare to work policies is that universal cash hand-outs are not maximally effective because some people in the target group would benefit more from human capital investment.

Therefore a more constructive response to diversity may be to exploit the concept of trajectories introduced above to elucidate different kinds of poverty and identify points for policy intervention. Even in the absence of extensive evidence, trajectories provide a useful heuristic device. For example, the kind of self-induced poverty that might be solved by enhancing a person's sense of personal and social responsibility would require, as a necessary if insufficient condition, a trajectory in which a low rating on social esteem preceded a long spell of low income. Policies to enhance responsibility should therefore be targeted at people before rather than after they become income poor. Then again, recall the health income spiral discussed above (Figure 2.4). Being able to claim a partial disability benefit when the person's health first deteriorated might have meant higher income when health eventually failed and prevented the spiral from becoming a vortex. Consider, too, the trajectory from income poverty to exclusion (Figure 2.5). Labour's New Deal for the Unemployed could have prevented the initial drop in morale, although the family might already have faced difficulties because of the two-year waiting period. Better still to offer services early if it was known that the breadwinner lacked skills and qualifications—good predictors of a long spell of unemployment.[6] If similar trajectories are common in a particular neighbourhood – a risk, perhaps, that the locality may be destined to become a 'poor place' – New Deal-like policies might be offered early to all unemployed residents. There could even be a case of extending services to those still working but fearful of losing their job: prevention might be less costly than cure (Walker, 1998b).

It is easy to illustrate the potential of being able to target proactive policies at the right point in the process. Implementation is more difficult. There is an obvious need for new data and better models to inform policy design. Execution may require collecting additional information from people. As with the New Deal, interventions may need to be more personalised than in the past and will often demand inter-agency liaison. But none of these problems is insuperable.

To conclude, there is no one policy, one big idea that will eradicate poverty. But there is new thinking that potentially offers real solutions. Think not of poverty but of poverties, processes rather than states, and prevention and intervention rather than poverty relief.

References

Abel-Smith, B, and Townsend, P, (1965), *The Poor and the Poorest*, London: LSE Occasional Papers in Social Administration.

Ashworth, K, (1997), 'Practical applications of longitudinal analysis in social security research', In *DSS Research Yearbook 1996/7*, London: Stationery Office.

Ashworth, K, Hill, M and Walker, R, (1994), 'Patterns of childhood poverty: new challenges for policy', *Journal of Policy Analysis and Management*, 13, 4, pp 658-680.

Atkinson A, Maynard A and Trinder C, (1983), *Parents and Children: Incomes in Two Generations*, London: Heineman Educational Books.

Baulch B (1996), 'The new poverty agenda: a disputed consensus', *IDS Bulletin*, 27, pp1-10.

Corcoran M and Boggess S (1994), *Intergenerational Transmission of Poverty and Inequality*, Ann Arbor: University of Michigan.

Dennehy A, Smith L and Harker P (1997), *Not to be Ignored: Young People, Poverty and Health*, London: Child Poverty Action Group.

Duncan G *et al* (1993), 'Poverty dynamics in eight countries', *Journal of Population Economics*, 6, pp. 295-334.

Ellwood D (1988), *Understanding Dependency: Choices, Confidence or Culture*, Cambridge Mass. Harvard University, Mimeo.

Ferrie J *et al* 'The health effects of major organisational change and job insecurity', *Social Science and Medicine*, 46, pp. 243-54.

Gershuny J (1998) 'Thinking dynamically: sociology and narrative data' pp34-48 in L. Leisering and R. Walker (eds.) *The Dynamics of Modern Society*, Bristol: Policy Press.

Gordon, D and Pantazis C, (1997), *Breadline Britain in the 1990s*, Aldershot: Ashgate.

Holmans, A, (1991), 'The 1977 national housing policy review in retrospect', *Housing Studies*, 6, pp. 206-19.

Jarvis, S. and Jenkins, S., (1996), *Income Mobility in Britain 1991-4: A First Look*, Colchester: ESRC Research Centre for Micro-Social Change, Mimeo.

Jarvis, S. and Jenkins, S, (1997), 'Low income dynamics in 1990s Britain', *Fiscal Studies*, 18, 2, pp. 123-142.

Kempson E, Bryson A, and Rowlingson K (1994), *Hard Times*, London: Policy Studies Institute.

Kiernan K (1997), *The Legacy of Parental Divorce: Social, Economic and Deomgraphic Experiences in Adulthood*, London: Centre for Analysis of Social Exclusion, CASE paper 1.

Lee P and Murie A (1997), Poverty, *Housing Tenure and Social Exclusion*, Bristol: Policy Press.

Leeming A Unell J and Walker R (1994), *Lone mothers coping with the consequences of separation*, London: HMSO, Department of Social Security Research Report, 30.

Mack J and Lansley S (1985), *Poor Britain*, London: Allen and Unwin.

McKay S, Walker R and Youngs R (1997), *Unemployment and Jobseeking Before Jobseeker's Allowance*, London: Stationery Office, DSS Research Report 73.

Mead L (1997), 'From welfare to work: lessons from America', pp1-50 in A. Deacon (ed.) *From Welfare to Work*, London: IEA, Choice in Welfare, 39.

Middleton S, Ashworth K and Baithwaite I (1997), *Small Fortunes: Spending on Children, Childhood Poverty and Parental Sacrifice*, York: Joseph Rowntree Foundation.

Middleton S, Ashworth K and Walker R (1997), *Family Fortunes*, London: Child Poverty Action Group.

Millar J and Glendinning C (1992) *Women and Poverty in Britain: the 1990s*, London: Harvester Wheatsheaf.

Morris J, Cook D and Shaper A (1994) 'Loss of employment and mortality', *British Medical Journal*, 308, pp 1135-9.

Piachaud D (1987) 'Problems in the definition and measurement of poverty', *Journal of Social Policy*, 16, pp 147-164.

Rowntree S (1901) *Poverty: A Study of Town Life*, London, Macmillan.

Rowntree S (1941) *Poverty and Progress: a Second Social Survey of York*, London, Longmans, Green.

Rowntree S (1922) *Poverty: A Study of Town Life*, London: Longmans.

Rowntree S and Lavers G (1951) *Poverty and the Welfare State*, London: Longmans, Green and Co.

Rowlingson K, Whyley C, Newburn T and Berthoud R (1997) *Social Security Fraud: the Role of Penalties*, London: Stationery Office, DSS Research Report 64.

Room G (1995) *Beyond the Threshold*, Bristol: Policy Press.

Shaw *et al* (1996) *Barriers to Moving Off Income Support*, London:

HMSO, Department of Social Security Research Report, 53.

Townsend P (1979), *Poverty in the United Kingdom*, Harmondsworth: Penguin.

Townsend P *et al* (1997), *Absolute and Overall Poverty in Britain in 1997*, Bristol: Bristol Statistical Monitoring Unit.

Vincent J, Deacon A and Walker R (1995) *Homeless Single Men: Roads to Resettlement*, Aldershot: Avebury.

Walker R (1998a) 'Does work work?', *Journal of Social Policy*, 27, 2, forthcoming.

Walker R (1998b) 'Positive welfare', *New Economics*, Forthcoming.

Walker R (1997) 'Poverty and social exclusion in Europe' pp 48-74 in A. Walker and C. Walker (eds.) *Britain Divided*, London: Child Poverty Action Group.

Walker R (1995) 'Routes in and out of poverty over the life course', pp32-4 in R. Bayley, A Condy, and C. Roberts (eds.) *Policies for Families: Work, Poverty and Resources*, London: Family Policy Studies Centre.

Walker R and Ashworth, K (1998) 'Welfare and recession in Britain', In L. Leisering and R. Walker (eds.) *Dynamics of Modern Society*, Bristol: Policy Press.

Walker R and Shaw A (1998) 'Escaping social assistance in Britain', In L. Leisering and R. Walker (eds.) *Dynamics of Modern Society*, Bristol: Policy Press.

Wandner S (1997) 'Early reemployment for dislocated workers in the United States', *International Social Security Review*, 50, 4, pp. 95-112.

Wilkes J (1997) *Poverty and Labour Market Policy in North and South*, Brighton: MPhil Dissertation, Institute of Development Studies.

Endnotes

1. It is sometimes argued that the fear of poverty acts to discipline the workforce (Mead, 1997).

2. They might prefer to focus on the third row, taking account of private consumption, common property resources and state provided commodities and transfers, but settle for the first alone on account of data limitations (Baulch 1996). For the same reason income replaces consumption as the principal metric.

3. Special thanks are due to Sharon Walker and Swells Hariman for translating the figures from all prepared sketches.

4. Unfortunately most British data-sets that facilitate inter-generational analysis have poor income data which means this finding should be treated with care (Atkinson et al., 1983).

5. Empirically severity has been shown to correlate with poverty differentiated according to number, duration and spacing of spells (Ashworth, Hill and Walker, (1994).

6. Client profiling has been shown to work in the USA (Wandner, 1997).

3. Comment: unravelling poverty

by Fran Bennett

Introduction

These two chapters perform different functions. They cannot therefore be compared and contrasted – although they are similar in emphasising the multidimensional nature of the problems they discuss, and the dynamic nature of the processes causing them.

Both chapters demonstrate that we live in interesting times. First, new data are now available – for example, combining longitudinal evidence about income mobility with small area information about income distribution. David Piachaud has even managed for the first time to forecast the likely numbers in poverty a few years hence.[1] Secondly, the rethinking of concepts is leading to more creative thinking about policy solutions. Thirdly, identification of a changed framework and different motors of causality is prompting the elaboration of a new model and rethinking of policy levers. Finally, a new government is in office, which can speak the name of poverty again; which promises a policy focus on social exclusion; and which is interested in the causes, not just the symptoms, of poverty (though both authors also identify the limits and problems inherent in its approach).

Definitions and measures

Both chapters tackle many problematic issues of definition. Walker unpacks the relationship of poverty with the dimensions of space, and especially time, to develop a model of transient, recurrent and permanent poverty, and explores its implications. His emphasis on the significant number of people touched by poverty helps to underline the extent to which poverty is a shared experience. John Hills suggested recently[2] that the new income mobility data have been used positively, to oppose the notion of a substantial 'underclass'; but that to go to the other extreme, and conclude that income mobility resembles a random lottery, would be mistaken. Most income trajectories are still relatively flat.

Walker's emphasis on the poverty threshold as essentially a political, rather than scientific, construct is welcome. The key to a definition of 'poverty' is that it is socially unacceptable; a poverty threshold must therefore be arrived at by consensus. However, we must be cautious in over-estimating public sympathy towards 'the poor'; once faces are put to the abstract concept, it may be people in poverty who are considered socially unacceptable, rather than poverty itself. Moreover, there is ample evidence that people living in poverty often do not want to label themselves as 'poor'; any explorations of definitions involving them must be conducted with great sensitivity.

We should also consider the difficulties of defining social participation, social inclusion and social norms in an increasingly differentiated and diverse society. Ruth Lister[3] discusses how to incorporate a politics of difference and identity into the citizenship debate. It is not clear whether these concerns could be reflected in Walker's 'poverties'.

Oppenheim usefully tries to distinguish between poverty, deprivation and social exclusion. However, she may not ultimately resolve the issue of whether poverty itself should be seen as multi-dimensional – or whether the primary characteristic of poverty is low income/living standards, with other features more accurately described as its effects, and social exclusion as the multi-dimensional experience.

With the creation of the Social Exclusion Unit, definitions of social exclusion are likely to become the next contested area of debate. Tony Atkinson argued recently[4] that the concepts of relativity, agency and dynamics are crucial to an accurate understanding. As yet, however, there has been little discussion of how to incorporate public opinion into this debate. Public views may not reflect the idea of social exclusion as a dynamic process, multi-dimensional in nature, and affecting communities as well as individuals and households.

Both chapters prompt questions about definitions of social exclusion shading into normative descriptions. Are socially excluded people located outside the rights and norms of society? Is one defining characteristic of social exclusion the social unacceptability of strategies adopted by people with limited resources? Neither author lays much stress on these aspects. But a government which has used the language of 'the benefit dependency culture', and even 'the underclass', may also be tempted to adopt normative explanations of social exclusion.

The Social Exclusion Unit is to draw up indicators of social exclusion and suggest how to track them, to monitor the effectiveness of government policies. Oppenheim asks whether the same people are involved on each dimension of exclusion; and both authors describe how one element of exclusion may either counteract or reinforce others. Existing work on the inter-relationships between different forms of deprivation might provide starting-points for considering such issues. New research on social networks[5] also explores a key component. Some people argue that the concepts of social exclusion and inclusion, however, are not all-embracing. They may not help in understanding inequality or polarisation, for example, because they do not encompass an analysis of processes affecting the upper end of the distribution.

Policies and action

The authors discuss action on different fronts (so many policy areas are relevant); at various levels (the individual, household and community) and using a variety of instruments (public and private).

Today's policy arena is more fragmented, with more actors – including public, private and voluntary sectors – and with different tiers of government having more influence. These developments widen the scope for action in a way which may be helpful for one topical debate, about the place of benefit increases within an anti-poverty strategy. The disposable incomes of people in poverty, for example, could be increased via a reduction in the costs they face for basic services and utilities. The responsibility of different actors to help create a fairer and more inclusive society can be seen as a shared task, rather than expecting the social security safety net to bear the burden of compensating for the impact of other policies.

The wide-ranging debates about social exclusion in these chapters contrast with the initial targets of the Social Exclusion Unit. Its focus on truancy and school exclusions, 'rough sleepers' and estates with multiple problems could be interpreted as targeting problem people, rather than seeing these issues as the end result of recent economic and social change, coupled with government policies implemented in an unequal society. Problems may be presented as 'anti-social' behaviour, or 'nuisance neighbours', rather than merely poverty or bad housing, precisely because 'more of the problems are piling up in the same places'.[6] Truancy and school exclusions should be set in the context of an increasingly competitive education system, and a government determined not to allow social disadvantage to be an 'excuse' for differential performance.

Conclusion

Some tensions within the new context have a familiar feel. Oppenheim acknowledges that 'rebuilding endowments' may be costly; it is not only traditional methods of redistribution which can be criticised as 'tax and spend'. She also notes the public ambivalence about traditional forms of redistribution (though Walker is more optimistic). As yet, we know little about public attitudes towards any additional expenditure involved in the new government's approach – or towards the possible displacement of some workers by subsidised young or long-term unemployed people, or the impact on differentials of a minimum wage. But the awkward political issues involved in redistribution do not disappear merely because a different mechanism is employed. The recent troubled history of child support demonstrates this very clearly.

Both authors also emphasise the importance of preventing poverty, facilitating change and mobility and enabling people to cope with risk. But such policies would not necessarily avoid the dilemmas about targeting and poverty relief which dog debates about benefits. Under the previous government, for example, European Union subsidies for retraining workers in industries with an insecure future (under Objective 4 of the Structural Funds) were rejected, because the government argued that it wanted to 'target' its training on the unemployed.

Finally, more detailed attention should perhaps be paid to the two extreme ends of the policy-making spectrum – both the potential for influencing the impact of globalisation, on the one hand, and the need to involve people in poverty themselves as active participants in the design and implementation of policies, on the other. If we manage to incorporate these two ends of the spectrum too, we will be approaching the creation of what the government likes to call 'joined-up policies'.

Endnotes

1. See Piachaud D (1998) "The Prospects for Poverty" in *New Economy* Blackwell, Oxford

2. Hills J (1998) 'Does Income Mobility Mean that We Do Not Need to Worry About Poverty?' in Atkinson A B and Hills J (eds.) *Exclusion, Employment and Opportunity* CASE paper 4 STICERD/LSE, London

3. Lister R (1997), unpublished paper delivered at conference on citizenship and the welfare state, organised by Oxford Brookes University and Ruskin College in mid-December 1997.

4. Atkinson A B (1998) 'Social Exclusion, Poverty and Unemployment' in Atkinson A B and Hills J (eds.) *Social Exclusion, Employment and Opportunity* CASE paper 4 STICERD/LSE, London

5. See, for example, 6 Perri (1997) 'Social Exclusion: Time to be Optimistic' in Christie I (ed.) *The Wealth and Poverty of Networks,* Collection no. 12 Demos, London

6. Barclay P (1995) *Joseph Rowntree Foundation Inquiry into Income and Wealth, Volume 1* Joseph Rowntree Foundation, York

II:
Poverty
targets

4. The case for an official poverty target
by A B Atkinson

The Labour Government has shown itself willing to set numerical targets against which its policy is to be judged. In Opposition, Gordon Brown announced a target for reducing the number of long-term registered unemployed aged 18-24. As Chancellor, he has followed the Conservative Government in setting a numerical target for the rate of inflation. There are national targets for the attainment of literacy and numeracy by the year 2002. The White Paper on *Eliminating World Poverty* has reaffirmed the UK's commitment to the 0.7 per cent of GNP target for development assistance.

In this chapter,[1] I argue that the Labour Government should set an explicit target for the reduction of poverty in the UK.[1] There should be an official poverty line, decoupled from social security benefit rates. Reducing poverty would become an explicit object of policy, and the Office for National Statistics would be requested to produce an annual *Poverty Report* assessing how far the target in the UK had been reached, just as the *Inflation Report* of the Bank of England assesses progress in meeting the inflation target.

My concern here is with poverty in the United Kingdom, which is very different from poverty on a world scale. It could well be argued that poverty in Africa and Asia is so important as to preclude any consideration of the deprived within OECD countries. While it is my own personal judgment that world poverty has priority, I do not accept that this leaves no room for consideration of poverty in the UK. A target for reducing poverty in the UK is fully consistent with meeting our international responsibilities. And many people must be asking themselves why a Labour Government can accept an inflation target but has not yet set one for poverty reduction.

Setting a poverty target

The Declaration at the 1995 Copenhagen Summit on Social Development committed countries to planning to

> establish ... strategies and affordable time-bound goals and targets for the substantial reduction of overall poverty and the eradication of absolute poverty.

Some countries have responded very positively to this commitment. The Irish Government set up an Interdepartmental Policy Committee charged with drawing up the National Anti-Poverty Strategy, which in 1997 produced a Strategy Statement. This concluded that what was required was

> the adoption of clear overall objectives, targets and policy actions ... designed to demonstrate to everyone the ongoing process (National Anti-Poverty Strategy Statement, 1997, p 4).

The reduction of poverty has to be an official ambition, just like the reduction of inflation, with quantitative targets:

> Over the period, 1997-2007, the National Anti-Poverty Strategy will aim at considerably reducing the numbers of those who are 'consistently poor' from 9 per cent to 15 per cent to less than 5 to 10 per cent, as measured by the ESRI (National Anti-Poverty Strategy, 1997, p 9, *the ESRI is the Dublin research institute which has carried out regular studies of poverty*)

The Irish are not, of course, the first to adopt an official poverty line. In the United States, when the War on Poverty was declared by President Johnson, the Council of Economic Advisers defined the poverty line as $3,000 a year for a family and $1,500 for a single person. A more refined version of the poverty line was adopted by the Office of Economic Opportunity as 'a working definition of poverty for statistical, planning and budget purposes'. Today, the United States official poverty line is the basis for the Bureau of the Census Current Population Report, *Poverty in the United States*.

Whereas the British government has no official poverty line, the European Commission (for example, 1981 and 1989) has applied such a criterion, stating that

> the poor shall be taken to mean persons, families and groups of persons whose resources (material, cultural and social) are so limited as to exclude them from the minimum acceptable way of life in the Member States in which they live.

This is the definition contained in the decision of the Council of Ministers when approving the first Community Action Programme to Combat Poverty. In its evaluation of the Programme, the Commission took as the concrete implementation of this definition a poverty standard of 50 per cent of the average disposable income per equivalent adult in the country in question, and this is used in Eurostat publications.

An official poverty target in the UK

My proposal is that the UK should set an official poverty target. While it is too late to abolish poverty for the Millennium, but this may be a reasonable aspiration for 2015 when the children born today will become adults. Moreover, we should introduce a regular *Poverty Report* on the extent and nature of poverty.[2] The Office for National Statistics should be charged with publishing annual statistics on the United Kingdom population with incomes below specified percentages of the official poverty line, and their relation to the national performance target. The calculations in the *Poverty Report* would be the responsibility of the Director of the Office for National Statistics, who would apply and develop the appropriate professional standards.

The nucleus of such a report already exists in the form of the publication *Households Below Average Income* developed by the Analytical Services Division of the Department of Social Security (for example, Department of Social Security, 1997). This documents the proportion of the population living in households with incomes below different percentages of mean income. If the official poverty line were to take this form, as with the European Union poverty standard, then we already have much of the necessary material.

The simple publication of statistics, however, is not enough. What is needed is a statement of intent. The *Inflation Report* acquires its special significance on account of the Government's inflation target (Bank of England, 1993). The reduction of poverty has to be an ambition of the Government, just like the reduction of inflation. The figures in the *Poverty Report* have to be seen as indicating how far we are from achieving a national goal.

Essential to the proposal is that the official poverty scale should be set independently of social security benefit rates. It is important to keep these separate. The poverty target is an *objective*; social security benefits are an *instrument*. As it is put by John Veit Wilson in his case for a Minimum Income Standard (MIS)

> setting an MIS is one thing. It depends on social values and political aspirations for social justice. Setting income maintenance levels is another and different procedure affected by other considerations of politics and economics (1994).

It is for this reason that I propose that the *Poverty Report* should be the responsibility of the Office for National Statistics, rather than the Department of Social Security. The setting of national objectives should not be a matter for the public spending round.

Equally essential is that the poverty estimates should be as up to date as possible. When Gordon Brown presented his March 1998 Budget, the most recent official low income figures were for 3 years earlier (1994/5). On this basis, we will not learn the impact of the new Working Families Tax Credit, due to be introduced in October 1999, until after the next Election. There is no need to wait for a new year's data to be collected: it would be possible to make estimates on a rolling basis. The careful processing of survey data takes time, but resources can in part be substituted for delay. It is a matter of priorities.

Could we agree on a poverty standard?

The first possible objection to the proposal is that we could not agree on the definition of a poverty line and the contents of the *Poverty Report*. Even among those who support the reduction of poverty, there is much disagreement about its definition. The academic literature is replete with discussion of the difficulties in defining a poverty line. From this literature, readers will recognise the problems with the European Union 50 per cent poverty line. For some, the definition will already have closed too many options. It may not be adequate to measure poverty in terms of income, rather than expenditure, or the consumption of specific commodities, such as food or shelter. Income may be an intermediate variable, rather than an end in itself, allowing people to achieve a certain level of functioning. For others, it will have left open too many questions. The '50 per cent of average income' criterion can be interpreted in different ways.

All of these pose formidable problems; at the same time, there is an important difference between agreeing on a criterion according to which benefits are to be paid and agreeing on a definition for purely statistical purposes. We do not have to worry about the feasibility of the administrative apparatus for determining benefit eligibility. If an aggregate poverty statistic is the end product, then a certain amount of approximation may be acceptable. There does not have to be the fineness of classification necessary to ensure horizontal equity in the payment of benefits. Members of Parliament will not find their constituents complaining because they have been left out of the poverty total!

What is more, it may be possible to identify common ground even where there is not complete agreement. People may prefer an imperfect measure to one that matches their ideal in all respects. They may agree that the poverty line for a single person should be at least £X a week, even if they do not agree how much higher it should be.

Finally, one of the objects of the *Poverty Report* is to divert attention from a single number. The *Report* should present a range of information, as well as an informed commentary. The range will no doubt include different poverty cut-offs: the U.S. Bureau of the Census shows people living at 50 per cent, 75 per cent, 125 per cent, 150 per cent and 175 per cent of the official poverty line. There will be different poverty indicators (for example with different equivalence scales, or different methods of up-rating over time). There will be poverty rates for different subgroups of the population, just as in the present *Households below average income* publication.

Would a national poverty objective be counter-productive?

A potentially serious objection to the proposed *Poverty Report* and official poverty standard is that they would be counter-productive. This is a standard criticism of performance targets, and we have to ask how far it applies in the present case.

Establishment of an official poverty line could be simply cathartic or it could deform decisions in a way that has a negative impact on anti-poverty policy. As in planned economies, targets could distort government decisions in favour of the chosen objective and against other worthy goals. There is a risk that the Department of Social

Security would minimise the poverty statistics to the disregard of all other functions. This is a major ground for concern, since the objectives of social security are much broader than the alleviation of poverty. social transfers are also intended to smooth income across the lifetime, to redistribute towards those with dependants, to provide for adversities such as sickness and disability which involve a loss of income but not necessarily poverty, and to provide a general sense of security. Although it would be small protection, I would like to see the terms of reference of the *Poverty Report* include a requirement to comment where an improvement in the poverty figures had been achieved at the expense of other social goals.

A narrower version of the same objection is that, if the government is to be judged on its poverty performance, then it may concentrate on those policies which lead to improvement in the particular chosen indicator (for example helping those who are just below the poverty line but not those more in need). It seems to me however that this is less potentially serious. The risk can be moderated by careful choice of the measure, by use of multiple indicators, and by allowing the Office for National Statistics freedom to choose alternative criteria where it feels that the picture is being distorted. The purpose of having a *Poverty Report*, rather than simply publication of the statistics, is that the commentary would draw attention to the limitations of the indicators and the emergence of new forms of deprivation.

The introduction of the *Poverty Report* could, alternatively, have a negative impact by crowding out substantive measures to help the poor. Is it a work-generation project for academics rather than for the unemployed? Whether this could happen depends on the constraints on government action. If the binding constraint is public expenditure, then it seems unlikely that this is a serious obstacle. Nor is Parliamentary time likely to be a problem, since the proposal is designed in such a way that the Chancellor of the Exchequer can request the Report without recourse to Parliament. The main issue is that of 'political capital', and this brings us to the question why the Government should agree to commit itself to such a target.

Why should the government accept a poverty performance target?

Governments do not like offering hostages to fortune. So why should they agree to a poverty target? The experience of the inflation target is instructive. This was introduced after the United Kingdom left the Exchange Rate Mechanism to help give credibility to the new economic policy. It was a signal to the financial markets of the Government's commitment to price stability, despite the dramatic shift in policy.

The parallel is far from exact. However, the present Government is making a major change in social policy, emphasising welfare to work rather than social transfers as the solution to poverty. Social Security ministers are arguing that funds should be used for training and job finding, abandoning Labour's past policy of raising benefits. Work is to be the main route out of poverty. On the other hand, social policy outsiders, while agreeing that work is an important part of the strategy, remain unconvinced that benefit levels can be forgotten completely. For groups such as pensioners, restoring benefits is seen as the only solution.

Social policy professors do not have the same political clout as financial analysts in the City, but they are nonetheless experts in their field, and the Government may need to reinforce the credibility of its new policy. Moreover, one cannot rule out the risk for Labour that the Conservatives may seek to outflank the Government. In 1970 the Conservatives made considerable play of Labour's failure to reduce child poverty; one might in the future observe an attempt by the Conservatives to steal this issue from Labour.

If there is a need for credibility for the Government's new approach to welfare, then this may be best achieved by the approach outlined here. The national performance standard, and the political commitment, would be set in terms of outcomes rather than social transfer policy instruments. The decoupling of the poverty commitment from benefit spending is in this respect crucial. The government would be committed, not to raising child benefit by £X, or pensions by £Y, but to reducing poverty. As Peter Mandelson has argued,

> the acid test is what you end up achieving. I say to the
> doubters, judge us after ten years of success in office. For one

of the fruits of that success will be that Britain has become a more equal society (1997, p 7).

As he says, this can be achieved by different routes. The attraction of the proposal made here is that it provides the 'acid test' as to whether the different routes do indeed deliver a reduction in poverty. If we are agreed on the objective, and the government is committed to such a target, then this provides the basis for assessing different policy mechanisms. If welfare to work is a better use of scarce funds, then this will show up in better poverty figures.

Conclusions

I have argued for the institution in the UK of an official poverty target, and suggested that this might help restore credibility to the Government's welfare policy. I accept that there are grounds for concern that such a target would focus attention on the anti-poverty function of social transfers to the exclusion of other functions, but I feel nevertheless that there is a good case for adopting in the UK an official poverty line which is decoupled from benefit scales, to which there is a national commitment, and for there to be an official *Poverty Report* documenting and interpreting performance in the light of this performance standard. The reduction of poverty should be an ambition of the Government just as much as the reduction of inflation.

References

Atkinson AB (1996) 'The institution of an official poverty line and economic policy' in ed. Muscatelli VA *Economic and Political Institutions in Economic Policy* Manchester University Press, Manchester.

Bank of England (1993) 'Inflation Report' *Bank of England Quarterly Bulletin*.

Barker P (1996) *Living as Equals* Oxford University Press, Oxford.

Department of Social Security (1997) *Households Below Average Income 1979-1994/95* Stationery Office, London.

European Commission (1981) *Final Report on the First Programme of Pilot Schemes and Studies to Combat Poverty* Brussels.

European Commission (1989) *Interim Report on the Second European Poverty Programme*, Social Europe Supplement 2/89.

Mandelson P (1997) *Labour's next steps: tackling social exclusion* Fabian Pamphlet 581.

National Anti-Poverty Strategy (1997) *Sharing in Progress* Stationery Office, Dublin.

Veit Wilson J (1994) *Dignity not Poverty: A Minimum Income Standard for the UK* Commission on Social Justice Issue Paper 6 IPPR, London.

Young M (1974) *Poverty Report 1974* Temple Smith, London.

Endnotes

1. The proposal builds on that made in my 1993 Stevenson Lecture on Citizenship at the University of Glasgow, published in Atkinson (1996) and in the Eva Colorni Memorial Lecture in 1996, published in Barker (1996).

2. Like many innovations in the UK, a Poverty Report was first conceived in 1969 by Michael Young, and *Reports* were published under his editorship in the 1970s – see, for example, Young (1974).

5. A Poverty Report
by Chris Trinder

Poverty must be prevented and not just cured. To do this effectively it is crucial to anticipate poverty occurring and intervene early. My aim in this chapter is to show how a *Poverty Report* which is regularly produced by an independent authority, comprehensive and forward looking, could play an important part in achieving this. The Prime Minister, Tony Blair, is not opposed to this idea in principle. In combination with an official poverty target (see chapter 4) such a report could be a powerful policy tool in the battle against poverty.

Background

It is useful to put the case for a *Poverty Report* in historical perspective. In the mid-1970s Michael Young pioneered annual *Poverty Reports* at the Institute for Community Studies. During the 1980s and 1990s there have been numerous reports by academics, commissions of enquiries, charitable foundations and the Churches. One of the most important contributions was the *Joseph Rowntree Foundation Inquiry into Income and Wealth* chaired by Sir Peter Barclay, drawing together a wealth of data and analysis of inequality in the UK and setting out policy proposals (Barclay, 1995). The Churches' salvos in this area have created political storms – beginning with *Faith in the City* and ending with the Churches Enquiry, *Unemployment and the Future of Work* published during the 1997 Election campaign. Despite the excellence and wide dissemination of this work, it still has had only a limited impact on the operations of government policy.

There is of course widespread official material which explores low income. The Department of Social Security's (DSS) *Households Below Average Income* is the most extensive official data source on incomes and benefits. The DSS's Annual Departmental Reports draw together many of the effects of its policies on the bottom end of the income distribution and its individual research reports provide vital material on the effectiveness of particular areas of policy. This is to name just some of the data emanating from one department. However, despite the quality and extensiveness of the material, it suffers from two principal limitations: first, the analysis is confined to one department, it must be interdepartmental if the combined effects of principal areas of policy are to be understood and measured; second and more problematic is the in-built dilemma that the originators and implementors of policy cannot objectively assess their own record. Other kinds of official report, such as those conducted by the National Audit Office or Ofsted, try to meet this last point. They operate in areas where there are central targets and often local delivery with sometimes inadequate mechanisms of accountability. These reports provide useful intermediary information about changing institutional mechanisms. They are however usually focused on individual areas and do not address larger issues such as poverty or social exclusion.

Overall this body of research provides rich sources of material, but it remains largely composed of atomised pieces of work which are not integrated into an overall economic context. Economic indicators pay little attention to the issues of poverty and the analysis of poverty pays only passing reference to the economic context. Another important gap in the existing data is the failure to look ahead. Take the following example. The relationship between earnings and prices gives us what we call 'real' wage growth and shows how much of the fruits of economic growth is being passed on to workers. 'Real' wage growth of about 1.5 per cent is occurring in 1998. Economic growth in 1997, although slowing down throughout the year, was 3 per cent higher than a year earlier. The relevance of this information for a *Poverty Report* is that it focuses attention on different trends in living standards for different groups in the population in a very current way. So, with the economy growing by 3 per cent last year, how much, if any, did the poor share of these extra resources? Are they keeping up with the average worker? Who is getting the extra? The bulk of research on poverty tends not be current but historical. There are no predictions of poverty rates. One important consequence of this focus on the past is that research about poverty is not integrated into the policy processes of government departments, in particular the Treasury.

The Advantages of an official Poverty Report

Debates about poverty in recent years have been highly charged with opponents throwing statistics and counter statistics at each other. The debate is both ideological and technical. The ideological debate has touched on fundamental issues about the goals of policy – are they to provide minimum living standards, address inequality of outcome or opportunity? The technical arguments centre on a number of key issues such as whether the focus should be on income or expenditure, living standards over time or on a cross-sectional basis and appropriate adjustments for family size.

Each time the government releases official data on poverty these debates come into the public domain, baffling many of uninitiated and crucially detracting from the main issues on the causes of poverty and possible policies. The persistence of these wrangles suggests that while there is no agreement on an acceptable way of measuring poverty, arguments will continue to obscure the real debate about the nature of poverty and what to do about it. It is not that the ideological and technical issues are not important – they clearly are – they shape the kinds of policies that are needed and that they are acceptable. What is deeply unsatisfactory is the way in which the debate is conducted.

In contrast a *Poverty Report* would be authoritative. It would be comprehensive, analysing the key determinants of poverty, providing an overall analysis of changes in trends in both an economic and policy context. It would therefore enable policy makers and the public to assess change in the nature and extent of poverty 'in the light of their own actions' – showing how far they were the result of extraneous factors or policy changes. The overview of such reports is important in trying to counter the tendency for policy making to be focused within individual departments.

Parallels with other kinds of reports

Now let us look in more detail at a parallel report the Bank of England Inflation Report. For the first time in October 1992 the Conservative government announced the creation of a target range for inflation for the remainder of the Parliament and for the longer term. This was to be measured in a precise and widely recognised way. It was argued that the credibility of the policy depended on an acceptable definition and target for inflation and that it was important to explain clearly to Parliament how progress towards achieving the target was being assessed. The government therefore proposed changes to make policy more transparent and decisions more accountable. Hence the creation of the

Inflation Report which first appeared in February 1993.

The Chancellor believed it marked 'a welcome shift away from excessive secrecy' and would 'lead to an improvement in the way economic debate is conducted'. The Governor of the Bank of England called it 'a giant leap'; *The Inflation Report:*

'will offer a comprehensive guide to inflation. It will discuss in detail the past performance of a number of measures of inflation. And it will analyse, within a well-specified economic framework, the behaviour of the key determinants of inflation. It will not be restricted to a discussion of the past. In order to arrive at well informed policy decisions we must also take account of likely future developments, in both the short and medium term especially in the light of our own actions. The report will do precisely that. Our aim will be to produce a wholly objective and comprehensive analysis of inflationary trends and pressures which will put the Bank's professional competence on the line' (London School of Economics Lecture 11 November 1992).

The Governor also told the House of Commons Treasury and Civil Service Committee on 28 October 1992 that the policy of greater openness was a means of building a 'track record' and credibility by setting out 'clearly the basis along which the policy will work and also to accept this degree of openness about how the policy is evolving at any given moment so that people from the outside can test the credibility of the policy by using the same material as we ourselves use in reaching our conclusions'. *The Inflation Reports* were therefore to be comprehensive, current, providing analysis of the past as well as the future; objective and authoritative documents and importantly they were to serve a democratic purpose – making the policy process more visible and thus accountable, stimulating informed debate.

The latest *Inflation Report* is now produced under the guidance of the members of the Monetary Policy Committee. A key feature is its projection of inflation. A Poverty Report would predict future poverty in a similar way. The Inflation Report recognises it is impossible to assess the probabilities of different outcomes with any precision, but still makes projections saying the central one is the Monetary Policy Committee's 'best estimate'. Moreover, the projection for inflation does not stop there.

There is a band, which goes slightly either side of the central estimate. In the latest report it is between 2.6 per cent and 2.8 per cent for inflation in the year 2000. The Bank of England report warned that further increases in interest rates might be necessary if the government's inflation target is hit.

A second important feature of the inflation Report is its objectivity. The Bank does not take the government's assessments at face value. It looks at what the markets say is the central estimate on short and long term interest rates, building societies, banks and other independent experts on house prices, labour market experts on earnings forecasts and it then places all this information clearly into its chosen framework and assesses the consequences. The Treasury is there as an observer, not to influence the proceedings. a poverty committee, underpinned by a quarterly poverty report could be set up to work in the same way?

Another type of report that is worth drawing on is the Pay Review Body Report. Pay Review Body Reports have been published each year since 1971 for the armed forces; doctors and dentists; since 1984 for nurses and professions allied to medicine; and for teachers since 1988 as an interim advisory committee and 1992 as a Pay Review Body. The purpose of the Independent Pay Review Body reports is to recommend pay rates, which are appropriate to recruit, retain and motivate people of appropriate quality. These Reports are independently constructed, well researched and confront the government with the facts about each of the groups covered, however unpleasant they may be. These are eminently appropriate goals for the poverty debate.

Reproducing in the poverty arena what is now accepted as normal practice in relation to the government's inflation target, and in relation to the regular Pay Review Body Reports could be expected to add a new dimension to the battle against poverty.

How a poverty report might affect decision-making

The *Poverty Report* would enhance the way in which poverty is discussed in a number of ways. Firstly, it would be regarded as objective. The Inflation and Pay Review Body Reports continue to cause argument, for example in relation to the importance attached to the anti-inflation objective of policy – but they cannot be written off as biased as happens with much of the material on poverty. Second, it would open up the research agenda to a wider group of bodies and organisations, Third, it could tackle difficult questions such as the dynamics of poverty – who is on benefit and for how long, the concentration of poverty and deprivation in certain geographical areas, differences within groups, and also broader questions of motivation and encouragement. Instead of these being used to undermine the existence of poverty they could be tools to develop well-grounded policies. Fourth, it would stimulate strategic debate rather than the political tug of war which has characterised so much of the discussion of poverty. The Poverty Reports would be part of the process of trying to unveil the long term and difficult thinking about what to do about poverty.

An important aspect would be why policies are not achieving their desired effect. The government may need advice on strategies that will work. In the case of preventing poverty it may involve ensuring distributional objectives are given the importance they deserve. The lack of power of poor people means that they often cannot offset the effects of policies in the same way the rich do. A *Poverty Report* would act as a focus for informing the public and bringing wider participation in the debate. It would contribute to our material on what would prevent poverty. An independent body might also have a useful role in helping to set targets.

Conclusions

In this chapter I have made the case for a *Poverty Report* which is comprehensive and forward looking and provides a framework within which decisions can be made which prevent poverty occurring. This might seem a radical proposal for poverty, but it merely reproduces what is commonplace elsewhere in the economy. For too long poverty has been the 'poor relation' of government policy. It is time it was elevated to the policy summit, a place which it deserves.

The regularity of *Poverty Reports* would also distinguish them from one-off inquiries which provide an in-depth focus but which can be shelved by government without feeding into the policy process on a regular basis. The regular production of *Poverty Reports* would provide a framework and a purpose for the producers of research and statistics. We can see the way the *Inflation Reports* have become richer, more thorough, and better presented over the course of the 20 so far produced. Finally, the *Poverty Report* would look at future developments in the short and medium term and thus break the traditional focus of much policy making that is short term and heavily influenced by the electoral timetable.

References

Bank of England (1998) *Inflation Report*, February 1998

Barclay P (1995). *Joseph Rowntree Foundation Inquiry into Income and wealth*. Vols 1 and 2, Joseph Rowntree Foundation

Church of England Archbishop's Commission on Urban Priority Areas (1985) *Faith in the City*, Church House Publishing

Council of Churches for Britain and Ireland (1997) *Unemployment and the Future of Work, An Enquiry for the churches*, Council of Churches for Britain and Ireland

DSS (1997) *Households Below Average Income,a statistical analysis* 1979-1994/95 HMSO

Review Body on Doctors' and Dentists' Remuneration (1998) *28th report* Cm 3585

HM Treasury, (1998) *Budget 98: New ambitions for Britain*, House of Commons Paper 620

Trinder, C (1974) 'Incomes policy and the Low paid' in M Young (ed) *Poverty Report 1974*, Maurice Temple Smith.

Trinder, C (1975) 'Disposable resources of the working poor' in M Young (ed) *Poverty report 1975*, Maurice Temple Smith

Trinder, C (1976) ' Incomes of those not at work' in P Willmott (ed) *Sharing Inflation: Poverty Report 1976* Maurice Temple Smith.

6. A multi-dimensional approach to social exclusion indicators

by Catherine Howarth and Peter Kenway

> In economic management, in international development, and increasingly in environmental assessment, indicators play a key role in informing decision makers and the public. What we urgently need now are new indicators in Britain which focus on the people who get forgotten by conventional indicators of progress.   Glenys Kinnock MEP[1]

In a major speech on the subject of poverty in Sheffield in March the Prime Minister spoke of developing 'an anti-poverty strategy of the same ambition and breadth' as that of the post-war government. The Chancellor of the Exchequer, echoing the phrase used by the reforming American President, Lyndon Johnson, has also described the government as being engaged in a 'War on Poverty'.[2] Government spokesmen now link poverty with poor health and poor education. For this to be the *official* view of poverty is a very great change indeed.

If the vision laid out by the politicians is to succeed, it needs to be shared and understood by society at large. Not just politicians, their civil servants and a handful of experts, but the public too needs some means of tracking what is going on and gauging both the successes – and the failures – of what is being attempted.

Regular and consistent assessment is especially important because reducing poverty and social exclusion requires fundamental reform which will inevitably take time to have effect. The Prime Minister emphasised this when he launched the government's Social Exclusion Unit in December 1997.

The fact that no one government department is responsible for the poor and excluded has in the past been an obstacle to progress. The launch of the Social Exclusion Unit, charged with 'improving mechanisms for integrating the work of departments' was therefore a positive development. Acting on particular problems in a co-ordinated fashion is a crucial first step, but unless we simultaneously start to research and report poverty and exclusion in a holistic way the impetus to co-ordinate may be weakened.

In this Chapter we argue that what is needed is a regular report using a wide ranging set of poverty and social exclusion indicators that will allow consistent tracking to take place.

The scope of a poverty and social exclusion report

The view taken of what actually constitutes 'poverty and social exclusion' is the fundamental determinant both of the scope of such a report and the selection of indicators within it.

We argue for a broad definition of poverty, as not simply an inadequate level of material resources but a cluster of disadvantages, a lack of social, cultural and physical resources, as well as material ones. Clearly, low income is an essential, or necessary, component of poverty, but it is not on its own enough to condemn people to poverty. The duration of time spent on low income and the frequency of such spells are factors that turns low income into poverty. The availability of other resources, financial or non-financial, from friends and family must also be considered.

This implies a need for a range of poverty indicators, stretching beyond low income. It will not be enough to see incomes at the bottom of the distribution rise, in absolute or relative terms, if other inequalities in health, housing and educational attainment persist. A *Poverty Report* focusing solely on changes in income would fail to represent the breadth of disadvantages that constitute poverty.

Social exclusion has come rapidly into common usage in Britain in the past year, though it is far from yet having a settled meaning. Many people see poverty and social exclusion as fundamentally similar, differing only in the degree of deprivation each represents. For some, the 'socially excluded' are a particularly disadvantaged sub-group of the poor; while for others, social exclusion is a less acute but more widely experienced condition than poverty. The fact that 'social exclusion' can apparently stand in two, quite different, relationships to 'poverty' may well explain its widespread appeal.

A second definition of social exclusion sees it as something fundamentally distinct from poverty. This more esoteric view regards poverty as an outcome and social exclusion as a process that has failed: 'the malfunctioning', as one recent report puts it, 'of the major societal systems that should guarantee the social integration of the individual or household'.[3] These systems may include the labour market, the welfare state, the legal system and the political system as well as family and the community.

This second definition of social exclusion has a number of advantages. First, it shifts the focus from effects (poverty) to causes (social exclusion), thereby drawing attention towards possible solutions. Second, the detrimental effects of particular 'failing social institutions' are often widely felt. Those living on low income are likely to suffer the greatest disadvantage from such failures and they may be likely, too, to gain the greatest benefit from remedying them. But where adverse effects are more widely felt, the extent of popular support for remedial action will also be broader.

Seeing social exclusion as something fundamentally different from poverty, rather than as a subset (or superset) of it, is crucial to our argument that any official report should concentrate on both. The concept of social exclusion adds a new dimension to the subject of deprivation and disadvantage. Not moving beyond poverty alone would, as we have already argued, be a missed opportunity.

Equally, however, we believe it is not enough to focus on social exclusion while ignoring low income and poverty more generally. The relationship between low income and other disadvantages such as poor health is notoriously complex. In the past governments have avoided exploring or confronting that relationship. Now that poverty and social exclusion have become matters of official concern it would be a waste to see a report on poverty and social exclusion in Britain not contribute towards a deeper understanding of the dynamic relationship between low income and other forms of disadvantage.

The DSS Green Paper, *New Ambitions for our Country: A New Contract for Welfare*[4] took a similar line in many respects to the one we argue for in this Chapter. The implicit view of poverty and social exclusion taken in the paper was a broad one, with chapters covering subjects from literacy and housing to disability and unemployment. By introducing a series of 'success measures' the paper showed that the government sees a diverse set of statistics as a useful means of monitoring progress. Conspicuously, however, the Green Paper had little to say about poverty itself, relative or absolute, or about a level of income the government regards as inadequate. This is a significant shortcoming of the Green Paper. To focus on the processes of social exclusion while disregarding poverty outcomes is to leave out of the picture what is in the end the purpose of the whole exercise. Any set of indicators which purports to monitor poverty and social exclusion must address directly and together both low income and a range of other deprivations.

What a poverty and social exclusion report could offer

A national *Poverty Report* would be a public document based around a set of key indicators. Its basic aim would be to serve as a framework for a public debate on poverty and social exclusion, providing a substantial amount of information in each edition cumulatively showing the pace and degree of change. To succeed in that, it must achieve three things.

- First, it needs to be published regularly, possibly every year, with each key indicator being updated in each edition.

- Second, since many indicators, especially those showing income distributions, are hotly debated by politicians and experts, the arguments around them need to be presented impartially. Contentious interpretation would need to be clearly sign-posted and separated from more basic descriptive passages.

- Third, as a document aimed at a wide audience including politicians, local authority councillors and officials, charities and pressure groups, public libraries, business, and private individuals, the report must use accessible language and present the basic data as clearly as possible using charts, maps and tables.

One of the most interesting perspectives to have emerged over recent years is the geography of poverty and social exclusion. From variations across regions, wards or parliamentary constituencies, we understand far better now how location affects people's experiences and the risks they face. A poverty and social exclusion report must provide a sense of how different areas compare both on an absolute level and in terms of rates of improvement.

Although the report we envisage here would be focused on Britain, it should be rooted in an awareness of developments abroad, both practical approaches to eradicating poverty and exclusion, and developments in academic thinking on these two issues (see chapter 4). An example would be the United Nations World Summit on Social Development in 1995 at which the UK, along with over one hundred other countries, signed up to reporting its progress on eradication of poverty. Other countries took the commitment more seriously than the UK and instituted well researched and planned anti-poverty programmes. Ireland is a good example where people living in poverty were involved in the development of the strategy and its targets.

The indicators themselves ought to be internationally comparable wherever possible, placing the British situation in context. The policy approach in this country has been very different in a number of areas from that of other Europeans, notably on labour markets and social security payments. A report could show different outcomes on an international basis and whether the differences are fading or growing over time. For example, the European Commission's statistical bureau, Eurostat, defines a person as being 'poor' if they have a net income of below 50 per cent of average income in his or her country. This threshold is the same as one in the DSS's *Households Below Average Income* report. Eurostat's data shows how Britain compares to her European partners in absolute levels of poverty, in levels of domestic inequality, and in some of the dynamic processes which affect the poorest, especially their experience of the labour market. A poverty and social exclusion report in the UK should make maximum use of these sources as well as domestic statistical material.

Examples of other indicator-based reports

Researching other countries' poverty reports, and indicator-based reports on other subjects in this country, shows the potential value of a poverty and social exclusion report in Britain.

The UN's *Human Development Report*[5] is a key model, showing how a wide selection of indicators can increase public understanding of the problems. This annual report presents international comparisons using a definition of poverty which focuses on 'denial of choices and opportunities' as well as lack of material resources. Its composite Human Development Index, made up of a broad group of variables, ranks the world's countries according to a weighting formula. The rest of the report is divided into chapters discussing measurement and definitions, discussions of countries which have moved up or down the ranking, economic causes of poverty, and the politics of poverty eradication. The way that the report ranks and marks progress over several years using a constant set of variables has gained it wide attention. Many poorer countries have focused great attention on improving their scores. The broad view of poverty developed in the Human Development Report has encouraged a more sophisticated understanding of how poverty operates as a process. Inclusion of indicators on educational imbalances, on social investment, and women's political and economic participation have provoked greater thoughtfulness on the role these elements play in alleviating poverty and promoting human development.

Another example is *Poverty in the United States*[6], an annual document, officially produced, showing the number of people below the US poverty line. Using a variety of absolute measures of poverty, this report breaks down the national figures by state, and also by individuals' age, race, place of birth, family composition and work history. It shows the ratio of income to the poverty line, demonstrating how far below it people fall.

The strength of the US report lies in its predictability and authority. Using the same definition of poverty each year has allowed meaningful comparisons to be made over a time span of more than thirty years. Journalists are aware of its publication date and are able to line up specialist commentators to discuss the significance and reasons for yearly changes. The variety of data breakdowns gives a picture of which groups and areas are falling behind or making progress. Analysis of the policies and circumstances which may have contributed to these changes can then be carried out independently.

In the UK, the Employment Policy Institute's quarterly *Employment Audit* has provided a focus for a more informed debate on unemployment. This is an alternative and independent report in which a new set of labour market indicators have been devised. Indicators, such as International Labour Organisation's unemployment measure, are used but they have been placed alongside alternative ones with different emphases. It shows how a mix of old, familiar indicators with new ones can be extremely effective. Some of its new indicators are now widely quoted in the media and by politicians.

Importantly, a report on poverty and social exclusion could both reflect and embody the importance which the government attaches to these problems. As both Atkinson and Trinder explain in their Chapters, the Bank of England's quarterly Inflation Report serves as an example of this. Introduced in 1992, the reports were part of an effort to improve policy making and accountability. The then Chancellor of the Exchequer argued that the report would raise the standard of economic debate in the country. What can be done for inflation can also be achieved for poverty and social exclusion. As with inflation, there are various ways of measuring income poverty, and these should be included in the report so that people can understand how they compare. In 1998, the government is not faced with a comparable crisis to the one which precipitated the Inflation Report, which is one reason why an initial poverty and social exclusion report should be developed independently of government. In time, however, it too could become an official publication.

Choosing the indicators

There are, of course, practical restrictions on the indicators which could be used in a poverty and social exclusion report. For example, all indicators must be capable of being updated regularly, which imposes limits particularly on any use of more 'subjective' indicators.

Table 6.1 shows examples of indicators that could be included in a poverty and social exclusion report. This broad range of indicators points up the fact that the report envisaged here would not attempt to produce a composite index that gives a catch-all definition of poverty or social exclusion. Neither would it suggest a poverty line. Instead, this approach is much more that of a 'scorecard' where each indicator appears independently instead of disappearing into an amalgam.

One advantage of this is flexibility, allowing new indicators to be introduced or others to be removed without damaging the integrity of the rest. Another advantage is that it lets people focus on what matters most to them: perhaps pensioner poverty, or long term unemployment, or child poverty. This approach makes it possible for particular details to emerge as well as an overall picture.

This approach varies considerably from that adopted by the

Table 6.1
Indicators for a poverty and social exclusion report

Chapter	Thematic Group	Description
Income	Distribution	% of individuals in households with < 1/2 average income.
	Missing the safety net	% of individuals entitled to but not taking up Income Support payments.
		% individuals suffering deductions from Income Support.
Children	Health	% of babies born underweight
		Rate of mortality due to injury and poisoning
	Education	% of eleven year olds failing to acquire basic skills in numeracy and literacy
		% of primary schools with high concentrations of poor children
	Social stability	% of health authorities with conception rates for girls under 16 > twice average
		% of children permanently excluded from secondary school
		% of children whose parents have divorced in the last year
Young adults (aged 16-25)	Economic circumstances	% of young adults on wage rates below the national minimum wage (to be set)
	Health and well-being	% of young people committing suicide
		% of young people who are drug addicts
	Barriers to work	% of 19 year-olds without a basic educational or training qualification.
		% of wards where 18-25 year-old unemployment rate > twice average
		% of young people in prison or young offenders institutions
		% of young people who are homeless
Adults	Health	% of adults reporting poor health
	Lack of work	% of households where no-one is in work
		% of the workforce unemployed one year or more
	Working conditions	% of the workforce working more than 48 hours per week
		% of the workforce on less than half the median male hourly rate of pay
		% of the workforce without employment rights
	Longer term prospects	% of adults without pension arrangements
Pensioners	Economic circumstances	% of pensioners on the state retirement pension and means tested benefits alone
		% of expenditure by pensioner households on essentials
	Health	% of pensioners reporting health problems that severely limit their activity
	Access to support	% of pensioner households without a telephone
		% of pensioners with no involvement in any civic organisation or group
		% of pensioners over 70 years old whom Local Authorities help to live independently at home
Communities	Economic circumstances	% of wards with > twice the average proportion of residents on Income Support
		% of mortgage holders suffering repossession
	Housing conditions	% of tenant households that are overcrowded
	Crime and its cost	Violent crime rates in Police Force areas

Department of Environment's Index of Local Conditions, which is a composite index. It was designed with practical functions in mind, particularly the allocation of resources to areas of high deprivation. A poverty and social exclusion report would need to include indicators which respond in sensible ways to government initiatives addressing poverty and social exclusion as they start to take effect, relating the effects of policies to wider changes in levels of poverty. For example, if training and basic skills improve through the government's initiatives, will that reduce poverty, and, if so, whose poverty? A poverty and social exclusion report could only make a start on this, partly because the impact of policies takes time to have an effect, and partly because they will in many cases require special studies by experts to establish the answers. But providing a public and accessible summary of the effects of policy is one of the most important things that a regular report on poverty and social exclusion would achieve.

Conclusion

Statistics are not value free. They change our perceptions and priorities however objective they are. By putting a spotlight on poverty and social exclusion a report such as the one described in this paper could deepen awareness of a broad set of interrelated problems, and in time increase the importance that society attaches to them.

Endnotes

1. Kinnock G (1998) *Preface to Monitoring Poverty and Social Exclusion: Why Britain needs A Key Indicators Report* New Policy Institute, London

2. Brown G (1998) Interview in the *New Statesman*.

3. Shucksmith M *et al* (1997) *Poverty and Exclusion in Rural Britain*, Joseph Rowntree Foundation, York

4. Department of Social Security (1998) *New Ambitions for our Country: A New Contract for Welfare*, The Stationary Office.

5. United Nations Development Programme (1997) *Human Development Report 1997*, Oxford University Press.

6. Lamison-White L (1997) *Poverty in the United States: 1996*, U.S. Department of Commerce, Bureau of the Census.

7. Comment: Poverty targets and reports
by Gerald Holtham

Tony Atkinson's proposition is that 'Reducing poverty would become an explicit object of policy'. I accept that as appropriate and discuss only whether and how an official poverty target is a good means to go about it. To buttress the target, a *Poverty Report* by the Office of National Staistics (ONS) is also proposed. The ONS would act independently and report on the extent to which poverty targets were achieved, quite separately from the operation of government policy.

A *Poverty Report* seems to be an idea with few drawbacks. It already has the support of the Prime Minister in principle. It is a useful means to focus attention and mobilise political will. It is a potentially potent 'self-embarrassment' instrument to ensure that government continues to take the problems seriously. It could inform the public and raise the quality of discussion about issues. The development of the report over time, in the hands of a competent and independent agency, could also refine and focus the collection and collation of data and so contribute a valuable resource for policy research and the design of policy itself.

The idea of a target, to accompany the report is attractive but raises some difficulties.

As Atkinson notes, a single target can distort policy by leading it to focus on the symptoms of the problem, relief of which would do most to achieve compliance with the target. There is no shortage of examples where the existence of a target distorts the behaviour both of policy-makers and those who are influenced by the policy in question, whether professionals or the target group. The practice of targeting hospital waiting lists may be a case in point, creating an arguably adverse incentive for hospitals seeking additional funds and focusing policy on measures that may be peripheral to public health.

The importance of an independent report is clear in that context. It can draw attention to any deleterious effects that stem from a wrong-headed focus on a single target. I would argue that one could have the report without the target but it would be a mistake to have the target without the report.

Another approach is to have not simply a poverty target, expressed in terms of absolute or relative income levels of the poorest but a range of targets. These could include other indicators of relative or absolute deprivation. It is well known, for example, that the poor often have worse access to public services like education and healthcare than the better off. While a range of targets lessens the risk of counter-productive policies, it also raises issues of its own. Will a multiplicity of targets obscure the political impact a single target could have? Will there be trade-offs among the targets and, if so, how would the different elements be weighted? How could government policy be assessed; would nearly hitting every target be better or worse than hitting some and missing others by miles?

It has been suggested that a consensus over the appropriate targets, perhaps resolving that sort of difficulty, could be obtained by invoking another quasi-independent body such as the Low Pay Commission. However, that seems even more problematic. Would the government be bound by a target set by another body? Would it not have an incentive to disparage the target as inappropriate? Self-embarrassment may work but the government could resist embarrassment by others.

There is also a danger in targets that are not hit within a few years. They can come to seem purely formal, even ornamental, an aspiration which everyone is supposed to profess but no-one is expected to fulfill. Consider, the UN target of giving 0.7 per cent of GDP in aid to poorer countries. The Labour government recently 'reaffirmed' this target. Yet it has never been achieved once in the thirty-odd years of its existence. Currently British aid is at less than half the target amount. The government has not announced any programme which suggests that it will reach the target and no-one expects it to do so. Even embarrassment fades with time so that the government is not apparently sheepish about its odd use of the word reaffirm.

This experience strongly suggests that the government must set any target and be seen to take responsibility for it. The target should also not be too ambitious or remote. If it is, no-one will expect it to be achieved in the short-term and its political potency may well have dwindled by the time a reckoning has to be made. Targets should be reasonably short-term and realistic. They can always be rolled out into a programme of successive targets for the elimination of poverty over the longer run. The inflation target, which Atkinson cites as an example of successful use of targets to build policy momentum and credibility, derives much of its force from the fact that it is annual.

One other criticism of the poverty target in comparison with the inflation target is that the latter is made the responsibility of a public body which is given control of a policy instrument to achieve it. However, there is no point in over-drawing the comparison. I see it as one of the advantages of the proposed poverty target that while it commits the government to seeking an outcome it does not foreclose its choice of strategy far less policy instruments to achieve it. On the evidence of the government's approach so far, it might prefer to target 'social exclusion' rather than poverty. That would surely commit it to a complex target or a range of simple ones, with the difficulties mentioned above but it would also force a practical definition of social exclusion, which could be no bad thing.

On balance, the idea of a *Poverty Report* seems clearly a good one. And the idea of a poverty target, or perhaps targets, certainly merits serious consideration.

III:
Employment, taxes and benefits

8. Taxes, benefits and paid work
by Eithne McLaughlin

For the purposes of this chapter, poverty is taken to mean that poor individuals have (too) low regular incomes, hold few or no material assets, occupy a poor quality physical and social environment (and therefore have few non-material, or social, assets), and experience all three simultaneously.

Such poverty, when it continues for more than a few months, will be 'felt' or experienced as restriction, exclusion, and alienation, and will cause poorer physical and mental health and lower educational achievement than would otherwise be the case for the individual concerned. It is traditional in both social democratic and modern liberal perspectives to argue that the role of the state – through the provision of cash benefits, tax exemptions and publicly funded services – is to both prevent and alleviate such poverty. If both aims are to be met, policy responses must be able to accommodate, and target, the complexity of people's lives. They can: grow up in poverty as children; 'grow into' poverty as young adults; fall into poverty later in adulthood; stay in poverty for substantial periods of their working age lives; and 'end up' in poverty (that is, when over retirement age); although these are not necessarily discrete.

This chapter is concerned more narrowly with the role of paid work, taxes and benefits in relation to social exclusion – or more precisely the interaction between these. The total absence of paid work can of course cause social exclusion if it continues for a considerable period of time and provided the individuals concerned are not independently wealthy. Certain types of paid work may also be associated with social exclusion or, more especially, the risk of social exclusion at some stage in a person's future life course (for example, after state pension age). The importance of paid work in relation to social exclusion is shown by the way that, over the last two decades, the poor have become increasingly likely to be in non-elderly households without a head in work. Nonetheless, falls in, or loss of, the earnings of a household head have explained only a minority of 'falls into' poverty in both the US and the UK. Nearly a third – 30 per cent – of events coinciding with the beginning of a spell of income poverty in Britain in the period 1990-1994 were of this type (Jarvis and Jenkins, 1997). Nearly half of 'falls' into income poverty in recent times have been due to changes in household composition in both the US and UK.

Whether there is a connection between these kinds of poverty-inducing changes in household composition and losses of earnings/unemployment, is something which has provoked emotional debate, but rather little rigorous research, on both sides of the Atlantic. In terms of preventing and/or ending long-term poverty and social exclusion, however, we do need to bear in mind that it has been earnings generated by more than one household member which has been the primary and most sustainable route out of poverty. In other words, if losses of earning/unemployment coincide with household dissolution, then, whether the relationship is causal or not, routes out of poverty will be difficult to find. Despite shortcomings in the research base, policy-makers should consider:

- the effect of the tax/benefit system on incentives and disincentives to take and keep any, or particular forms of, paid work in the short-term;

- the influence, *if any*, of the particular labour market/tax/benefit regime on patterns of household formation, maintenance and dissolution.

The provision of social security/income maintenance benefits is not, in terms of social exclusion and inclusion, for the foreseeable future, a substitute for labour market participation among those of working age. But this leaves open important questions about the relative balance between market-generated income and social security-generated income over the 45 or so years of an individual's working-age life. The question of balance is not just about individual circumstances, or the social necessity of the unpaid work many people provide, important as these are. It is also about changes in the labour market itself; changes which have reduced the opportunity for some social groups to participate substantially. These include sustained periods of low levels of labour demand in specific localities and regions, and the development over the last 20 years or so of 'non-standard' or 'atypical' jobs – some of which (for example, 'part-time' jobs) are now so significant a part of the labour market that they can no longer justifiably be termed 'atypical'. This chapter is concerned with tax/benefit reform in relation to access to paid work and the next section notes the nature of labour market developments which have implications for such reform. For reasons of space, I have been unable to include discussion of the special needs and circumstances of jobless people who have disabilities. (Howard, 1998).

Labour market developments

There have been three main labour market developments which have radical implications for tax/benefit policies. Firstly, rises in women's participation, secondly, the development of non-standard forms of employment, and thirdly, decreases in men's employment rates and the decline of the male family wage. While the average hours worked by both men and women have not changed a great deal in the past twenty years, traditional work patterns are now less common. As The Treasury recently noted: 'only 10 percent now work... a 'standard' 40 hour week, compared to 25 per cent in Germany and 45 percent in France and Italy.' (HM Treasury, 1997).

Such labour market developments are well-known but three difficulties stand out. First, the growth in non-standard forms of work has been more 'gendered' or sex-segregated in the UK than elsewhere (Gornick and Jacobs, 1994). Second, given the development of 'bits' of jobs, no one of which provides enough for the individual to subsist on a long-term basis, how can we define the appropriate balance between, and respective obligations of, capital and state in the future? Thirdly, what are the implications of the growth of non-standard employment and the decline of standard/male employment for the economic security and maintenance of households? It is these three issues which tax/benefit (and other policy) reforms need to address.

The gendered nature of non-standard work in the UK may be partly to do with the preferential treatment the tax/benefit system provides to households with a full-time and part-time earner. 'The incentives for second earners to take jobs, particularly [small] part-time jobs, are large' (Meadows, 1997). This effect of personal taxation has been reinforced by the national insurance system which involved neither employer nor employee payments below a certain earnings threshold. In contrast, for those relying on social security benefits (for example, lone mothers, unemployed couples), there has been no similar preferential treatment of 'small' jobs. However, also of importance has been continued gender inequality in wage rates and lower hourly rates among part-timers than full-timers, even if both are of the same sex. Both of these problems may be eased by the introduction of a national minimum wage, discussed in the next section, as well as reforms of the tax/benefit system.

To turn to the second issue (the growth of 'small' jobs), the labour market flexibility signified by the development of non-standard forms of work has been advocated as a means of improving economic competitiveness, reducing unemployment, and enhancing equal opportunities through the possibilities flexible forms of labour may offer for reconciling work and family life. Yet numerical flexibility (forms of flexibility designed to enable employers to match their workforce more closely to peaks and troughs in demand, such as temporary, fixed term, subcontracted, unsocial hours, part-time work, annualised hours, zero hours contracts and term-time working), cannot be assumed to make a positive contribution towards all these different policy goals. Much numerical flexibility presupposes the existence of a second source of income – another job, a partner or social security income. As Rubery (1997) put it, subsistence has become divorced from the pay for individual jobs. As a result, it is possible that some or all of these forms of flexibility shift some of the burden of maintenance of labour used onto either the state or indeed other employers (via the wages paid to employees who are themselves the partners of someone in a 'flexible' job; see McLaughlin, 1995). Neither the implications for economic competitiveness nor for the 'public good' have so far been thought through.

The third issue – the 'construction' of economic viability and sustainability of households in a labour market where entrance and re-entrance is skewed towards non-standard forms of paid work – is more of a problem in some localities and regions than others, and for some social groups than others. There is some evidence that decisions about marriage, relationships and having children may be deterred or deferred by job insecurity and of course long-term unemployment. 'Household strategies' are interdependent with 'employment strategies', with gender roles mediating between these (Bradley, 1997; Crompton, 1997; Gershuny et al, 1994). In addition, labour market trends unfriendly to household formation and maintenance have probably been exacerbated by two decades of heavy reliance on means-testing.

In the UK more of the unemployed are means-tested, and means-tested earlier, than in continental European countries and in the USA (for opposite reasons, of course). The impact of such extensive means-testing has, again, spatial features – just as long-term unemployment is unevenly distributed both regionally and at the level of localities, so too is means-testing. Such means-testing has extended to low-paid people in work as well (Evans, 1996b). As Parker (1995) notes, the 1970s tax/benefit experiments in the US suggested increased rates of marital dissolution accompanied increased rates of means-testing, but the converse – increased individualisation in tax/benefit regimes – has not so far had sufficient attention paid to it in UK policy-making and debate. Increased 'individualisation' is also of course effected by increased participation of women in employment. The gap between those couples affected by extensive means-testing on the one hand, and those whose lives are 'individualised' through dual participation in the labour market, on the other, has never been greater; a gap often described in terms of the growing concentration into workless and work-rich households.

Wage rates, a national minimum wage and the tax/benefit system

The nature of deregulation of the labour market pursued in the UK for the last two decades, has given rise to a significant proportion of jobs, the pay rates and weekly wages of which are low relative to social security benefits, even though the level of the latter has been reduced in relative terms.[1] (It is, however, easy (and common) to over-estimate the effect such factors have in the causes and continuation of unemployment over time, a point to which I will return later.)

Low wage rates have been more common than often thought, partly because the most commonly used source of earnings data – the New Earnings Survey – excludes those earning too little to pay national insurance contributions. Close to one in eight employees in the Labour Force Survey[2] – 11.2 per cent in Great Britain and 12.4 per cent in Northern Ireland – had weekly earnings below the lower earnings limit for national insurance contributions during the 1993-1996 period. Among this group of employees, median hourly rates of pay among adults (19 or more) were £3.00 in Northern Ireland and £3.25 in Great

Britain among women, and £2.00 and £3.00 in Northern Ireland and Great Britain respectively among men (McLaughlin *et al*, forthcoming).[3] The introduction of a National Minimum Wage (NMW) should begin to stem this particular tide. In addition, a NMW allows a reconsideration of the relationship between earnings and tax/benefit support. A NMW cannot itself 'fix' the problem of jobs whose aggregate, rather than hourly, earnings are too low to sustain individuals or households (because of low number of hours of work). On the other hand, its introduction does permit serious discussion of what constitutes being 'in-work' from the point of view of income maintenance policy.

Social security policy uses 16 hours a week of paid work as the boundary between classifying someone as 'in work' and 'out of work' with the treatment of earnings being very different on either side of this boundary. A further boundary exists at 30 hours, where Family Credit, and now the Working Families Tax Credit, gives an additional 'incentive' payment to those working more than 30 hours. Neither the use of 16 hours, rather than 15 or 17 or whatever, nor 30 hours, has been the result of applying logical considerations. Indeed, that would have been impossible in an environment without a NMW. Thus, the introduction of a NMW calls for an informed policy debate to begin about whether 16 hours is the best boundary to use as the dividing line between people being in or out of work for social security purposes (and whether the 30 hours additional boundary serves a sufficiently useful function to justify the additional expenditure involved). Such discussion will revolve around the number of hours of work at the NMW which are judged, post-tax, to provide a minimally acceptable income for an individual adult.

Tax/benefit reforms and the 1998 budget

Tax/benefit reforms cannot single-handedly solve problems of poverty and social exclusion, but must be part of wider change. Even in relation to the specific issue of paid work (in contrast to, for example, policies about unpaid work), the role of tax/benefit reform should not be overestimated. Firstly, a nationally applicable tax/benefit system is inevitably a blunt instrument with which to tackle the consequences of widely varying labour markets at local and regional level. Secondly, spatial

---

Table 8.1
Working families tax credit

The example below compares outcomes for a one earner and two earner cohabiting couple under WFTC, given the published features of the scheme at the time of writing (March 1998; see HM Treasury, 1998). Personal tax liabilities are estimates, given that these depend on taxable income other than earnings, and assets. In addition, housing costs and benefits are ignored for reasons of simplicity. CB below denotes child benefit. Disposable income refers to net income after childcare expenditure. The difference between the disposable incomes of the two cases is £219.35 – £182.90, or £36.45 per week. In the first couple, therefore, the second earner is employed for 38.5 hours at £4 an hour for a net gain of about £1 per hour.

A. Two earners, cohabiting, one pre-school child, each working 38.5 hours a week at £4 an hour. Child care costs of £75 a week.

Earnings	£153.85 each gross
	est. £131 each net per week
	£262 joint net earnings
WFTC	+32.35
Made up of:	+48.80
	+14.85
	+10.80
	+52.50 (70% of £75)
	−94.60 (55% of 262-90=172)
Gross income	£262 + 32.35 + CB = 294.35 + CB
Disposable income	£294.35 – £75 childcare expenditure + CB
	= £219.35 + CB

B. One earner, cohabiting couple, one pre-school child, one working 38.5 hours a week at £4 an hour; other partner at home full-time.

Earnings	£153.85 gross per week
	est. £131 net per week
WFTC	+51.90
Made up of	+48.80
	+14.85
	+10.80
	-22.55 (55% of 131-90=41)
Gross income	£131 + 51.90 + CB = £182.90 + CB
Disposable income	£182.90 + CB

---

programmes of social and economic development and high quality public employment services probably have far more importance in relation to reducing long-term unemployment than tweakings of the tax/benefit system. The latter, however, dominated the 1998 Budget because of the announcement of the Working Families Tax Credit

(WFTC). The WFTC should be regarded as a supplement to the New Deal, not a centrepiece. In addition, the 1998 Budget contained a national insurance reform intended to increase job-creation. Nonetheless, some of the language used to announce WFTC could be criticised as misleading since it implied that a tax/benefit reform like WFTC could 'solve' unemployment.

The working families tax credit

The usual area of concern in reform of the tax/national insurance/benefit systems has been the incentives of actual or potentially low earners (especially unemployed men, though also in more recent years, lone mothers) to supply labour to 'full-time' jobs. There is, however, little evidence to suggest that disincentives have been the principle cause of either unemployment generally or long-term unemployment (although they may contribute to a general sense of alienation, low expectations and hopelessness among long-term unemployed people).

The 1998 Budget's principal reform – the WFTC – has, nonetheless, continued this pattern of concern. The WFTC will, compared with its predecessor family credit, reduce marginal tax rates for both first and second earners in, or moving into, low-paid jobs, move the highest marginal tax rates further up the income scale, and extend assistance with childcare costs. As such it probably represents the furthest one could go, in terms of redressing the decline of the economic viability and security of low income households, using a 'means-tested' type of approach. The additional assistance with childcare costs should reduce the depressive effect of family credit on second earners (full-time) labour supply, but the 'means-tested' nature of the measure means the challenge of 'individualisation' has been avoided. WFTC also does little to address the 'gendered' growth of non-standard forms of work, particularly given: the continuation of the 16 hour rule for the main earner; the availability of childcare assistance only when the second earner also works at least 16 hours; and the failure to introduce reforms in the way earnings are treated on the out-of-work side of the 16 hour divide. Finally, a great deal of the effect of the WFTC will rest on the extent to which it really can be marketed as an 'income guarantee'. The level of any form of financial support which depends on detailed assessment of income and assets can never be guaranteed in advance of the assessment. This was true of family credit and it remains true of WFTC. The complexity of WFTC means that unemployed and jobless individuals are very unlikely to be able to work out for themselves what level of support they would recieve if they found a job. Thus, the 'guarantee' element will have to come from aggressive marketing and careful presentation rather than the features of the scheme itself, and from the quality and availability of advice to potential WFTC claimants.

National insurance contributions

The other reform in the 1998 Budget of interest to the theme of this chapter concerned national insurance contributions. The level of wages at which employers pay national insurance contributions was raised from £64 in 1998/99 to £81 in 1999/2000. Together with the removal of what has been called 'the entry fee' (that is, the conversion of what was the lower earnings limit into a national insurance free allowance of £81 for all), the assumption is that this reduction in non-wage costs will lead to employers creating more jobs. Obviously any increase in labour demand is to be welcomed. However, the type of demand most likely to result will entail a heavy commitment from the public purse through WFTC if these 'extra' jobs are to support previously unemployed couples or lone mothers.

The issue of employees' national insurance contributions needs to be considered separately, given the implications of non-payment of contributions for individuals' social security both before and after retirement age. My own view is that the payment of national insurance contributions on all earnings should be reconsidered as an option. It opens the possibility, both politically and in technical ways, for the extension of social insurance protection to at least some of those currently excluded from it. The more ephemeral effects on personal, social and political identities, too, of being 'included' through even small payments of national insurance, should not be overlooked.

The national insurance system, before the 1998 Budget, had a graduated basis so that contributions were charged at 2 per cent on earnings up to £62 a week (1997/8 figures), if at least £62 was earned. It is difficult to see what harm would have been done to employees by introducing the payment of 2 per cent of earnings below £62 for those who did not earn more than £62 a week since the maximum contribution required would have been £1.24 a week. Given the calculation of WFTC (and previously other means-tested benefits) on net, not gross, earnings, if contributions were required on all earnings, earners in the WFTC net would have their contributions in effect rebated by 45 percent. For others, the amount of contribution required, if set at a level like 2 per cent, is too low to pose a serious disincentive problem, and must be set against the benefits accruing from national insurance scheme membership. The only real disadvantage is that employers would incur the administrative costs of 'returning' all employees, rather than only those earning above £81 a week, to the Inland Revenue.

The alternative is to introduce 'credits' of national insurance contributions for those on low earnings, and this seems to be the direction currently being investigated by government – the 1998 Budget declared an intention to pursue, though only for those earning between £64 and £81 a week, protection of the benefit entitlement of employees when the threshold for payment of contributions rises from £64 to £81. It is difficult to see how such protection or crediting could operate without administrative costs for employers, leaving this proposal with little advantage over the levy of a small proportional payment of contributions by employees on all earnings. In addition, if protection / crediting is only introduced for those earning between £64 and £81, new equity issues arise. There will be those earning less than £64 a week and not being credited with contributions through any other route, those earning less than £64 and being credited through another route (for example, child benefit), and those earning between £64 and £81 a week who are protected or credited in some way. Crediting of national insurance contributions is a much bigger issue than merely protection of the benefit entitlement of those directly affected by an increase in the threshold for contributions from £64 to £81.

What other tax/benefit reforms could promote social inclusion?

The previous section has reviewed two areas of reform in the 1998 Budget. This section comments on other measures which could usefully be considered in the interests of the promotion of social inclusion. These are: in the longer-term, a reduction in the low income population's exposure to 'means-testing' (which means consideration of reform to the WFTC); and in the shorter-term, changes in the treatment of earnings for those deemed to be out of work and transitional financial arrangements for those moving between unemployment/jobless and 'full-time' paid work.

Reducing means-testing

Leaving aside the issue of housing needs and support, there are two principle ways of reducing the extent of means-testing – firstly, expansion of the national insurance system and secondly reform of the pattern of support for children. To take the latter, the Canadian experience documented by Mendelson (1998) suggests directions in which the WFTC, child benefit and income support could evolve in the UK. Over the next few years, the Canadian Child Tax Benefit (CCTB) will create a situation where the level of (income related) cash support received by families when out of work is the same as the level of support (also paid in cash) received by families when one or both parents are in work. The CCTB will replace all three of the previous Child Tax Benefit, Working Income Supplement (WIS, modelled on the US Earned Income Tax Credits (EITC) and introduced in 1993), and the 'scale rate' allowances paid in respect of children on welfare benefits. The reasons for the quick demise of the WIS in Canada in favour of the CCTB are instructive. They included the problems: that high marginal tax rates have to continue up to some point of the income distribution under schemes like the US's EITC and the UK's WFTC; poor 'additionality' (that is, very few people were in work who would not have been but for the existence of the WIS);[4] and poor redistribution.

The CCTB will provide benefits to about 85 percent of Canadian families, extending well into the reaches of the middle income groups, with the level of support gradually declining until it ends at around $65,000 of earned income. It is intended to be, and will be, an income which will transfer 'seamlessly' from the out-of-work to the in-work state and so assist people in making these transitions with a modicum of security. The new Canadian system has many similarities with proposals in the UK for increased levels of child benefit, particularly those proposals which incorporate an element of vertical redistribution through taxation or withdrawal of all or part of child benefit from those on high income.

The second way to reduce exposure to means-testing in the population as a whole, rather than those with children specifically, concerns expansion of the national insurance system. The individualising effect of a greater role for national/social insurance remains an important issue to be considered in tax/benefit reform and its connection to labour market issues, both directly and indirectly (i.e. through household effects). Such expansion involves the conversion of the UK's national insurance system into a social insurance system and has three main elements – expansion of the 'risks' included under a collective insurance system, the introduction of a full-scale system of crediting, and the introduction of part-time benefits. There is insufficient space here to set out either the full justifications for such expansion or the details of such an expanded system, and I believe the justifications and detailed proposals of the Commission on Social Justice (1994) remain valid. Here I will only note that the expansion of 'risks' and the development of a fully-fledged credit system are imperative if women's greater risks of poverty and social exclusion are to end; while the development of part-time social insurance benefits – such as unemployment benefit, incapacity benefit and perhaps a new carers benefit – involves the removal of sharp discontinuities between hours for out-of-work and in-work benefits, without all the risks of an unlimited removal of in-work/out-of-work conditions in benefit support.

The treatment of earnings of those out of work

The problem of the exclusion of those on out-of-work benefits from 'small' job opportunities suggests that earnings disregards under income support should be increased and/or that income support and WFTC should be merged into a single system without hours thresholds (see also Oppenheim, 1998). The principle alternative to either of these involves very complex forms of disaggregation of parts of the earnings of each partner from the other within means-tested support for unemployed claimants and their partners (as in the Australian system). The complexity of such alternatives is likely to undermine their objectives, since if we know one thing from social security research in the UK, it is that most people do not understand complex social security provisions.

The merits of merging WFTC and income support provision for

those of working age are probably not so great to make such a reform preferable to the other possibilities which exist; particularly, given the potential, even in a post-NMW environment, for further transfer of responsibility for the physical and social costs of labour used from employers to the state. Instead, I have argued above that the introduction of a NMW facilitates an informed debate about where out-of-work status ends and in-work status begins. Such a debate would then in turn permit reasoned discussion of the extent of earnings which it is fair and efficient for those deemed to be out-of-work to be permitted to retain. The objective should be an increase on the present situation where individuals may retain only £5 a week of any earnings (and couples £10), before pound for pound benefit reductions and should include active promotion of the rights of claimants to have some earnings on top of out-of-work benefits. Such earnings play an important role in encouraging the development of social networks (and hence awareness of job opportunities and the potential for re-integration into more full-time employment) and reducing the anxiety and depression associated with living on out-of-work benefits at their current levels (see also below). The greater generosity of the WFTC over family credit, and the introduction of a national minimum wage, should permit increases to, for example, £30 a week. In addition, it would be valuable if the nature of the earnings disregard changed to allow small amounts of earnings to be 'rolled up' (or assessed) over a longer period than one week, in order to facilitate casual and seasonal work.

Moving into work – transitional financial arrangements

One element of tax/benefit reform which should be an integral part of active labour market programmes – that is, New Deal – are 'transitional assistance measures' which seek to facilitate the movement from a state of worklessness to a state of participation in employment (or educational and training provision, if these are not funded through the social security system). At present these include Jobfinder's Grant, Benefit Run-On, Back-to-Work Bonus and Child Maintenance Bonus, though Jobmatch and Work Trials could also be said to share some of the attributes of transitional assistance measures. Evidence of effectiveness is not in the public domain for all of these, but Gardiner (1997) found that Jobfinder's Grant has twice as much additionality as

Training for Work for a tiny fraction of the cost, while Workstart and Jobmatch both offered twice or three times as much additionality as Jobfinder's Grant though for double or treble the costs.[5] Transitional assistance measures, seem then to have a role to play within active labour market programmes.

One of the reasons why such transitional assistance is necessary is, of course, the meagre level of out-of-work benefits, which leave no scope for coping with change within the household budget (see for example, Kempson, 1996). Another is the absence of significant amounts of 'portable' income which crosses the out-of-work/in-work divide (at present, only Child Benefit). Increases in both would reduce the need for transitional assistance measures. Increases in out-of-work benefits should not be seen as somehow in conflict with a welfare-to-work approach – structural change to the tax/benefit system of the types outlined in this chapter will be far more important to improving the employment prospects and social inclusion of poor people than holding down out-of-work benefit levels. As well as the transition problems caused by the latter, low out-of-work benefit levels have serious negative effects on the physical and mental health (and hence capacity for proactivity (Fryer, 1992), autonomous action (Doyal and Gough, 1991), and therefore employability of adults. In turn the negative effects of low out-of-work benefit levels on the health and educational attainment of the children of poor adults, are effects which will hamper and disadvantage those children for the rest of their lives, laying the seeds of future social exclusion.

References

Bradley H (1997) 'Gender and change in employment: feminization and its effects', in Brown, R. (ed) *The Changing Shape of Work*, Basingstoke: St. Martin's Press.

Commission on Social Justice (1994) *Social Justice: strategies for national renewal*, London: Vintage

Crompton R (1997) *Women and Work in Modern Britain*, Oxford University Press

Doyal L and Gough I (1991) *A Theory of Human Need*, Houndsmill: Macmillan

Eissa N and Liebman J (1996) 'Labour supply response to the EITC', *Quarterly Journal of Economics*, 111, pp. 606-637

Evans M (1996a) *Means-testing the Unemployed in Britain, France and Germany*, London: WSP/117 STICERD, LSE

Evans M (1996b) *Giving Credit Where It's Due? The success of family credit reassessed*, London: WSP/121 STICERD, LSE

Fryer D (1992) 'Psychological or Material Deprivation: why does unemployment have mental health consequences?' in McLaughlin E (ed) *Understanding Unemployment*, London: Routledge

Gardiner K (1997) *Bridges from Benefits to Work: a review*, York: JRF

Gershuny J, Godwin M and Jones S (1994) 'The domestic labour revolution: a process of lagged adaptation', in Anderson, M, Bechhofer F and Gershuny,J (eds) *The Social and Political Economy of the Household*, Oxford University Press

Gornick J and Jacobs J (1994) *A cross-national analysis of the wages of part-time workers: evidence from the US, UK, Canada and Australia*, Working Paper No. 113, Luxembourg Income Study

Howard M (1998) 'Disability Dilemmas: Welfare to Work or early retirement', in McCormick J and Oppenheim C (ed.), *Welfare in Working Order*, London, IPPR.

HM Treasury (1997) *Employment Opportunity in a Changing Labour Market. The modernisation of Britain's Tax and Benefit System. I.*, London

HM Treasury (1998) The Working Families Tax Credit and work incentives, No.3, The Modernisation of Britain's Tax and Benefit System, London: HM Treasury.

Jarvis S and Jenkins S (1997), 'Low income dynamics in 1990s Britain',

Fiscal Studies, 18, 2, pp. 123-142.

Kempson E (1996) *Life on a Low Income*, York: Joseph Rowntree Foundation.

McLaughlin E (1995) 'Gender and egalitarianism in the British welfare state', in Humphries, J and Rubery J (eds) *The Economics of Equal Opportunities*, Manchester: EOC.

McLaughlin E, McCay N and Trewsdale J (forthcoming) *An Investigation of Earnings Below the Lower Earnings Limit for National Insurance Contributions*, Belfast: EOC.

Meadows P (1997) *The integration of taxes and benefits for working families with children: issues raised to date*, York: JRF/York Publishing Services.

Mendelson M. (1998) *The WIS that was: replacing the Canadian Working Income Supplement*, York: JRF/York Publishing Services.

Oppenheim C (1998) 'Welfare to Work: taxes and benefits', in McCormick J and Oppenheim C (eds.) *Welfare in Working Order*, London: IPPR.

Parker H (1995) *Taxes, Benefits and Family Life*, London: IEA

Rubery J. (1997) 'Wages and the Labour Market', *British Journal of Industrial Relations*, 35, 3, pp337-366.

Endnotes

1   Evans (1996a) gives the example of how in 1995, the minimum rate of pay at 16 hours of work a week which would provide an income greater than basic Income Support rates was £2.86 an hour for a single adult over 25, but £4.48 for a couple in which only one partner was seeking or offered work (1996a).

2   Employees of working-age, excluding those on government training and employment programmes. This discussion relates only to those employees in the LFS who provided earnings data.

3   The median hourly wage rate of young people earning less than the Lower Earnings Limit for national insurance contributions was £2.00 in Northern Ireland and £2.83 in Great Britain among young (16-18) women, £2.50 among young men in Northern Ireland and £2.67 in Great Britain.

4   The problem of poor additionality is, of course, shared with the EITC where about 94 per cent of recipients would have been working

anyway (Eissa and Liebman, 1996; Mendelson, 1998). In the Canadian case, Mendelson estimates that the cost of each additional person in work because of the WIS was a staggering $700,000 (1998).

5   I have seen no evidence on the effectiveness of Back-to-Work and Child Maintenance Bonuses but they seem to have limited take-up so far (150,000 and 40,000 beneficiaries respectively in 1995/6, Gardiner, 1997).

9. Employment and social inclusion
by Peter Robinson

> For too long we have dealt only with the consequences of poverty and inequality and not with their causes – unemployment, lack of skills and education and an unreformed welfare state. (Gordon Brown, The Second John Smith Memorial Lecture, 19 April 1996)

If there is one central idea which apparently defines the new approach to social policy of the Labour Government elected in Britain in 1997, it is the belief that social inclusion is best promoted through enhanced employment opportunity and not the redistribution of income through the tax and benefits system. Increased employment opportunity is to be achieved by improving the skills of the workforce, through active labour market or 'welfare-to-work' policies to enhance the employability of the workforce, and changes to the tax and benefits system and a minimum wage designed to improve work incentives.

This strategy is contrasted with what is perceived to be the traditional 'welfare' approach, which saw a more significant role for taxes and benefits to substantially modify the primary income distribution derived from the market. However, this traditional approach always saw a commitment to full employment as central to the goal of promoting a more equitable society.

This chapter aims to assess the likelihood of success for the strategy of tackling social exclusion through promoting employment. Traditionally, keeping the distribution of final household income within 'acceptable' bounds has been seen as one of the best indicators of a more inclusive society. One way of achieving this could be through higher levels of employment. However, a low level of unemployment is also rightly seen in its own right as a vital means of promoting inclusion. High levels of unemployment are associated not only with poverty, but with physical and mental ill-health and social isolation. Reducing the incidence of poverty and reducing the incidence of unemployment might be seen as equal objectives. Of course problems arise if the two objectives are seen to conflict.

Employment and social inclusion in the industrialised countries

There are two key dimensions of labour market performance which have been the focus for discussion in Britain and other industrialised countries:

● the trends in employment and unemployment, and

● the trends in real wages and wage inequality.

From the end of the second world war until the late 1970s all Governments in the UK were formally committed to the objective of full employment, usually defined as a claimant unemployment rate of around two per cent or so, using a definition of claimant unemployment consistent with current coverage. The relationship over time between the claimant unemployment rate and the internationally agreed ILO definition of unemployment derived from the Labour Force Survey has remained stable, but with the ILO measure always higher than the claimant measure during economic upturns (Robinson, 1996). In 1979 the ILO measure of unemployment would have been about two percentage points above the claimant measure, a little higher than the gap which existed in 1997. This suggests that if the correct benchmark for full employment in the post-war period was a claimant unemployment rate of two per cent, then on the ILO measure the correct benchmark for full employment would be around four per cent.

Figure 9.1 plots three different measures of labour market exclusion in the UK over the period 1979-97. The ILO unemployment rate in this period averaged over nine per cent. An alternative measure of the performance of the labour market over this period is the trend in the employment-population ratio, that is the proportion of the working age population (16-59/64) in employment; figure 9.1 reports its converse, the non-employment rate. In 1979, 26 per cent of the adult population was not in employment, falling marginally to 25 per cent by 1990, but ending the period at 27 per cent, that is an employment-population ratio of 73 per cent. A final measure of the employment problem is given by the workless household rate, that is the proportion of all households headed by someone of working age where no-one is in employment. Aside from the period 1987-90 and again in 1997, this measure has risen consistently, more than doubling over the period.

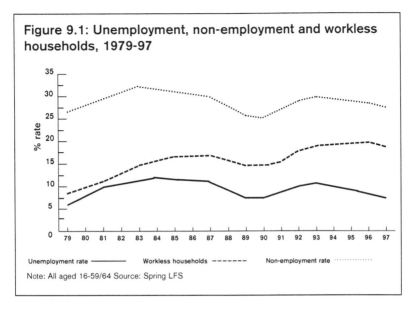

Figure 9.1: Unemployment, non-employment and workless households, 1979-97

Unemployment rate ———————   Workless households — — — — — —   Non-employment rate ·············
Note: All aged 16-59/64 Source: Spring LFS

Over the same time frame in which all the measures of labour market exclusion showed a deterioration there was also a sharp increase in relative poverty and income inequality. How much of this increase in inequality was due to unemployment and have periods of strong labour market performance reversed or at least tempered this growth in inequality?

A decomposition of the growth in income inequality between 1979-88 suggested that around one-third of the increase could be put down to the fall in economic activity (Johnson and Webb 1993). Between 1986 and 1990 all the measures of labour market exclusion reported in Figure 9.1 showed a significant improvement. However, the same time period also saw one of the most substantial increases in income inequality. This suggests that the link between labour market exclusion and income inequality is not as clear cut as one might think.

Other things being equal, a sustained improvement in employment will reduce income inequality. However, in the late 1980s other things were not equal.

Over the period between the late 1970s and the mid-1990s there was a significant increase in wage inequality in the UK, which was out of line with both historical experience and the experience of other European countries, though not the United States. Average real wages in the UK economy increased at a healthy rate over this period. Real hourly wages for men at the lower decile also increased, but at a significantly slower rate than for men at the median and at the higher decile. The increase in wage inequality amongst women working full-time was just as great. However, the male-female wage gap narrowed. It is noticeable that wage inequality continued to grow in the late 1980s even when aggregate unemployment fell sharply. There is some indication that the growth in wage inequality may have come to a halt in 1997.

The growth in wage inequality in the UK (and the US) has produced a large literature (reviewed by Atkinson, 1997). Two main hypotheses have been put forward, one focusing on changes in the demand for labour biased against unskilled workers and the other on changes to the institutions which determine pay and the attitudes which underlie that institutional framework. Amongst those who have focused on changes in the demand for labour there is a further sub-division between those who blame skill-biased technological change and those who blame increased competition from developing countries. This latter division of opinion is of second order importance as both put the focus on the problems faced by the less skilled and make the same recommendations about the need to enhance 'skills'.

In the 1980s there was a modest increase in the pay premium attached to holding higher qualifications, but for British men increased returns to education and experience accounted for only one third of the overall increase in wage inequality after 1979 (Schmitt, 1996). There is little doubt that institutional changes have also contributed to the increase in wage inequality. The decline in unionisation, the reduction in minimum wage rates and the eventual abolition of most minimum wage protection in 1993, the abandonment of incomes policies for the private sector after 1979, and the increased decentralisation of pay bargaining, will all have played a role.

However, there has been no full accounting for the increase in wage inequality in the UK. In particular one of the most difficult features of the growth in wage inequality to explain is that the greater part of that growth has occurred within occupational or educational groups.

The increase in wage inequality played an important role in explaining the overall growth in income inequality between 1979 and 1988, accounting for around one-sixth of the overall increase (Johnson and Webb, 1993). The continued growth in wage inequality between

1986-90 is part of the reason why overall income inequality continued to grow over this period despite the sharp rise in economic activity.

Overall, about half of the increase in income inequality in the 1980s can be put down to changes in the labour market, that is growing wage inequality and unemployment and inactivity. A progressive tax and benefits system would have acted to offset these changes in the primary distribution of income. In fact in the UK reductions in average tax rates for high income households combined with the policy after 1980 of uprating benefits in line with prices rather than earnings, meant that growing inequalities in the primary distribution of income were magnified. Indeed, changes to the tax and benefits system were at least as important as changes in the labour market in explaining growing income inequality across all households. Far from compensating the losers in the process of labour market restructuring, tax and benefits policy further rewarded the winners. Regressive changes to the tax and benefits system was the other main reason, along with growing wage inequality, why falling unemployment in the late 1980s was not accompanied by a reduction in income inequality.

The weaker than expected link between the labour market and income inequality or social exclusion is confirmed by looking across countries. Table 9.1 reports the ILO unemployment rate, employment-population ratio and workless household rate for seven major western economies. On all three measures the United States had by the mid-1990s the best performing labour market, with the lowest

Table 9.1
Different measures of labour market inclusion, 1994

	ILO Unemployment rate		Employment/ population ratio		Workless household rate	
	1983	1994	1983	1994	1983	1994
US	9.6	6.1	68.0	74.2	13.1	11.5*
UK	11.8	9.6	67.0	69.9	16.0	18.9
Canada	11.9	10.4	64.8	68.2	15.2	15.1
Germany	7.9	8.4	62.2	65.4	15.0*	15.5
France	8.0	12.4	62.0	58.7	12.5	16.5
Italy	8.6	11.3	55.0	51.7	13.2	17.2
Spain	17.0	23.9	49.5	47.0	19.4*	20.1

Notes: * US 1993, Germany 1984, Spain 1986.
Sources: Gregg and Wadsworth (1996). OECD Employment Outlook (1997).

unemployment rate and the lowest workless household rate, along with the highest employment-population ratio. Yet it also had very high levels of income inequality and could hardly be argued to represent the most socially inclusive society. The overlap across countries between any of the measures of labour market exclusion and income inequality is rather limited. Atkinson (1998) argues that several European countries experienced increases in unemployment from the late 1970s to the early 1990s which were as severe as in the UK, but without the same dramatic increase in relative poverty seen here.

The limited overlap over time and across countries between trends in poverty and in unemployment is not meant to imply that low unemployment and high employment rates are not desirable – they clearly are. However, they are clearly not sufficient in themselves to solve the problems of poverty and inequality.

The Anglo-Saxon jobs miracle?

The United States and to a lesser extent the UK have had a better employment record in recent times than the bigger continental European economies, which is often ascribed to their less regulated labour markets. It is also believed that there is a trade-off between employment generation and inequality, in that the better employment performance of the US and the UK has been bought only at the expense of greater wage inequality. If this is true then it could pose big problems for a strategy of trying to reduce both unemployment and poverty.

However, a major difficulty with this explanation is that the UK labour market has always been less regulated than the labour markets of other European economies, yet through the 1980s Britain's unemployment performance was not any better. Moreover, it is by no means obvious that all labour market policy after 1979 was in the direction of 'deregulation'. The most significant aspects of 'deregulation' in the UK have occurred in the fields of collective industrial relations and pay determination. However, this has been matched by some moves to greater regulation in the field of individual employment rights as a result of EU Directives and the Courts' interpretations of the provisions of the Treaty of Rome with respect to equal opportunities.

Moreover, if we look at the parameters of the growth in wage inequality, one of the most significant changes has been between age groups, with a sharp decline in relative youth wages. However, this has not been associated with any improvement in relative youth employment rates (Blanchflower and Freeman, 1997). There is no evidence that the employment protection legislation which was in place in 1979 had any significant adverse impact on employment and no evidence that the changes to that legislation significantly boosted employment. The abolition of the Wages Councils clearly led to an increase in wage inequality but there is no evidence for any boost to employment (Dickens *et al*, 1995). Beyond any simple apparent correlation between the growth in wage inequality in the US and the UK and their better employment performance, there is little direct evidence to back the argument that greater inequality has bought greater employment opportunity.

Increased product market competition (as a result for example, of privatisation and the phasing out of industrial subsidies) in the UK since 1979 does represent a more decisive break with the past and with the experience of other European countries. This may be part of the explanation for the UK's relatively better employment performance in the 1990s. However, the other competing explanation is that it has been the astute handling of monetary policy in the UK after 1992 (and by the Federal Reserve in the US in recent years), in contrast to the relatively tight monetary policy across Europe in the mid-1990s, which has helped foster the recent impressive employment growth in the Anglo-Saxon economies. Britain's experience between 1992-97 also makes it clear that 'globalisation' does not preclude a medium-sized country from pursuing a successful independent monetary policy.

Labour's strategy for employment and social inclusion

If the emphasis of the Labour Government on tackling social exclusion through improving employment is thought to represent a new departure, its analysis of why unemployment remains high largely follows the conventional wisdom. The Government has inherited a belief that the natural or structural rate of unemployment remains too high, at over seven per cent of the labour force on the ILO measure and six per cent on the claimant count (that is higher than the actual rate in early 1998). This high natural rate is in turn blamed on insufficiently 'flexible' product and labour markets, the lack of employability and the lack of skills of those not in work, and a tax and benefits system which harms incentives to work (HM Treasury, 1997). From this analysis flows the Government's five-pronged employment strategy:

1. If unemployment is structural then *macroeconomic* policy has little role to play in its reduction, rather the goal of macro policy is to foster stability by avoiding both sharp recessions and unsustainable booms.

2. Product and labour markets need to retain their *flexibility*, with further measures to promote product market competition, and the keeping in place of many of the labour market reforms of the previous administration, while at the same time strengthening *minimum standards* in the labour market through such legislative measures as the minimum wage.

3. Enhancing the *employability* of those not in employment through active labour market or 'welfare-to-work' measures.

4. Improving the skills of the workforce with education and training initiatives.

5. Restructuring the tax and benefits system and introducing a minimum wage to sharpen work incentives.

This combination of policies has been given the collective label of 'flexibility plus'. Any usage of the 'f' word seems designed to distance the Government from the policies perceived to be characteristic of the continental European model.

As has already been discussed, in the period before 1973 the traditional commitment to full employment could be expressed in terms of a quite precise numerical objective: a claimant unemployment rate of around two per cent. The new policy objective is framed in terms of 'employment opportunity for all' rather than full employment. What does this mean in terms of specific targets?

On a positive level the new objective focuses not just on the unemployed, and certainly not only on the claimant unemployed, but on other groups with a more marginal attachment to the labour market. These include the spouses of the unemployed, the long-term sick and disabled and lone parents. The initial stated aim is to extend to these groups the information, job search and counselling facilities long available through the Employment Service to the registered unemployed. Currently, however, there is no stated intention to make job search compulsory for these groups as it is for the registered unemployed.

There is a great deal of concern for those suffering prolonged spells of unemployment (that is the long-term unemployed) and those suffering repeated spells (the recurrently unemployed). The long-term unemployment rate appears to have borne a very stable relationship to the aggregate unemployment rate over the post-war period, so that it is not clear how far a policy for tackling long-term unemployment needs to differ from a strategy to tackle overall unemployment (Webster, 1996).

In the period 1991-95 around one-seventh of the workforce had suffered either prolonged periods of unemployment or recurrent spells, cycling between relatively low paid and insecure jobs and periods out of work (HM Treasury, 1997). There is no evidence that this proportion has increased since the mid-1980s and the data is lacking to know what kind of churning occurred during the era of full employment. However, as the Treasury itself has emphasised, a focus on the dynamics of unemployment and low pay would tend to tilt the focus of policy towards older members of the workforce, who suffer the sharpest declines in wages when they lose their jobs, and away from younger workers for whom some churning is inevitable as they search for their best match in the labour market. However, the Government's active labour market or 'welfare-to-work' policies remain heavily weighted towards the young.

How far does a focus on the problem of workless households lead to a different set of policies? To answer this question we need to look at the composition of workless households (Table 9.2). The single most common type of workless household, accounting for around 30 per cent of the total, consists of one adult of working age living on their own, including the single unemployed, the single disabled and the single divorced. One fifth are lone parent households, and altogether two-thirds of workless households have just one adult of working age. Only just over one-quarter consist of a married or cohabiting couple with or without children, and for many of these households, one partner was inactive before the other lost their job, so that the actual magnitude of the problem of work incentives for the spouses of the unemployed is unclear. In two-thirds of workless households the adults are inactive rather than ILO unemployed.

Table 9.2
The composition of workless households, 1996

	%
Single adults	29.4
Single parents	21.5
One working age adult + pensioner	14.6
Two working adults, no children	13.7
Two working age adults, with children	14.0
Two working age adults, with pensioner	1.3
Three or more working age adults	5.5

Source: Labour Force Survey, Spring (Hastings, 1997).

Indeed it is unclear how far the groups identified by the 'new' approach, with its focus on lack of employment opportunities, differs significantly from the groups which would be identified by 'traditional' poverty researchers. The traditional focus has always been on five household types ranging from low paid workers to the unemployed, lone parents, the long-term sick and disabled and pensioners on low incomes, ranked in order of their attachment to the labour market. Single pensioners and lone parents are most likely to suffer from persistent low incomes and they are also the demographic groups with the highest poverty rates when comparing Britain with other EU countries. For pensioners an 'employment' based strategy for alleviating poverty is by definition irrelevant and for lone parents it raises issues relating to the balance between work and child care responsibilities.

The new commitment to 'employment opportunity for all' is not accompanied by any specific targets. There is no commitment to reduce ILO unemployment to, say, four per cent which might equate with the post-war definition of full employment, and no commitment to a specific target for reducing the workless household rate. There is mention of the need to increase the employment-population ratio by five percentage points by the year 2050 to keep the ratio of dependents to those in employment constant (HM Treasury, 1997). However, it is not clear that maximising the employment-population ratio either in aggregate or for any specific group such as lone parents, represents a sensible policy objective. One specific target which was set before the election to reduce youth long-term unemployment by 250,000 was already dated at that time because of the sharp fall in youth unemployment brought about by the labour market recovery between 1993 and 1997.

The lack of any specific targets for any possible intermediate employment objectives is of course matched by the lack of any specific target for reducing poverty. In which case how will we measure whether the Government has achieved its aim of 'employment opportunity for all' and a reduction in social exclusion?

There are doubts about the effectiveness of the different policy instruments which form the new agenda. The downplaying of the role of macroeconomic policy, while in tune with the conventional wisdom, seems unwarranted if it is true that the better employment performance of the UK and the US in the 1990s is as much to do with astute handling of monetary policy as with any supply-side reforms.

There is a considerable literature on the effectiveness of active labour market policies such as wage subsidies and assistance with job search (Robinson, 1996, McCormick 1998). Simple initiatives such as Work Trials which offer an improved match with employers, or assistance with job search, can be shown to have a significant if generally modest impact on participants' job prospects. The evidence for the effects of training and work programmes is much more mixed. Work programmes can help tide people over while the regular jobs market improves, but there is little evidence that they significantly improve the chances of participants finding regular jobs. Only small scale and relatively expensive training programmes seem to deliver clear positive results in terms of higher earnings for participants. Wage subsidies generally suffer from high levels of deadweight (that is employers use the subsidy to employ people they were going to take on anyway) and do not create many new jobs, but they can tilt recruitment towards the target group.

If the aim of work programmes is to re-integrate the unemployed back into the mainstream labour market, then caution about the expansion of such programmes is warranted. Participants who had a placement on a work project with a public or voluntary agency on the programmes which were eventually merged to create the Training for Work scheme did not see an improvement in their subsequent employment rates (Payne *et al,* 1996). Similar results were also found for the Community Programme which ran in Britain in the mid-1980s. The apparent success of the Intermediate Labour Market approach, pioneered in cities such as Glasgow, may be the result of specific features of the programme design such as its relatively modest scale, the payment of the rate for the job, a duration of up to one year, its very high cost, and its lack of compulsion. It is not clear how far any of these features would be replicated if this approach was attempted on a much larger scale.

Job search and placement initiatives do feature strongly in the various 'New Deals' and have been modestly successful in improving employment rates, though of course they are not intended to lead to improvements in earnings. This suggests that active labour market or 'welfare-to work' policies may make only a modest contribution to mitigating earnings and income inequality. The Government believes that its measures will significantly, and quickly, reduce the natural rate of unemployment, a belief based on the view that the long-term unemployed are effectively cut off from the labour market. However, this view is difficult to reconcile with the sharp fall in long-term unemployment in the late 1980s and again in the mid-1990s during periods of strong employment growth.

Some focus on helping individuals to access education and training opportunities must be welcome, though if only a modest part of the increase in wage inequality from the late 1970s to the mid-1990s was due to increased returns to educational qualifications, then increased education and training may also make only a modest contribution to reducing wage inequality.

Clearly the introduction of a minimum wage will help to reduce wage inequality and will make a modest contribution to reducing poverty, lowering the numbers in low income households by around 300,000 (Piachaud, 1998). The Government has signalled its commitment to achieving a better balance in terms of labour market regulation by signing up to the Social Chapter of the Maastricht Treaty. However, the Social Chapter itself is a modest instrument which, in common with other EU legislation, will push the UK in the direction it has already been going, in terms of codifying and extending individual employment rights. In the areas where the EU has no competence, such as union rights, the

Government's agenda is a cautious one. There is no clear commitment to reversing the changes in employment protection legislation introduced by the previous Government. The Government aims to strike the right balance in the field of employment regulation, but its specific policy agenda does not, with the exception of the minimum wage, look radically different from that of the previous administration, which was anyway heavily constrained by the direct and indirect effects of being a signatory of the Treaty of Rome.

Conclusions

Will a commitment to a strategy of 'employment opportunity for all' and the policy instruments which underlie that strategy, be sufficient to reverse the trend towards greater relative poverty and income inequality in the UK?

There are three reasons for being cautious:

1. The growth in income inequality in the UK in the 1980s was in part linked to the fall in economic activity. However, in the labour market boom of the late 1980s, when all indicators of labour market exclusion moved in the right direction, income inequality continued to grow. The United States has the best aggregate employment indicators and the sharpest income inequality of any major industrialised nation.

2. The increase in wage inequality did make an important contribution to the growth in income inequality in the 1980s. However, the growth in wage inequality is itself an ill-understood phenomenon, which in turn makes it hard to tackle directly.

3. The policy instruments available to tackle directly the inequality which comes from the labour market may not be powerful enough to make more than a modest difference. A minimum wage will make some contribution. However, it has yet to be demonstrated that active labour market or 'welfare-to-work' policies can have more than a modest influence on overall employment rates, or any significant influence at all on earnings potential.

If we combine these reservations about how successful a direct attack on the inequalities which come from the labour market can be, with the observation that the single most important contribution to the growth in income inequality in the 1980s came from changes to the tax and benefits system, then this suggests that redistribution through the tax and benefits system has to remain one of the main policy instruments which the Government must use if it wants to significantly reduce income inequality.

For all its rhetoric, it seems that the Government pragmatically accepts this. The March 1998 Budget was straightforwardly redistributive. Between 1998-2000 higher taxes on married couples, home owners and motorists will pay for a more generous working families tax credit to supplant family credit, higher child benefit and income support payments for children and a child care tax credit. The impact of this package on labour supply incentives is hard to ascertain, but its impact in terms of redistributing income from higher income households to low income households (with children), is clear.

There are also indications that the Government will institute a minimum pension guarantee for the elderly on low incomes, which would also be a straightforward act of redistribution. Phasing out tax expenditures so that average tax rates rise on high income households, and using the resources to improve benefits for groups such as low income pensioners and families with children, is precisely the strategy long argued for by those concerned with the growth in income inequality and relative poverty.

A market economy will always produce significant inequality as some people are unable to obtain a market income or are able to earn only a small income. So long as the employment-population ratio does not approach one-hundred per cent, either in aggregate or for any group such as lone parents, the issue of the generosity of benefits for those currently not in employment will remain an important one. It is vitally important to pursue policies which will reduce unemployment, a point always recognised by the 'old' consensus with its strong commitment to full employment. However, unemployment is not 'solved' by 'job creation' programmes or 'new deals'. It will be solved by the combination of a modestly expansionary macroeconomic policy and the right supply-side framework. Moreover, in itself falling unemployment will not be sufficient to significantly reduce income inequality. An improved labour market will need to be matched by a more strongly redistributive tax and benefits system designed to offset inevitable market inequalities.

References

Atkinson A B (1997) 'Bringing income distribution in from the cold' *Economic Journal*, Vol. 107, No. 441, pp. 297-305, March 1997.

Atkinson A B (1998) 'Social exclusion, poverty and unemployment', in Atkinson A B and Hills J (eds.) *Exclusion, employment and opportunity* Paper 4, Centre for Analysis of Social Exclusion, London School of Economics.

Blanchflower D and Freeman R (1997) 'Creating jobs for youth' *New Economy* 4.2, pp 68-73, Summer 1997.

Dickens R, Machin S, Manning, A and Wilkinson D (1995) 'What happened to wages and employment after the abolition of minimum wages in Britain?', *mimeo*, Centre for Economic Performance, London School of Economics, March 1995.

Gregg P and Wadsworth J (1996) 'It takes two: employment polarisation in the OECD', OECD 1996.

Hastings D (1997) 'Economic activity of working age households' *Labour Market Trends* 105.9, pp 339-345, September 1997.

McCormick J (1998), 'Brokering a New Deal: the design and delivery of Welfare to Work' in McCormick J and Oppenheim C (eds.) *Welfare in Working Order*, London, IPPR

HM Treasury (1997) 'Employment opportunity in a changing labour market'.

Johnson P and Webb S (1993) 'Explaining the growth in UK income inequality: 1979-88' *Economic Journal*, Vol. 103, No. 417, pp 429-435, March 1993.

Piachaud D (1998) 'The prospects for poverty' *New Economy* 5.1, pp 8-13, March 1998.

Payne J, Lissenburgh S and White M (1996) 'Employment Training and Employment Action: An evaluation by the matched comparison method', Research Series No. 74, Department for Education and Employment, March 1996.

Robinson P (1996) 'Labour Market Studies: United Kingdom', Directorate General for Employment. Industrial Relations and Social Affairs, European Commission, December 1996.

Schmitt J (1996) 'Education isn't everything' *New Economy* 3.4, pp 204-8, Winter 1996.

Webster D (1996) 'The simple relationship between long term and total unemployment and its implications for policies on employment and area regeneration', *Working paper*, Glasgow City Housing, March 1996.

10. Comment: Employment, taxes and benefits
by Paul Gregg

Taxes, benefits and work

McLaughlin's starting point is that the labour market facing those out of work barely resembles that of the mainstream labour market. It is dominated by part-time working, unstable jobs and low pay. Evidence from the labour force survey supports this view. The Employment Audit reports that entry jobs (taken by those out of work) typically pay around £4 per hour or £110 a week.[1] Around 40 per cent of these positions are part-time and over 30 per cent are temporary contracts. Moreover, some 35 per cent of jobs have ended within 9 months without another job lined up for the individual to go to (see Employment Audit No. 4 and other Issues). The problems this causes for the transition into work have been drawn out before. Issues of work incentives and income uncertainty have been discussed widely.

A second strand of McLaughlin's piece introduces the argument that poverty and financial uncertainty also damages family formation. Given that it is noted that there is no clear causal link from the labour market to family formation, this is a strong claim to make. I was left curious about the relative importance of correlations between family formation or dissolution and labour market opportunities. As well as assessing the relative role of changing family formation or changing economic opportunities in driving entry to and exit from poverty or exclusion, it is vital to know how far these components of the dynamics of poverty can be influenced by policy. If family break-up results in entry into poverty by a previously non-working mother should the policy response be to financially penalise break-up, to support the non-working residual family through increased benefits or to encourage a move out of poverty through maintenance, wages and income supplements? The government has sent clear signals it supports the last option. The merits of this approach depend on how sensitive family dissolution is to financial incentives.

The third strand of McLaughlin's reasoning is how the tax/benefit system reinforces the dual earner model, particularly households which combine an individual in a full-time job with someone in atypical employment.

The benefit system supports both the poverty trap and unemployment trap for jobs paying over £77 a week. Furthermore the National Insurance (NI) system of entitlement to benefits via contributions is biased against those using 'bits of jobs' as a method of supporting oneself. Access to contributory job seekers allowance or state pensions is likely to be reduced because of multiple part-time job holding within the household or intermittent employment. This feature of the system clearly derives from the gendered model of male bread winner which is now, at best, anachronistic.

I thought one central area of concern was not discussed here. The *duration* of exclusion that individuals and households face. It is implied, but not verified, that lack of access to benefit eligibility is becoming concentrated on a minority of individuals for long periods. A focus on the duration and repeated experience of exclusion is central to the debate about how to address and tackle problems.

The debate of ideas for reform in this paper is extremely timely in a number of ways.

1. Gordon Brown's first full budget addressed a number of the concerns raised in McLaughlin's chapter, although not necessarily in ways she would support. The Working Families Tax Credit (WFTC) with its new Childcare Credits is focused on improving incentives in non-standard employment. The minimum wage will set the boundary between the burden of family support that falls on the state or on the employer. Keeping the 16 hour rule for entitlement also limits the state's share of the burden. The ending of distortionary incentives to create jobs just below the NI Lower Earnings Limit (LEL) is also central here.

2. The Budget also raises the profile of the debate on the role of the NI system. The employer's NI LEL will now start at £81 a week but at £64 for employees. This split is ungainly and has come about because of the contributory regime. If the LEL for employees was raised large numbers of workers, mainly women, would lose benefit rights. This goes to the heart of McLaughlin's concerns. She clearly wants to preserve the contributory link. This gives benefits by individual right rather than by family means test. Her lead proposal here is to create part-time benefits for those below the LEL. Reduced contributions

for reduced entitlement is plausible, however, some entitlement without any contribution may face legal challenge unless it applies to all workers. If very low paid, mainly women, workers are exempt from eligibility but another predominantly male group slightly better paid, have rights without contributing there is a danger of allegations of discrimination. Hence to move from the proposals outlined in the Budget to McLaughlin's system involves increasing NI charges on lower paid workers and enshrining a separate LEL for employers and employees. Reduced benefit rights to all lower paid workers would be consistent with much of McLaughlin's agenda but would represent a downgrading of entitlements for those between the old and new LEL. A credit system with no costs would breach the connection between personal contributions and personal entitlement. There are also difficulties with establishing eligibility where no records are kept. Employers would not welcome the increase in the administrative burden implied by recording all employees even where no contributions are made. This is thorny stuff and requires a wide debate on what the NI system should be doing and who it should include.

3. The Budget raised child benefit, a non-means tested benefit that crosses the work divide. McLaughlin notes that this could be developed into something more akin to the Canadian system of a super child benefit taken away from higher earning families in the form of an affluence test. However, withdrawing child benefit is clearly sensitive, even if the money is recycled to increase its value. The idea of an expanded child support system that is not linked to the parents' benefit entitlements would open up the possibility of individualisation of the parents' entitlements. McLaughlin focuses on the NI system as the route for this but it is not clear that this is the only alternative. Other approaches such as a partial individualisation of means tested benefits undertaken in Australia and Basic Income ideas have been around for a long time. Mclaughlin's contribution is topical and informative and feeds into key policy concerns of the new government.

Employment and Social Exclusion

This Chapter addresses the debate on how to tackle poverty and inequality in Britain that has become personified in the exchanges between Roy Hattersley and the Chancellor Gordon Brown. Robinson's Chapter starts with two assertions, the first that social exclusion can be usefully equated with income inequality. Robinson obviously recognises there is more to exclusion than income but believes it is one useful benchmark. While allowing him this, it is still worth noting that the link between exclusion and income is predominantly about poverty not overall income inequality. At a number of points the Chapter would have benefited by focusing explicitly on poverty rather than the whole of the income distribution.

The second assertion is that the Brown emphasis on the primary distribution of income (ie before the secondary redistribution through the tax and benefit system) and the Hattersley emphasis on tax and benefit generosity have the same aim with different means. Hence they can be evaluated against each other on efficiency grounds alone. This is patently wrong. The Brown approach to equality of opportunity is about tackling *life-time inequalities* whereas the Hattersley's approach focuses on *a single point in time* (cross-sectional inequality). Whereas greater lifetime equality will in time also produce cross-sectional equality the reverse is not true. The redistribution of income through taxes and benefits does little to raise the future earnings potential of the current poor and extended duration and repeated unemployment reduce future earnings potential. The failure to address the central issue here, namely can a strategy to reduce lifetime inequality be effective and what should happen while it comes on stream, clouds much of the analysis in the Chapter. Thinking about how events and actions now change future trajectories is at the heart of other Chapters in this book (see Chapter 2), its absence here is an important omission.

Robinson goes on to assert that a test of the current government's focus on the labour market as a means to tackle inequalities is whether high levels of employment reduces inequality when studied across countries or across time. He notes that countries with high employment rates are not always those with low inequality (it is true of many Scandinavian countries but not the UK or the US). But this is a travesty of the government's case which empasizes the distribution of work by individuals (long-term unemployment and inactivity) and households rather than aggregate levels of employment. When expressed in terms of income this distinction is obvious. Raising the aggregate income tells you nothing about its distribution and inequality is all about distribution. Equally, raising aggregate employment says nothing about inequality in the distribution of employment. The story with regard to the distribution of employment is clear. Over half of the poorest people (bottom decile) live in workless households, up by half since 1979. The declining group amongst the poorest are pensioners. The big losers have been children, nearly one third of children live in poor households (up from 1 in 8 in 1979) and 60 percent of these children in poor families are in workless households (up from 37 percent in 1979). Just 11 percent of the children in poor families are poor despite a full-time job which is not low paid (ie at wages above the bottom quartile of all wages). In general, for non-pensioner households, poverty occurs because of the absence of a full-time job which is not low paid. Current pensioner poverty can not be addressed by access to employment, but clearly the next generation of poor pensioners will be poor because of extended periods without work or on low pay which prevented adequate contribution to second tier pensions.

It is obvious that increased benefit payments to these poor families would reduce the depth of poverty and if the system became dramatically more generous would lift substantial numbers out of poverty. However, as the overall tax burden has not fallen, a large increase in benefits would require a substantial increase in taxation relative to that in 1979. The shifts in the distribution of labour market opportunities over the last twenty years have been so large that they would require the tax and benefit system to work much harder for inequality to stand still. Either the tax system of 1979 or the benefit system had to give and the Conservative government chose in relation to its priorities. In my view tackling the primary distribution of work and wages is central to rebuilding a viable welfare state.

Robinson's Chapter then looks at wage inequality and suggests that we do not understand fully what lies behind its rise since 1978 and so it is difficult to fully address it. Whilst clearly true, there is a substantial body of work suggesting that rising returns to education and experience and the decline of formalised wage setting by trade unions and Wages Councils account for large slices. So there is clearly room for some policy developments here.

Only very late on does the Chapter discuss the new government's declared strategy which is broadly that product and labour market regulation are not the main agenda (although minimum wages, trade union representation rights are far from trivial) and the main focus is to tackle the inequalities that shape people's experience of the labour market and through it on into retirement. It is here that the discussion should focus on the growing evidence of what happens to people as they move through the labour market. The scarring effects of extensive unemployment, the evidence of declining wage mobility and the exit rate from the labour market into inactivity which is now centred on women without a working partner and older men is central to this analysis. There is a background academic debate on whether unemployment is most usefully thought off as an individual experience with detrimental effects from long duration and increased likelihood of unemployment in the future or as an area phenomenon. However, at one level this government is developing attempts to reduce concentration on areas, groups and individuals whether through the New Deal, 'worst' estates policy and reducing educational inequalities. It is also clear the young are the focus of policy if you are trying to address the lifetime inequality that enduring and intermittent unemployment produces.

In the end the Chapter cannot really explore the differences approaches between the cross-sectional single snapshot approach of Hattersley and the lifetime picture of Brown because it only looks at the snapshot evidence. This is a missed opportunity to illuminate readers about this highly topical and interesting area of the current debate.

Endnotes

1. Source for these figures are own calculations from Family Expenditure Survey (1979 to 1995/6).

IV:
The Public
Sector and
social exclusion

11. Tackling poverty at its roots? Education
by Howard Glennerster

Social Exclusion

Education is clearly central to the whole concept of social exclusion. It is impossible to be a full citizen without enough education to be a participating member of that society. That was the basis of Tawney's writing and it is important to Sen's notion of entitlements. A mother's education is crucial to the health of both mother and child, in a developing country especially, but in the UK too. One of Rawls' primary goods is self respect and without an education that is appropriate for the society in question no individual can ever feel full self respect. The more sophisticated our interactions with each other in modern society the more this holds true. Such a canvas is too vast for such a short contribution. Here, I am addressing a narrower but still important issue – how far can education hope to combat widening income inequalities? Other contributors have documented the problem amply. Benefit strategies alone will never be able to compensate for the severe stretching in original income distribution the UK has experienced, along with many other countries, in the past two decades and the worrying geographical concentration of that poverty.[1] Can education policy play any part in mitigating these trends?

What we know

- Poor educational performance has become increasingly associated with low earnings and with unemployment not only in the UK but in other advanced economies.[2] Even in the mid-1970s those men who left school at the first opportunity with no or few qualifications did relatively badly in the job market. In the UK they were one third more likely to be unemployed than their better qualified school mates. By 1990 they were two thirds more likely to be unemployed. This ratio eased back again a bit as the labour market tightened in the 1990s but, come another recession, it will worsen again. In the United States, which seems to be an early warning station of these things, the likelihood of poorly qualified school leavers ending up unemployed was very similar to that in this country in the 1970s. Now, in the US, this group of poorly qualified high school leavers is twice as likely to be unemployed as the rest of the population. They are much more at risk.

- Technological change within industries as well as changes in industrial structures are producing a wider distribution of rewards for those in work.[3] Rising demands for more highly skilled people have pushed up rewards at the top and the relatively reduced demand for low skilled people has reduced rewards at the bottom of the labour market. This is something that holds across all kinds of industry and services here and abroad.

- In America there is also evidence that falling educational attainments at the very bottom of the education ladder have made things worse. They have been associated with an absolute fall in real earnings at the bottom of the income distribution.[4] We have not experienced this in the UK, which is at least something to be grateful for.

- World trade has also affected the relative demand for labour in advanced countries though there is a dispute about the size of this affect. It has increased the supply of less educated labour 'available' to a country like the US or the UK relative to the supply of more educated workers. This has tended to push down the price of that labour. Those at the bottom have suffered most. Global trade and this labour supply effect, has, on one estimate, accounted for half of the relative decline in the earnings of high school drop outs since 1980.[5] In the UK where we are more dependent on world trade we might expect the effect to be greater.

- England has one of the widest dispersions of educational attainments in the advanced world, only the US outstripping us in this dubious achievement. This was true in the 1960s when we put it all down to the 11 plus and secondary modern schools. There may have been some narrowing since then but a significantly wide spread of attainment remains.[6] That is true not only of the dispersion in maths scores, where we do relatively poorly in international rankings, but also for science where we do well in our average levels of achievement. There must be an interaction effect at work here. Once a country or an area has a large supply of poorly educated people it is likely to attract firms looking for low skills.

● Poverty and deprivation in children's families and in their neighbourhood is associated with their performance in school. The striking analysis produced for the Catholic Bishops by OFSTEAD last year illustrates the point only too clearly (see table 11.1).

Table 11.1 Poverty and School Performance
Free school meals take up and GCSE results: 1995

Pupils with free school meals %	Number of schools	GCSE %5 A-C	GCSE %5 A-G
0-10	987	58	95
11-20	894	42	90
21-30	453	31	84
31-40	231	25	79
41-50	169	22	76
51-60	98	20	73
over 60	74	18	70

Surely some fairly simple policy prescriptions follow. Improve education and training and we can improve the lot of the poorest. Increase the incomes of the poor and their schooling will improve. Unfortunately nothing in social science is that simple. Education on its own is not going to solve the problem any more than benefit increases on their own are going to. We need to operate on both cylinders.

What we don't know

● Economists are still in dispute about how far investing more in education improves an individual's earnings capacity as opposed to giving signals to the employer that he or she is an able motivated person.

● Virtually all the evidence suggests that spending more money on schools or on reducing class size beyond their present levels is a waste of money. Recent suggestions to the contrary in the US have been effectively refuted, at least on my reading of the evidence.[7]

● Recent studies in the UK have confirmed the old negative evidence using more elaborate analysis than was possible before. It seeks to link children's later earnings to the 'quality' of the schools they attended. Neither more spending nor more teachers seem to make any difference.[8,9]

● Despite the fact that we have a much more even spread of spending on schools in different areas than in the USA the spread of school performance seems to be nearly as wide[10] (though we may be legitimately worried about poor response rates to the survey from poor areas here).

● Training and education programmes for those who are out of work have produced some gains in the UK but they are varied and can be costly.[11] Much better evaluations have been done in the US where basic training and job search help has been shown to have a positive effect in getting people back into work and off benefit. But the story about poverty reduction is less clear. A review of US experiments makes the point:[12]

The evidence from these evaluation studies shows that good employment and training programs can significantly raise the earnings of welfare recipients and can do so in a cost effective way. But the evidence offers a more depressing lesson as well. Even the most successful programs fail to raise earnings enough to make a large difference in the poverty status of poor mothers and their children. The reason is simple: people on welfare earn very little money. A number of programs have been found to work but none has been found to work miracles. pp100-1

● Claims that improved basic education levels will transform economic performance overall are not born out by the evidence.[13]

● While poverty is associated with poor school performance much of that association is accounted for by the low levels of parents' education. This will not be reversed by raising parents' income through benefits or otherwise.

It is easy enough to get one's self into a torpor of complete pessimism here. Nothing works. But there is research evidence that does point to more positive and practical interpretations.

What matters and what we might try

Higher basic skills matter

1. If we are concerned to modify the distribution of earnings at the very bottom, as opposed to transforming the UK economy as a whole, and we are prepared to play a very long game, then education and training may have an important role to play in raising the bottom end of the income distribution. But this strategy must be a general one not just targeted on the few who are on social security benefit. Nor must it be targeted on schools alone. Adult literacy and maths levels must be tackled too. If the general skill levels of the lowest qualified are raised this could have two effects. It will reduce the supply of low skilled people competing for the supply of jobs at this level. This will tend to raise their wages as well as improving the prospects of those who have gained the extra skills. In the absence of such a strategy boosting the supply of low skilled people through welfare to work incentives will drive down wages at the low end even more. In the very long run, a higher distribution of skills in the population could affect the structure of the economy as a whole.

2. The higher chances of unemployment suffered by the least qualified seem to be worse in countries that have the lowest levels of basic education and training. Workers at the bottom are least well able to adapt to change. [14]

Both points suggest the need for a general improvement in the skills of the least advantaged. This is not something that can be done quickly. Education policy has actually succeeded in reducing the gap in qualifications achieved between the least and most advantaged in the past twenty years.[15] The social class gap has narrowed compared to twenty years ago but the achievements at the very bottom still lag far behind. Moreover, the problem has been that the labour market has changed even faster.

Locality matters

The skill mix of the local labour market affects where firms of particular kinds locate. I talked recently to a large enterprise which was planning to expand within reach of a community with high unemployment. Their experience of recruiting skilled people had been so disappointing that it was a serious impediment to further expansion there. A lot of American studies suggest that the spatial mismatch of local job opportunities with local schools produces a powerful negative feedback. Limited opportunities reinforce the message that effort is not rewarded. School to work programmes that have been successful have physically transported children to selected employment schemes over long periods, as well as training some children for the kinds of jobs that the very local labour market offered.[16]

Education and mobility matters

The follow up of the 1958 Cohort study by various authors shows that educational achievement is important in explaining movement out of the cycle of poverty of those children's parents.[17] Declining school performance of girls is important in explaining teenage pregnancy and the later poor performance of those mothers' children.[18] If the danger signals of declining performance can be picked up and addressed early enough there is the possibility of tackling not only the poverty of one generation but of two or more.

Peer groups matter

Though crude measures of additional school inputs show little correlation with school outcomes or later earnings, who you are at school with does matter. Past educational research had suggested that a mix of abilities and backgrounds was beneficial to school performance overall and especially for the least able and poor children. Now a recent follow up of the NCDS 1958 cohort has suggested that being educated with more able and motivated children translates into higher earnings later in life as well.[19] This seems to be true for all children so it creates a problem for education policy! Selection helps the winners but worsens the chances of the losers. However, there are decreasing returns to being educated with more able children. Thus, able children will gain from being educated with more able children – the pull-up effect – but they will gain far less than the less able will. We have a hard choice here. If we care about the pulling apart of our society – social exclusion in short – we must do what we can to ensure that the poorest are indeed pulled up. All the current forces are in the opposite direction. We can see the results of letting it run away from us in America. This suggests that avoiding the re-emergence of selective or socially cream skimmed schools is especially important for poor children's capacity to climb out of poverty. It also suggests that in our performance indicators for schools we should set a goal of reducing the spread of performance not just the average results.

Maths matters

While it may be difficult to show a simple link between the performance of a whole economy and the average maths scores of the population, being poor at maths does seem to be bad news for individuals in the income distribution. A study undertaken by economists at Harvard and MIT has shown that the achievement of basic mathematical skills at school has become an increasingly important predictor of later wages.[20] A nation-wide follow up survey of high school graduates graduating in 1972 was compared with one graduating in 1980. Their earnings were measured at the age of 24. Basic maths proved important across the board. "Basic" meant skills taught no later than eighth grade – basic arithmetic, and shape – not knowledge of advanced algebra, for example. For women the whole of the extra earnings previously associated with their going to college can be accounted for by their higher maths scores gained at school. The longer out of school the more important this basic competence seemed to be.

If we probe further into the reasons for the relatively poor performance of English school children at maths it has something to do with the sheer time they spend on maths compared to children in other countries. For example, French students doing the maths / physics / science Baccalaureate spend nine hours a week on maths in their final year and six the year before that. In England the overwhelming number of maths students do no more than 4-5 hours a week for both years.[21]

Teacher quality matters

Most of the studies that are negative about the effects of more spending on schools do agree that the quality of teaching matters. Getting more good teachers into schools in poor areas will cost money especially to recruit outstanding heads and pay high performing teachers to stay in the classroom. One of the best things we could do to help children in poor areas would be to make sure that each primary school in such areas had at least one first rate maths teacher who would make maths rewarding and exciting and help the other teachers to do so too. At the moment primary schools are full of dedicated young teachers many of whom are terrified of maths!

Ensuring that schools in poor areas are as well endowed with good teachers more generally will also cost money. This is not positive discrimination, just paying what it takes to get the same quality of teachers in front of all classes. This is scarcely a new idea but the last Government actually restricted local authorities' capacity to concentrate budgets on poor schools by restricting the needs based element in school budget allocations. Targeting schools in poor areas with a top class core of maths specialists good at getting maths across would not be a bad place for a Secretary of State to begin in the Education Action Zones. It would also help to keep bright children in those schools.

In the 1970s when I was a member of the ILEA we devised a system of targeting resources on schools in deprived areas. Over the 1970s and 1980s those children from other countries, who form such a large part of London's school population, steadily caught up and began to achieve as well or better than the indigenous population. This was an unsung but very important achievement.

Adults matter

Most political attention concentrates on schools and school performance. Yet, to make the obvious point, most people with low skills are not school children but adults. Older cohorts have much lower levels of qualifications than our present school leavers. Teenage culture and the earlier age of sexual maturity made it difficult for schools to succeed with many of their unmotivated children. Once an adult, however, it becomes very difficult to 'come out' and reveal illiteracy or the incapacity to add up. Incentives to get back into the labour market must be linked to sensitive programmes to help those who are suffering under this particular and highly stigmatic disadvantage.

Parental time matters

So far we have been discussing formal education – schooling and qualifications gained in some educational institution. But it is becoming increasingly clear that we have been disinvesting in children in other ways and that it matters. There is some evidence that where parents work full time this has an impact on the educational attainments of the young child and even on the future earning capacity of the child. The whole issue and the evidence are contested. The results seem to vary by the income and kind of family circumstance. Children in poorer families may gain if both parents, or the mother on her own works, because of the income effect but overall the parental time variable does seem to matter – indeed it would be very odd if it did not! For very poor parents, where mothers work and bring in more money this helps raise the quality of the home environment, which in turn compensates for the loss of time spent with the child, but the effect remains.[22, 23, 24] There are all kinds of incentives that encourage parents to invest less time with their children. Those in full time work are working longer hours and both parents now work more than they used to. We know much less about this than we should but it seems a fair guess that parental investment in children is less in quantity than it used to be though it is probably more in quality. As a colleague has put it:[25]

> What is needed to support these families is not rhetoric, condemnation or disinvestment, but high quality pedagogic

and educational investment from the earliest age for children alongside opportunities for parents to redress any shortcomings or opportunities foregone in their own education and training careers.

All of this has implications for the welfare to work policy. Part of our concern must be to help parents invest enough time in their children or provide adequate substitutes as well as being good working role models. More than this it has implications for the whole role of work in a modern society. It is forcing parents to disinvest in their children's future and probably especially better educated parents. This should be as much a worry as the problems of the poor.

We know that young girls are most at risk of becoming teenage mothers if they have suffered a steady decline in their educational performance at school. This then has an effect on the performance of the children they have.[26] Schools thus have a double responsibility to track and be alert to the needs of this vulnerable group.

Quality pre-school time matters

There has been a great deal of controversy over the years about the contribution pre-school education can make. Pre-school interventions with poor children in the USA in the 1960s had disappointing results blamed on the very limited scale and quality of those programmes. More recently some high quality interventions with deprived children in the USA have attracted a lot of attention because of their apparently good long term results. The best known is the Perry Pre-School Programme in Ypsilanti, Michigan.[27] This was available mainly to young black children from poor homes and it was an intensive experimental intervention. The experimental programme was run by staff trained in child development, classes had two teachers and less than twenty children. It was targeted on social interaction rather than highly formal education. Above all there was close involvement with parents. The follow up of young adults aged twenty seven suggested those in the programme had done better than those who had not experienced this education in the control group. They not only had higher levels of education on leaving school but were less likely to offend and they got better paid jobs and their earnings were higher.

This is the most striking and best known of the American studies. However, it is an experimental result obtained from a very small sample of very deprived children in one town in Michigan. In this country we do not have equivalent long term experiments but we do have very good national longitudinal studies – the National Child Development Study of children born in 1958 and the 1970 British Cohort Study. These have recently been reanalysed by colleagues working at the LSE ESRC Centre for Economic Performance and they produce some very interesting results.[28] There was a three fold increase in pre-school participation of children in these two samples – from 20 per cent to 60 per cent. If pre-school education were that important we should be seeing a big improvement in British children's educational performance, which we do not. More directly the authors look at the association between time spent by children in formal pre-school facilities, in informal child care eg child minders, and time spent with mother. A whole range of other variables are tested and their effects held constant. What emerges is that for the 1958 children time spent in pre-school was very positively associated with school achievements at seven but so was time spent with mother. One seemed a good substitute for the other. Informal care was much less effective than either. Positive results remained until eleven but had mostly disappeared by the time the children were sixteen. Those spending more time with their mothers, however, were better at maths at sixteen!

The really disturbing results relate to what has happened to the 1970 cohort. They have, as an age group, had much more experience of pre-school or nursery education but it has served them less well. At ten such children were no better at maths and significantly worse at reading compared to others. This was especially true of those from lower social class homes. We can only speculate on the reasons for this but it may well be that as we expanded pre-school provision the quality suffered. The policy conclusion is that if pre-school provision is to expand still further as women work full-time earlier in their children's lives the quality of pre-school provision becomes critical. Another important finding of the study is the importance of fathers' interest in their children's educational progress. It was shown to be highly significant. That, too, is something we could try to foster.

Other British evidence on pre-school is mixed but is consistent with the theme of pre-school quality being important.[29, 30] One recent retrospective study[31] of primary school children's performance under the new National Curriculum suggested that both nursery and play group experience was beneficial compared to non attendance. Similarly there is encouraging news from Tower Hamlets which is one of the most deprived areas in the country and has had a long history of low achievement in its schools.[32] The borough has substantially increased its nursery provision and has tested children's performance over time. At key stage 1 in English, Maths and Science pupils with nursery provision did significantly better than those who had not had it. The result was especially strong for those who did not have English as their only language. There has been a steady narrowing in the gap between pupils in the borough and the rest of Inner London. A gap of six points on the London reading test between Tower Hamlets children and the rest of Inner London in the 1980s has been reduced to one point in 1997. Progress can be made, even where social exclusion has been at its sharpest. How much of this can be put down to pre-school is not deducible from the overall figures we have.

In brief

We should be extremely careful about offering easy solutions or suggesting that education can solve the problems of poverty. But carefully thought out quality interventions targeted at low performers, both adults and children, especially in poor areas, could, over the long haul, make a difference.

Endnotes and references

1. Hills J (1996) *New Inequalities* Cambridge: Cambridge University Press

2. See Blanchard O J and Zoega's discussion of his paper 'Shifts in the relative demand for skills' in' D Snower and G.de la Dehasa (Eds) *Unemployment Policy Government Options for the Labour Market* Cambridge: Cambridge: Cambridge University Press 1997

3. Schmitt J *The Changing Structure of Male earnings in Britain 1974-88* Centre for Economic Performance Discussion Paper No 122 London: LSE/ CEP 1993

4. Murname R J, Willett and Levy F 'The Growing Importance of Cognitive Skills in Wage Determination' *Review of Economics and Statistics* 1995 pp 251-64

5. Borjas G J, Freeman R B and Katz L F 'How much do immigration and trade affect labour market outcomes?' in *Brookings Papers on Economic Activity* No 1 1997 Washington: Brookings Institution

6. Keys W Harris S and Fernandez C *Third International Mathematics and Science Study: First National Report Part 1* Slough: National Foundation for Educational Research 1996

7. Burtless G (Ed) *Does Money Matter? The Effect of School Resources on Student Achievement and Adult Success* Washington: Brookings Institutuion 1996

8. Robertson D and Symons J 'Do Peer Groups Matter: Peer Group versus Schooling Effects on Academic Achievement' Centre for Economic Performance paper S 129 London : LSE /CEP 1996

9. Meghir C ' The Effect of School Quality on Educational Attainment and Wages ' Centre for Economic Performance Paper No S.169, London: LSE, Nov 1997

10. Keys W, Harris S and Fernandes *op cit*

11. Gardiner K *Bridges from Benefit to Work : A review* York: Joseph Rowntree Foundation 1997

12. Burtless G 'Employment Prospects of Welfare Recipients' in Nightingale D S and Haveman R H (eds) *The Work Alternative: Welfare Reform and the Realities of the Job Market* Washington: Urban Institute 1995

13. Robinson P *Literacy, Numeracy and Economic Performance* London: Centre for Economic Performance LSE Sept 1997

14. See Blanchard and Zoega *op cit*

15. Glennerster H 'Education and the Welfare State' in *The State of Welfare, Second edition*, H Glennerster and J Hills (Eds) Oxford: Oxford University Press 1998

16. Pouncy H and Mincy R B 'Out of Welfare Strategies for Welfare Bound Youth' in *The Work Alternative* Nightingale and Haveman *op cit*

17. Johnson P and Reed H *Two Nations: The Inheritance of Poverty and Affluence* London: Institutue of Fiscal Studies 1996

18. Kiernan K E *Transition to Parenthood: Young Mothers, Young Fathers – Associated factors and later life experiences* Welfare State Dicussion Paper No 113 London: LSE also 'Family Change, Parenthood, Partnership and Policy' in *Options for Britain A strategic Policy Review* Ed Halpern D, White S and Cameron G, Dartmouth Press 1996

19. Robertson and Symonds *op cit*

20. Murname, Willett and Levy *op cit*

21. London Mathematical Society *Tackling the Mathematics Problem* London: Royal Statistical Society 1995

22. Michael R T, Chase-Lansdale P L, Desai S 'Mother or Market? Effect of Maternal Employment on the Intellectual Ability of 4 year old Children' *Demography* Vol 26 No4 Nov 1989

23. Desai S Michael R T and Chase-Lansdale P L. 'The Home Environment: A mechanism through which maternal employment affects child develpoment' Paper given to Population Association of America Sept 1990

24. Robertson and Symons *op cit*

25. Kiernan K E. *op cit*

26. Kiernan K E *op cit*

27. Schweinhart L J and Weikart D P (1993) *A summary of Significant Benefits the High/Scope Perry Preschool study through age 27* High Scope Press Michigan 1993

28. Feinstein L, Robertson D and Symons J *Pre-school Education and Attainment in the NCDS and BCS* Centre for Economics Performance LSE 1998

29. Jowett S and Sylva K 'Does kind of Pre-school matter?' Educational Research 28: No 1 p21 1986

30. Osborn A F and Milbank J E *The Effects of Early Education,* Oxford Clarendon Press 1987

31. Daniels S 'Can Pre-school Education Affect Children's Achievement in Primary School?' *Oxford Review of Education* Vol 21 No2 1995 pp 163-178

32. *Achieving Against the Odds,* Research and Statistics Education Strategy Group Tower Hamlets Borough Jan 1998

12. The Case for Civic Entrepreneurship
by Charles Leadbeater

(This Chapter is based on Civic Entrepreneurship: the people creating the new public sector, by Charles Leadbeater and Sue Goss, published by Demos, with the Public Management Foundation.)

When Norma Redfearn became head teacher at West Walker primary school in Newcastle in 1986 she took over a school in a state of near collapse. About three-quarters of the children were on free school meals. A majority of the parents were unemployed single mothers, who had grown up in workless households. Most of them had hated school as children and had low expectations for their own kids. On any one day about a fifth of the children were not at school. Quite a few of those who did make it to school came late and without having had anything to eat. Only a handful of the West Walker's 18 classrooms were occupied. The school seemed to be dying a slow death. Norma Redfearn set out to revive it.

In a decade she has transformed it, with the help of the governors, staff and most of all, the once demoralised parents. Norma Redfearn realised that to educate her kids she had to educate entire families. To get the parents involved the school had to become more than a set of classrooms: she turned it into a catalyst for community renewal. The school's attendance record is now in the high 90 per cent range and its scores in national tests are improving. Its classrooms are full. But it is much more than that. The school is home to a thriving adult education centre. It has a lively cafe, which provides breakfast for scores of kids each morning. Parents who met while building a nature garden, went on to form a housing association, which has built an estate of new homes opposite the school. Norma Redfearn understood from the outset that to revive her school she had to be much more than a head teacher, she had to be civic entrepreneur.

Norma Redfearn realises how a public organisation needs to win a mandate to innovate to meet changing demands. She is not alone. All over the public sector, and especially at the front-line, innovators and entrepreneurs are developing new services, often by breaking out of professional and administrative straitjackets. There is a huge amount of creativity and intelligence distributed at the edges of the public sector, where providers meet consumers, teachers meet parents. Take Bob Gregory as an example, a sergeant in the Thames Valley police. Bob Gregory is a long serving officer. He is an imposing figure with a booming voice, the antithesis of trendy, right-on policing. Yet Gregory has pioneered one of the most innovative approaches to youth crime in the country – the Thames Valley restorative justice programme. Instead of a traditional caution for first-time offenders, usually delivered by an inspector, the Aylesbury scheme asks the young offender to attend a conference, along with the victim of the offence. The offender attends with a parent, grandparent or teacher. The victim also comes with friends or family. The meeting is mediated by Gregory. The aim is to allow the victim to voice their hurt and to get the offender to understand the consequences of their actions. Initially most officers in the Thames Valley force were sceptical. They thought it sounded soft. But it has proved hugely effective. The re-offending rate under the traditional caution is 35 per cent. In the Aylesbury scheme's first year, the re-offending rate was just 4 per cent. Gregory reckons the long term re-offending rate is likely to be about 10 per cent. The new caution takes far less time to deliver than the traditional caution, which took five hours of paperwork. Gregory explained :

> Courts do virtually nothing for victims. They are largely left out of the process. Yet people leave our conferences not feeling like victims anymore. They have been able to confront the offender, voice their feelings and invariably they leave feeling better. For offenders a court appearance is technical, distant, they don't have to engage with it or explain themselves. A caution delivered by an inspector is often something they do not have to engage with. It's like being told off by a headmaster. They grit their teeth and get through it. In our approach they have to look the victim in the eye. Most of them break down. It's much tougher than court.

Civic entrepreneurship will be vital if the public sector is to renew itself to meet the pressures from clients and users for better services and the demands of politicians for greater efficiency and effectiveness.

Civic entrepreneurship is particularly important to the issue of poverty and social exclusion for three reasons. First, poverty has become entrenched in some areas and for some groups despite the existence of the welfare state. Second, many of the most disadvantaged parts of the UK are precisely those places where the public sector is the predominant source of employment, service and infrastructure (see Chapter 16). Third, the multi-dimensional nature of social exclusion demands an innovative response which challenges old models of public provision.

The public sector has undergone dramatic change in the past two decades. The Conservatives shook up public provision through compulsory competitive tendering, privatisation, restructuring and the introduction of businesslike management methods. Challenged to become more efficient, to produce more "output" from finite resources, most public sector organisations have responded. Management systems and training programmes have been introduced. Public organisations now go in for strategic business planning, re-engineering, downsizing, unit cost analysis, performance measurement and quality assurance.

These changes have undoubtedly brought benefits. In many public agencies customer service has improved. Working practices are more flexible. Organisations are more open to partnerships. Service costs at the best public sector organisations often compare well with those of private sector competitors. Yet despite these improvements, the public sector still often falls well short of its potential and of public expectations.

Barriers to innovation in the Public Sector

In the past few years bodies such as the Audit Commission have started to map the gap between performance and expectation. Its recent report on the youth justice system, *Misspent Youth*, found that an overwhelming majority of the resources were spent on processing crime, after the event. Very little was spent on prevention, rehabilitation or victim support. The youth justice system is processing a social problem but doing far too little to solve it. The reasons for this failure are common to many public institutions: they are focused on outputs rather than outcomes; people and budgets are departmentalised rather than integrated.

One of the main reasons that the public sector's performance falls short of expectations is that it is slow to learn and change. The most admired private sector companies, Tesco, British Airways, Intel, Hewlett

Packard, innovate to create change in products, markets and industries. Traditionally public sector organisations have done the opposite: they have held on to ways of doing things until they are so clearly obsolete that they are doing harm, and only then, often in the face of a crisis, do they begin the painful process of developing alternatives. The public sector has consistently underestimated the speed of change in the society around it and has been slow to use new technologies. Investment in public sector research and development is pitifully low compared with the private sector.

The history of public organisations makes them ill-equipped for learning, as well as to play new roles. Most were designed as large bureaucracies, capable of processing large numbers of cases in identical ways to achieve equity of treatment, with audit trails designed to prevent fraud but which do not encourage experimentation and risk taking. They are divided into professionally dominated departments and concentrate activity into narrow specialisms, with little cross-fertilisation of ideas or practices. Public organisations generally have heavy handed management systems, which provide limited autonomy or responsibility to front-line staff. These constraints make it difficult for the public sector to learn, even from itself, and to create more effective services.

The Way Ahead

We do not need to further restructure or rationalise the public sector, but to revive and revitalise it. The Labour government has set itself ambitious social goals in education, employment, crime, health and social exclusion, which it will only achieve if it can galvanise the public sector to new levels of effectiveness. Civic entrepreneurship will be vital to that revival.

The starting point for renewing the public sector must be a renewal of its relationship with the society it serves. It must proceed from a renewal of purpose. Outputs matter, but only in the context of the wider outcomes that society wants. The pursuit of greater efficiency within the public sector needs to be set within a larger goal of creating a more effective public sector. It needs to move away from transferring resources from one group to another and towards creating lasting social value by investing in social capital. We need a value creating public sector, which is capable of resolving complex social problems, such as educational underachievement, rather than simply processing it. That change in emphasis means shifting the terms of the debate about the future of the state, away from an obsession about its appropriate size and structure and towards an examination of the capacity and skills it needs to learn.

The idea of civic entrepreneurship might strike people as odd. Entrepreneurs are generally thought to be bucaneering, egotistical, profit seeking, business people, quite unlike the average public sector manager. Yet there is a growing recognition that the skills of entrepreneurship can be applied in different settings, for non-business goals. Take social entrepreneurs, often working in deprived communities or in innovative voluntary organisations who are entrepreneurial because they develop imaginative ways to satisfy unmet social needs by using under-utilised resources, such as derelict buildings or people written off by the education system (Leadbeater, 1997). They are social rather than business entrepreneurs because their main assets are social, in the form of relationships with supporters, partners and users and their main goals and outputs are social – a more educated, healthier, safer community.

Civic entrepreneurship combines some of the ingredients of social entrepreneurship and entrepreneurship in the business sector. Entrepreneurs in most walks of life are restless, creative, lateral-thinking, rule-breakers. They are frequently storytellers and risk-takers, who combine a capacity for visionary thinking with an appetite for opportunism. Many entrepreneurs in the public sector have these characteristics. But civic entrepreneurship requires distinctive skills because public sector organisations are so different from businesses or voluntary bodies. Public organisations are usually larger than most voluntary bodies; they have statutory responsibilities and use public money, for which they are held to account. They often have a more formal governance structure, in which managers have to answer to elected members. For these reasons, entrepreneurship in the public sector must be different from entrepreneurship in the business or the voluntary sector.

Three ingredients mark out civic entrepreneurship:

1. It is necessarily as much about political renewal as it is about managerial change. Public organisations cannot be revitalised unless

they renew their sense of purpose: that is a largely political process. Entrepreneurship requires risk taking to back experimentation and innovation. In the public sector managing those risks requires political skill and leadership.

2. It is necessarily collaborative. In the private sector the entrepreneur is a mythic heroic figure. Entrepreneurship in the public sector is essentially about collaborative leadership, working across boundaries within and beyond organisations.

3. It is about more than individual acts of innovation. Civic entrepreneurs often create new products and services, or find the space for others to do that and in turn disseminate those innovations.

A working definition of civic entrepreneurship then is:

> the renegotiation of the mandate and sense of purpose of a public organisation, which allows it to find new ways of combining resources and people, both public and private, to deliver better social outcomes, higher social value and more social capital.

We are not suggesting that all public sector managers, in all public organisations need to become entrepreneurial overnight. Nor are we proposing that public sector funding and regulation should in future ignore probity in favour of risk taking. We need a much healthier balance in the public sector, so that a far stronger, more widely spread capacity for entrepreneurship goes hand in hand with sound administration and good operational management.

Promoting Civic Entrepreneurship

The public sector needs much more effective mechanisms to promote, finance, reward, recognise and spread civic entrepreneurship. It is difficult to distil civic entrepreneurship into a replicable form. Entrepreneurship cannot be instructed from on high. It cannot be delivered by systems or structures, although it can be hindered and encouraged by them. Government policy should create spaces in which civic entrepreneurship can flourish.

National policy

National policy can help innovation and entrepreneurship by focusing managers on outcomes rather than outputs. Instead of judging the efficiency of an organisation by its throughput – for instance arrest warrants issued by the police, or beds occupied in hospitals – it would be better pinpoint the outcomes that they should be seeking: safer communities, lower waiting times, improved personal care. How organisations went about delivering these outcomes would then be open to innovation and local discretion.

National policy may be one of the few tools strong enough to break the stranglehold that producer interests can exert over public sector organisations. This is perhaps clearest in education, where the combination of centralised target setting and local management of schools, has shifted power away from local education authorities and trade unions and towards parents and head teachers. Just as national policies can enable innovation, they can hinder it. Budgets are often too departmentalised to encourage integrated solutions that involve cooperation between agencies. Central regulation of performance targets and spending can be too tight and detailed to allow the flexibility needed for innovation to thrive.

- Central government can lead by example, by developing a more integrated, holistic, approach to policy making, by pulling together departments into cross-functional teams to address common problems. The Social Exclusion Unit is one example of such integrated policy making unit, which could be applied to other areas such as youth policy and aspects of crime. Policy making, target setting and funding can be integrated around particular issues (youth crime) ; particular client groups (the under-eights) or around particular areas (the creation of health, education and employment zones may help this.)

- These experiments with a more integrated approach to policy making could lead to an even more radical overhaul of central policy making. The best councils, like Kirklees, are well ahead of central government in creating organisations capable of focusing both on strategy and operational delivery. Under a Kirklees style approach to central policy making, cabinet members would be given responsibility for strategic issues and social problems, which cut across departments, such as community safety, or the elderly. They would then call upon the resources of various 'back office' departments to solve the problems. This could help to produce more integrated solutions and reduce turf wars between cabinet ministers.

- Policy making to promote imaginative and integrated solutions to problems is one thing. Funding these is another. The government could create an Innovation Fund from a levy on all departmental budgets to finance projects which cut across departmental budgets.

- Another approach would be to extend the role of funding by bidding, along the lines of a simpler, less expensive form of City Challenge funding. Central government could specify the range of issues and outcomes it wanted tackled – for instance inventive approaches to youth crime, early release from prison or joint social services and health service initiatives – and seek bids from partnerships created to experiment with new solutions.

Rewarding and Recognising Entrepreneurship

Civic entrepreneurs are not in it for the money. Financial incentives, such as performance related pay for senior managers might play some role in promoting entrepreneurship. We need to find other distinctive ways to reward and recognise public sector entrepreneurs.

The financial incentives for innovation in the public sector are not powerful enough. In one large regional office of the Department of Social Security staff said they could identify ways to save several million pounds a year, without making any redundancies. However, there was no incentive to make the changes because the savings would not benefit their organisation but the DSS budget as a whole. Incentive structures to reward local offices and staff for their initiative, would help spur innovation by ensuring that some of the efficiency gains made were ploughed back into the work of that office.

Public sector managers are often motivated by esteem rather than financial reward. The creation of a Queen's Award for Public Excellence, to stand alongside the awards for industry and export, would recognise the achievements of the best public organisations and managers.

Public sector entrepreneurship could be rewarded through a scholarship or learning programme, in which recognised innovators and entrepreneurs at all levels of the public sector were helped to learn and study more about entrepreneurship in other walks of life.

Spreading Entrepreneurship

The public sector lacks effective mechanisms to spread the innovative approaches created by civic entrepreneurs. Dynamic regional economies such as Silicon Valley thrive on the rapid translation of bright ideas into entrepreneurial businesses, supported by venture capitalists. To create lasting social value on a significant scale we need to turn isolated cases of best practice into common practice.

Each government department should have a Lessons Learned unit, whose job would be to find and disseminate innovative best practice, in the UK and internationally. The US Army's system of after action reviews, and its small but highly effective central Lessons Learned unit is one model of how a public organisation can learn systematically from its own mistakes and successes. These departmental structures could be coordinated by a central Lessons Learned unit, whose main role would be to promote similar units throughout the public sector.

There are important questions about the effectiveness of much of the machinery which monitors the public sector. The National Audit Office, which tracks central government spending, is more narrowly financially oriented than the Audit Commission, which deals with local government and health. The Audit Commission is increasingly concentrating on lessons learned, innovation and auditing the public sector's approach to complex problems, such as youth crime, rather than simply auditing discrete organisations. Individual departments have their own auditors such as Ofsted in education, the Social Services Inspectorate and Her Majesty's Inspector of Prisons. This diverse public sector audit machinery could be developed in several ways. The first would be ensure more information sharing across these different auditors, to gather and promote best practice. The second would be to encourage more joint working, for instance bringing together Ofsted, the Audit Commission and the Social Services Inspectorate to examine policies towards the under eight year olds. The third, would be to develop and spread an approach to auditing, which augmented the traditional stress on probity and financial accountability, by paying more attention to the management of innovation and entrepreneurship. The fourth, would be to examine ways that these audit bodies might go beyond auditing to develop a public sector management consultancy to help managers to translate ideas into practice.

Public sector entrepreneurship is not simply a product of the interaction of national policies, however enlightened, and local management of service delivery. A wide range of intermediate bodies, which stand between central government and the school, police station or benefits office, play a vital role. This web of intermediate bodies is complex. The public sector needs a thinking, creative middle layer, which is able to promote and spread best practice innovations as one of its tasks. These institutions, local education authorities, health authorities, regional development agencies, could act as civic venture capitalists, spotting and then spreading good ideas.

Regulating for entrepreneurship

Too much top down, uniform standard setting will inhibit local initiative. The public sector needs a system of oversight which evaluates not just compliance, but the capacity of organisations to achieve the outcomes they have set for themselves.

Future developments might include:

- Learning audits, which go beyond assessing success and failure, to help schools, hospitals, police forces, to devise alternative strategies to improve performance. Seeing through this process of improvement needs local commitment, knowledge and support. That is a job regional and local bodies can do far more effectively than experts from Whitehall.

- Extend the use of joint user and peer audits, in which organisations can offer independent evaluation and advice to each other. Most companies of any size draw on ideas and advice from competitors, suppliers, customers and partners as well as paid advisors and non-executive directors. Each public sector organisation should develop a comparable web of contacts to promote learning and adaptation.

- The direct involvement of users in more formal processes of auditing an organisation. In all our case studies users played a vital role in providing a benchmark for organisational purpose and performance. This involvement could be formalised in the form of user's panels, focus groups and advisory panels.

Commissioning for entrepreneurship

It is likely that the strategic commissioning role of regional and intermediate bodies will become more not less important. They could encourage entrepreneurship through several roles:

- *Licensing:* strategic commissioning bodies, such as health authorities, could create licenses to operate, specifying outcomes to be delivered and baselines of performance, but leaving it up to local management as to how they deliver.

- *Market making:* by changing the purchasing patterns for public services, bringing in new providers for instance, intermediate bodies can engage in active market making to create new sources of supply. For instance they could help to promote new forms of self-help in housing, health and community safety by "preserving" part of their funding for these under-funded sectors.

- *Learning:* intermediate bodies such as health and local education authorities should be a conduit for new ideas to come from outside the locality they serve. Often it is difficult for an individual head-teacher or hospital manager to raise their heads from their immediate tasks to scan for new ideas.

Local politics

Service innovation in the public sector invariably goes hand in hand with political innovation in democratic machinery. A creative alliance between political leaders and senior managers is vital in several of our case study organisations. Political leaders play a vital role in helping to create a sense of direction and in managing the risks associated with change, particularly public disquiet and disapproval. They help to confer legitimacy on innovation. Yet politics often stands in the way of innovation. It is difficult for even the best public sector manager to be inventive in the face of political instability or opposition. Senior managers in innovative public sector organisations excel at managing the political alliances needed to safeguard their freedom of manoeuvre. To promote more entrepreneurship in the public sector we need to create a local politics which is more conducive to innovation and risk taking.

Traditional departmental committees, overly formal meetings and an almost total separation of political and management responsibility are not conducive to change. There has been widespread discussion of the merits of new forms of public participation in decision making – citizens juries, user panels and local referenda have been suggested as methods to augment representative democracy (see Delap, 1998). The main criteria for judging any democratic reform is whether it expands accountability and involvement in decision making. Yet in addition political reform should be judged for the contribution it could make to a more innovative, value creating public sector. Several questions could be used to assess the potential for political reform to promote public sector entrepreneurship:

- One might be to test ways of providing users with more direct involvement in decision making about specific services, along the lines of parental involvement in the management of schools. One possibility would be to pilot experiments with a form of 'democratic service' as a parallel to jury service.

- The growing dependence of the public sector on partnerships with the private sector raises important questions of governance and accountability, which may require novel approaches to community involvement.

- Another possibility would be to create local versions of the challenge funding being developed in Whitehall. Kirklees Council is developing one model in which ward level partnerships between councillors, community groups and business are being created to bid for money from a council wide community innovation fund.

Experiments with more direct forms of user involvement in decision making, such as the direct election of mayors, should be closely evaluated to assess the contribution they make to civic entrepreneurship.

Public Sector Management

Creating organisations which are capable of delivering higher standards of performance, learning and adapting swiftly and renewing their sense of purpose, is the job of senior managers in the public sector. There are not yet enough high quality innovative senior managers. We don't just need them at the very top of organisations. We need middle managers with creativity and imagination, with the capacity to work in partnership with users and local people. If there is a single new imperative for public organisations it is to build the capacity of managers to be entrepreneurial.

One way to do this is to draw managers from different sources. Public sector managers in the past have been predictably male, white and middle class. Their skills and management style and their ways of seeing the world can be very similar and sometimes create organisational blindspots. Women, black managers, people with disabilities, people who have lived abroad, worked in the private or voluntary sector, had divergent career paths, are needed not just to demonstrate a commitment to equal opportunities but to draw on a more diverse pool of knowledge and skills.

The Case for the New Public Sector

It is still deeply unfashionable to praise the public sector. It has become a convenient whipping-boy, frequently offering itself up for punishment. The state is still largely seen as a slow moving, bureaucratic, hierarchical and unfriendly obstacle to improving living standards. In the 1980s the public sector was repeatedly attacked for falling short of private sector standards. The private sector was seen as efficient, responsive, well managed. The public sector was seen as inefficient, unresponsive and managed in the interests of producers rather than consumers. The new Labour government marks a sharp break with that approach. It clearly believes that government has a vital role in reviving a sense of civic spirit in Britain. The public sector will be central to the delivery of many

164 An Inclusive Society

of the government's pledges on crime, education, employment, health and poverty. Yet that does not amount to an endorsement of the traditional public sector. Far from it. The government clearly wants to promote a role for the central state as a strategic commissioner, enabler and regulator of public services, not necessarily as a funder or provider. It wants a mixed economy of provision, in which the public sector is joined by the voluntary sector, business, social enterprise and new hybrid institutions created through partnerships. There is every sign that it will be impatient with those parts of the public sector unwilling to change fast enough. The public sector will continue to be under pressure, from politicians and the public, to respond more quickly to change and to become more effective. Civic entrepreneurship is not a panacea. Not all public sector managers can or necessarily need to become civic entrepreneurs. Probity and sound administration are vital components of public management. Public sector renewal can be driven by policy innovation and energetic leadership from the centre. The government's unfolding literacy programme in primary schools is an example of that. Yet civic entrepreneurship must be a central ingredient in the creation of the new public sector that people want. Without a much broader and deeper capacity for entrepreneurship within the public sector efforts at renewal will prove much more difficult.

For much of the 20th century the public sector has been associated with modernisation, social improvement and rising quality of life. It is only in the last two and a half decades that it has become publicly associated with decline and under-achievement. Despite two decades of cuts and restructuring the public sector remains central to British society and touches most people's lives. It can once again become a source of renewal in British society but only if it taps the spirit of civic entrepreneurship within it.

References

Delap (1998) *Making Better Decisions: Report of an IPPR Symposium on Citizens' Juries and other Methods of Public Involvement* IPPR, London.

Leadbeater C (1997) *The Rise of the Social Entrepreneur* Demos London

V:
The role of the
private sector

13. Private interests and public purposes: exclusion and the private sector[1]
Gavin Kelly and James McCormick

Introduction

New strategies to tackle social and economic exclusion will require a significant role for the private sector. This is an important development as traditional accounts of poverty have fallen into the trap of either omitting the private sector altogether or simply seeing it as part of the problem. Ignoring the potential contribution of business makes little sense in a world in which many of the goods and services which are key to the question of exclusion are now supplied privately. Recently most attention has focused on the provision of employment, for good reasons: one of the most powerful routes to inclusion is a job paid at a decent wage. However access to and the affordability of basic services such as fuel, telephone and water along with insurance coverage, pension provision, and access to a bank account and credit need to be central to programmes aimed at reducing exclusion.

Even in areas not normally associated with private sector provision there are plans to allow private firms to play a significant managerial role in combating exclusion. The escalation of the number of arenas in which business is perceived to be competent and have a legitimate role is breathtaking. Fifteen years ago the business-led Urban Development Corporations (UDCs) were highly contentious. Now the private sector has become formally involved in the design, delivery and governance of public policy across a range of areas which are relevant to the exclusion debate2. Indeed it is this involvement of the private sector in the policy process that has caught the headlines in recent months. This Chapter has a slightly different emphasis. It is concerned with the role that government can play in partnership with business in increasing access to certain privately supplied goods and services. So rather than focusing on the role that the private sector can play in reducing government failure, we consider the role that a light-footed government can play in altering market outcomes so as to reduce exclusion.

Despite the increased recognition of the potential role of business, much of the recent debate on exclusion has focused exclusively on the role of public sector agencies. Inherent in these contributions are judgements as to where responsibility for reducing exclusion should be located, as well as a view of the appropriate policy tools for bringing about change. Broadly speaking this identification of the public sector as the ultimate site of responsibility is inevitable and desirable: the widening reach of the private sector does not alter the basic fact that most businesses have little incentive to involve themselves directly in the alleviation of exclusion. But recognising the primacy of public responsibility in this area should in no way deter us from looking for new ways of using the private sector as a policy tool, or expanding the role that it plays in reducing exclusion.[3]

Unpacking exclusion and the private sector

In this Chapter the term exclusion has a variety of overlapping meanings in the current debate and can take a number of forms.

- The most common understanding concerns access exclusion which results from outright refusal to provide services to the highest risk-households (for example red-lining of particular neighbourhoods by insurance companies).

- A more subtle form of exclusion is condition exclusion. For instance a bank might offer an account that is suitable but not accessible because a minimum monthly balance must be maintained to avoid charges. An insurer might be prepared to offer an affordable policy but only if minimum (and expensive) home security requirements are first met.

- A third type of exclusion is price exclusion which can exist even where services are widely available and there are no prior conditions. The same insurer may offer policies even in high-risk neighbourhoods but at a price which is unaffordable. Exclusion on the grounds of cost can also reflect payment options (which is also a form of condition exclusion). While bills might be affordable if they are paid weekly in cash, monthly or quarterly payment may be the only options.

- In addition there is the less familiar problem of self-exclusion. To some extent this can be the result of other forms of exclusion (the price of fuel leading to self-disconnection when finances are low), but it also refers to the problem of individuals choosing of their own accord to be excluded in a particular context (for example, unskilled men in economically-depressed areas who fail to apply for new jobs which they think of as 'women's work').

In addition to these distinctions between different types of exclusion it is also important to recognise the interdependency between different forms of exclusion. Typically this is done with regard to services which are provided by public authorities but a similar point needs to be made (but rarely is) with regard to problems arising from the private sector. For instance the real cost of domestic fuel depends in part on access to a bank account which will be influenced by the branching decisions of the banks (or access to a telephone). The price of food depends upon consumer mobility which may in turn depend upon access to the service provided by private bus companies. These interdependencies reinforce another strand of thinking on exclusion, which is essentially community-focused. Rather than emphasising the problems that individuals face in accessing services and networks, this approach concentrates on the policies that encourage regeneration and growth within excluded communities. The objective is then to identify public or public-private initiatives that will spur revitalisation of particular localities, the view being that community regeneration and local economic development are the best way to reconnect such areas with the mainstream economy[4].

The multi-faceted nature of exclusion indicates the range of economic interests that are relevant to addressing it and the breadth of areas where government-private sector collaboration could be advantageous. Moreover the role that any one company may play will be sensitive to key economic characteristics (including firm size and degree of market competition) as well as the nature of the goods and services supplied. Government agencies may wish to enlist the co-operation of companies ranging from British Telecom to local community enterprises, underlining the need to move beyond catch-all generalisations about the role that 'the private sector' can play. New thinking on the role of business in shaping and tackling exclusion needs to register this diversity and be alert to the different possibilities that exist for various segments of the private sector.

Intellectual / political context

The range of ideological and political perspectives on business involvement in policy is broad and confounds traditional political alignments. The ascendant view within the current debate (spanning the centre-left and right) is that government should encourage private sector involvement as it represents the most innovative and forward looking sector of the economy. It should therefore have a role to play in addressing what are often portrayed as intractable social and economic problems. From government's perspective it represents the belief that by working with the private sector it will improve the design and implementation of key policies. The flip-side of this perspective – why business should agree to play this role – is somewhat less clear. At one level it is nothing more than the commonplace view that the private sector will respond to public incentives or regulation: the role of government is thus to construct incentive structures which ensure that private actors bring about public ends. But many politicians (and some business leaders) appear to supplement this narrow incentive-based argument with a hazier notion of corporate responsibility. This maintains that private sector companies should be willing to be 'public spirited' in order to fulfil the terms of their implicit 'license to operate'.[5] It must be emphasised, however, that in terms of what business is obliged to do the notion of a license to operate (for example, over and above conforming to existing laws, paying taxes) is generally associated with an extremely thin notion of social responsibility. Essentially it relies on voluntary behaviour by businesses who wish to play their role as good corporate citizens, though as discussed later, this may in itself constitute an important first-step in reducing certain types of exclusion.[6]

Against this is the view that the role of the private sector in dealing with issues of social policy and exclusion should be severely curtailed. Although this perspective has been very much on the retreat in recent years, a broad political alliance can be found which supports it. The core belief is that business will be exclusively concerned with commercial criteria, such as profitability or shareholder value. To try and alter this would be to undermine the basic nature of the company and would pose a threat to both social policy and free enterprise – predictably those on the left emphasise the former, those on the right the latter.[7] Clearly right-wing versions of this see an extensive role for the private sector in providing goods and services that left-wing critics would expect the state to supply: the two versions of this approach differ as to where the public/private boundary should be drawn, but both agree on the fundamental point that there should be a clear boundary. Accordingly, both views also oppose business involvement in the policy process and would be sceptical of the notion of public-private partnerships. Those on the right predict that these will lead to the ever growing encroachment of government regulation (in order to legitimise business involvement in public interest matters) while those on the left anticipate the spread of commercial values within the public sphere and the undermining of popular support for state funded services. In short business and public policy make bad bed-fellows, and it is in the interest of both sides to keep their distance.

Private interests and public purposes

We argue that both of the above positions need to be subject to critical evaluation. Though it is not taken as axiomatic that private sector led initiatives are necessarily the correct approach, the idea that business involvement inevitably undermines social policy or lacks legitimacy, is firmly rejected. Current private/public initiatives on exclusion are self-evidently structured by the wider political and economic context: shifts in the public-private balance within the economy, changes in the patterns of private ownership, along with the work of corporate public relations departments, have to a considerable extent altered the acceptability of business involvement in government initiatives. The simple fact that many providers of key services are now in the private sector inevitably has implications for the methods by which government attempts to address exclusion arising from service provision. However the widespread political enthusiasm for expanding the role of the private sector that this has engendered (the 'partnership' phenomena) has not been matched by greater conceptual clarity as to the merits and limits of this new role.

One of the central issues concerning the government-private sector relationship is the extent to which economic regulations shaping the behaviour of firms in sectors characterised by restricted competition (such as the utilities) should be used to pursue social objectives. This question has acquired increased importance as another public policy objective agenda in this area – increasing competition – inevitably leads to pressure for 'cost-reflectivity' in pricing. This restricts the scope for cross-subsidisation between low-income and high income consumers, or between domestic and industrial consumers. At the same time as these transfers have become more difficult, the lack of public legitimacy associated with some private sector utilities confers upon government a considerable amount of leverage to impose (redistributive) universal service obligations.[8] The 'license to operate' for firms in this position is clearly granted on very different terms to that for firms operating in highly competitive market structures and providing 'non-merit' goods and services. Hence many argue that it is reasonable to use the regulatory framework to pursue issues of social equity. Against this stands the conventional wisdom which maintains that the regulation of business to secure social objectives is costly in efficiency terms and makes for poor regulatory (and social) policy. According to this view, social objectives should always be achieved through other instruments such as 'upfront' redistributive fiscal policy or direct public provision. Government support for introducing social objectives into economic regulation is said to be based on the opportunistic desire to shift responsibility onto the private sector, since the consumer cross-subsidisation that this entails is less costly in political terms than highly visible redistributive payments by the state.

Underlying some of these (often oblique) debates on utility regulation is a very basic democratic issue. Should the state seek to resolve issues of disposable income/earnings potential solely through public initiatives (that is, redistibutive transfers through the tax-benefit system) or should it be willing to unbundle this redistributive process, using policy/regulation to increase the number of sites at which issues of exclusion and distribution are addressed. A key consideration for a government serious about combating exclusion (whilst retaining its pro-business credentials) is the extent to which it should seek to share responsibility for issues of exclusion more broadly, incorporating those (regulated) private sector suppliers of key services who operate in non-competitive markets.[9]

Unbundling partnership

If the private sector is to become involved in tackling exclusion it has to have reasons for doing so. This section will briefly map out some of the broad motivations for private sector involvement (these will be illustrated in more detail in the next section which considers a few examples of public-private initiatives). A starting point in this typology is to move beyond the catch-all phrase of 'partnership' in order to focus on the particular forms of relationship, the types of incentives, and the points of leverage, that government can use to affect the behaviour of private sector enterprises. Implicit in our argument is the belief that there is no blueprint for successful partnership between government and business. At the same time we also consider initiatives which companies may undertake of their own accord.

i) coercion / provision of financial incentives

Government can in theory oblige companies to provide services for certain groups or satisfy performance criteria for a given segment of the market, though often there are strong political obstacles to this approach. A more open-ended issue concerns the levers (short of outright compulsion) that can be used to prompt the private sector to perform functions or alter behaviour in a way which is thought to reduce exclusion.[10]

ii) pre-emptive strike by business to avoid the imposition of costly regulations

Another motive for private sector action is that of persuading government that proposed regulatory changes (or equally rumoured or perceived regulatory initiatives) do not come about. This is particularly relevant to large companies in industries which are either subject to particular regulations (for example, utilities, banks and emerging industries in which government licenses individual operators) or those sectors where government agencies confer particular benefits which might be withdrawn (for example, the charitable status of independent schools). There are recent examples of private sector companies seeking to barter with government by offering enhanced compensation for customers if their service agreements are not fulfilled in an effort to head off tighter regulation; this type of initiative can doubtless generate favourable PR spin-offs for companies who market such action as 'consumer responsiveness'. It also seems likely that community and public relations departments within large companies use these arguments to make the case for their projects through intra-company negotiations. Clearly government agencies, knowing that certain companies are sensitive to these issues, might play a proactive role in persuading companies of the benefits of voluntary action. Government may perceive that there are benefits from being unclear about their intentions, signalling that the choice may be between voluntary action and tougher regulation, rather than no action. This approach, of course, offers no guarantees for either side, fosters uncertainty, and suffers from a lack of transparency.

iii) coincidence between social objectives and commercially profitable opportunities

Where companies undertake new initiatives they may discover that it is possible to make a commercial return in market sectors/areas which were previously thought unviable. There are a number of areas of service provision where it is currently argued that private companies could make a commercial return at the same time as reducing exclusion. The frontier of profit-making activity can shift as a result of improved information, or changes in the management and perception of risk. Yet change does not lead only in more socially-inclusive directions; this argument cuts both ways. Just as some companies see new market opportunities which reduce exclusion, so other businesses (or indeed the same ones) decide that the provision of different services to particular consumers or localities is no longer commercially viable. This can be seen in the increasing retrenchment of bank branches within middle and high-income localities and away from low income areas, occurring at the same time as some of the banks are exploring new ways to extend financial services to currently excluded groups. Finally, it should be emphasised that the process by which the boundary of profit-making activity shifts is susceptible to public policy interventions and social entrepreneurship. There may be an important and much under-utilised role for government and other intermediaries in organising fragile markets in such a way that they become viable for the private sector to enter.

iv) corporate citizenship and the other regarding objectives of management

Another category concerns the direct role that business could play voluntarily in reducing exclusion. Clearly the private sector has through ventures such as Business in the Community chosen to undertake 'community work' which both combats aspects of exclusion and can be of positive benefit to the firms in question. Some concern has been voiced concerning the durability of these initiatives over the economic cycle. However, the fact that business itself designs these projects should help increase their resilience.

Examples of public-private initiatives which could promote inclusion

Gas regulation: competition and social equity

Greater competition in the domestic fuel market, while delivering clear benefits to the average consumer, has had highly uneven distributional consequences for different types of consumer. Since privatisation there has been a general trend towards greater dispersal in utility charges to consumers both across localities[11] and between different groups of consumers. Supplying pre-payment or late paying consumers is expensive and is a cost which has previously been shared across all consumer groups. Competition has reduced these cross-subsidies leading to concerns over the price paid by low income groups. For instance, the higher administrative costs of pre-payment customers has meant that they have received far smaller gains from greater competition. Indeed it may be the case that the more severe competition for 'commercially attractive' customers has led gas companies to pile some of the transitional costs of competition and a disproportionately high ratio of overhead costs onto commercially 'less attractive' customers.

These distributional effects of competition pose a fundamental question for government, regulators and the private suppliers: what type of responsibility, if any, should the privatised utilities have to ensure that low-income groups benefit from competition even if this is costly to the firm and shareholders?[12] Should a form of universal service obligation be imposed, and if so, what type? This issue (along with many others) is being considered in the Department of Trade and Industry (DTI)'s Review of Utilities Regulation. In its submission the regulator OFGAS rehearsed the conventional argument against broadening the objective of regulation beyond narrow 'economic issues', and augmented this with the view that wider discretionary powers required to deal with social issues would exacerbate existing concerns over the legitimacy of the regulator.13 Consumers groups, such as the Gas Consumers Council take a different view.

Clearly any meaningful form of social obligation will have resource implications. To some extent a financing mechanism is already available in that OFGAS can currently make provision for a fund to compensate those gas companies who supply markets with a disproportionately high share of high cost customers. Arguably though this approach suffers from a moral hazard problem – gas suppliers have an incentive to exaggerate the costs of supplying these customers (as this lets them raise prices or enhances their bargaining position with the regulator) which may have the counter-productive effect of deterring potential competitors from entering the high-cost end of the domestic market (Waddams-Price, 1997). Alternative funding arrangements have been proposed including a tax on gas companies (effectively reintroducing a cross-subsidy) or compensation through the social security system.

Exclusion from basic financial services

Financial exclusion has attracted greater attention in recent years following studies of the number of households in Britain without access to a bank account[14] (Kempson, 1994), and bank branch closures especially in low-income urban neighbourhoods (Thrift and Leyshon, 1997). Because a household is without a bank account it does not however mean it has been denied one or would even prefer to have one. Younger households may eventually join the financial service networks when the need arises. Older households may have used cash all their lives and see little reason to change now. These groups may be outside the banking system but not excluded. But others will find themselves facing a series of barriers which leave them excluded from the savings and insurance system because they are unable to meet the various conditions imposed by providers.

Here we discuss the specific situation of low income households without bank accounts, assuming that for many of them savings and credit facilities could reduce their financial vulnerability. Some lessons may be learnt from the US where the Community Reinvestment Act (CRA) imposes an obligation on all banks to endeavour to meet the credit needs of their local communities. Though controversial and not without its own faults, the CRA has led to a high level of awareness of the issue of financial exclusion and has encouraged US banks to undertake a series of community banking experiments. (It should be noted however that the CRA does not impose an obligation to meet the needs of each individual or household within low-income communities.) When considered from this perspective what is notable about the UK is not so much that it lacks a CRA, but the erosion of any notion of responsibility (whether residing in the public or private sector) for meeting the basic financial needs of all households. The tradition of what has become known in North America as 'financial citizenship' is much weaker. Critics of the CRA approach, or other more burdensome universal service obligation (USOs) on banks, argue that they constitute an essentially arbitrary burden on one segment of the financial sector without covering other 'near-bank' financial institutions.

Another complexity in designing new policy initiatives is in identifying the right balance between the costs and benefits of greater competition in the supply of credit to low-income communities. For instance, should public policy try to make all banks more active in deprived areas, or should it focus on identifying 'lead' lenders ? Where there are (relatively) high fixed-costs alongside 'increasing returns' to lending in low-income areas3, then greater competition may undermine the willingness of banks to make the initial investments required to make lending in these 'thin' markets worthwhile. If so, more competition will increase the risk of rationing (and even red-lining) in low-income localities. However these risks need to be traded-off against the benefits which greater competition would bring to those who are successful in gaining access to credit.[15] The implication for policy-makers is clear: do not oversimplify the impact of greater competition on some fragile markets.

Though policy debate in this area has a short history in the UK, it is currently rapidly evolving with a number of different schemes being proposed. In terms of the earlier 'typology', this is an issue where a number of different motivations for private sector innovation seem to coexist. At one level the banks are keen to ward off calls for heavy handed regulation aimed at increasing access. But some banks also wish to be seen as leaders in the debate, and are finding from their experiments in the field that – given the right framework – it is possible to make an acceptable rate of return on lending dedicated to previously excluded groups, such as community enterprises.

One approach is to encourage or oblige the banks to provide universal access to low-cost and basic accounts (current accounts with low charges and a low rate of interest). Though there is a clear need for such a product (and banks may seem like obvious suppliers) the banks themselves may well oppose this, and even if this resistance can be overcome, it is unclear how this option would get around the problem of access to banks in localities without a branch bank, or even a Automated Teller Machine. Proposals which pick up on this problem of local access have focused on the potential of Automated Cash Transfers (for benefit payments) to help entice local non-bank outlets such as supermarkets and post-offices to provide basic financial services to claimants (Kempson, 1994). A different tack is taken by those who emphasise that high-street banks could play an important role in the development of the existing (uneven) network of credit unions in low-income areas if they were given the right incentives (Conaty and Mayo, 1997). On its own, however, it is unclear how far this approach will go in addressing the problem of financial exclusion, particularly if it maintains the separation between excluded groups and mainstream providers. A further proposal is that banks could themselves issue a dedicated 'community bond', partially guaranteed by government, which mainstream savers could choose to invest in. This would provide capital which would then be directed to community enterprises, third sector organisations, and individuals in low-income neighbourhoods. Clearly this latter approach does not benefit from the comprehensiveness of a broad USO on banks (indeed it could complement rather than substitute it), but investment vehicles of this type have provided a substantial boost to inner city housing, small business and service developments in the USA.

Risk-pooling and market making:

There is an increasing awareness of the capacity of intermediaries, on an affinity group basis, to play a key role in making services available to groups of consumers that would not be available to them as individuals, or at least not on the same terms. In essence these intermediate organisations (for example local authorities, housing associations, or trade unions) can organise some consumer markets in such a way that transaction costs and information problems are reduced and scale economies achieved, to the extent that private sector provision becomes viable.

There are numerous local examples of these principles being applied to the home insurance market in low-income/high-risk communities (Whyley *et al*, 1998). The insurance industry has developed increasingly sophisticated ways of measuring the risk of theft using post code data. The result, once again, has been an unravelling of implicit cross-subsidies, pricing insurance policies beyond the reach of the most vulnerable households. Despite this, affordable cover is now being offered even in some of the highest-risk neighbourhoods as a result of innovative agreements between local authorities or housing associations and private insurers. Social landlords act as 'gatekeepers' to large numbers of uninsured households – a group for whom the highly competitive insurance market has failed to offer appropriate choices. Rather than providing a general subsidy through housing benefits or placing an obligation on insurance companies to provide policies to all, intermediate insurance markets have emerged.

Around half of Britain's local authorities share the costs of collecting insurance premiums alongside rental payments. In return for access to a substantial untapped market, participating insurers are willing to reduce entry and payment conditions. Tenants thereby gain access to comprehensive insurance policies from mainstream companies with premiums payable in cash on a regular basis. While this end of the market is likely to return low profits, many insurers conclude that 'insure with rent' schemes are viable provided they reach a critical mass of households and as long as schemes are well-managed. They are able to extend insurance to groups of tenants they would otherwise be reluctant to cover as individual households. In this way the dominant market trend can be bucked, financial exclusion reduced and private companies move into new market niches. Similarly housing associations are increasingly capable of offering low-cost services to residents, such as savings schemes and access to small pools of credit. The principle is similar in that a partnership between an affinity group and commercial firm (say the housing association and a building society) results in the extension of new services to low-income groups.[17]

Business in the Community: taking corporate citizenship seriously

Most business in the UK will not be affected by what we have discussed so far which has been oriented towards particular firms (often very large) who supply goods and services which are either a basic requirement (fuel, pension, home insurance) or form the basis of a pathway out of exclusion (skills, credit, transport). The first and most obvious point to make is that all businesses play a key role by providing employment. In localities of high unemployment this is their primary role: corporate citizenship probably means nothing more than what businesses are doing anyway. In these cases the need for government and business groups to provide a supportive institutional framework which seeks to assist the creation and survival of small firms is self-evident. But in most cases there is considerable scope for companies (and local business associations) to develop a 'thicker' notion of corporate citizenship and a range of motives for choosing to do so.

It is increasingly understood that motivation, trust, and high aspirations are needed to make businesses successful. The same is true of other civic institutions such as schools. Moreover, the insights of far-sighted business people can be effectively deployed to improve skills to the advantage of children struggling to learn. Where community affairs budgets are tight or do not exist even small businesses can provide time, expertise and role models. The idea of associate teachers in the classroom is not new. It involves training employees to bring new skills to schools, freeing teachers to give more of their time to those who most need it. The Prince's Trust – through both its Young Business and Volunteers programmes – applies the same principle more broadly. Companies which strive to be competitive and inclusive find that such initiatives have a hard economic value as well as a series of community benefits. A period spent helping to teach in an inner-city primary school is likely to provide a more demanding management training method for graduate-trainees than residential weekend courses spent with people like themselves. It is also cheaper and provides clear benefits to others.

But regeneration strategies involving the private sector also focus on employment creation and training. One issue surrounds the depressingly low levels of participation by local businesses in local employment initiatives in deprived localities. For instance, a recent survey of a low-income district of Sheffield demonstrated that there is a persistent lack of awareness of these initiatives among local firms, but that many firms (once informed) were keen to become involved.[18] Businesses who are never asked are unlikely to do more than the bare minimum in support of regeneration initiatives. Another more controversial initiative is the use of local labour clauses on public contracts.[19] The dangers inherent in this approach range from local clientilism to the concern that 'best value' is not being obtained from public funds. A key lesson from (often unsuccessful) experiments with these contracts in the 1980s is that they only work if employers are convinced that residents are job-prepared. It seems that a new model of local-contracting is emerging based on this insight. In the construction industry for example, some employers are negotiating their own local labour policies (including a pre-vocational training phase) driven by the realisation that the active participation of residents is likely to reduce the costs of maintenance. It is an investment in community ownership as well as skills enhancement.

Conclusions and Policy

Enduring need for government activism

This chapter has tried to demonstrate some of the ways that different public-private initiatives can help address forms of exclusion which arise as a consequence of market failure, government failure, and/or the distribution of income. The central argument made is that there is a role for government in seeking to maximise access to key goods and services supplied by the private sector, just as there will be a continuing role for different parts of the private sector in minimising inefficiency in the design and delivery of aspects of government policy. In terms of the organisation of central government's overall strategy towards exclusion the implication of this argument is straightforward enough: issues of economic and social exclusion should pre-occupy those in the DTI as much as those in the Department of Social Security.

Involvement in public-private initiatives can enhance the reputations of companies, and may have a more direct impact on profitability by opening up new market opportunities which would otherwise have been neglected. As has been emphasised government's role in this is often to co-ordinate and organise rather than to subsidise. However, we should not be too starry-eyed about the cumulative impact of such efforts. For many companies our discussion will be of dubious relevance. Though there is an impressive range of initiatives which the private sector can and does play a constructive role in, it would be foolhardy to exaggerate the aggregate impact of these: a leading role for government therefore remains both inevitable and entirely appropriate. Indeed there is a strong interdependence between the case for an expansive role for the private-sector and that for government activism. As a greater emphasis is placed upon the private suppliers of key services (as with stakeholder pensions) the regulation and monitoring of the quality of services will become a more important government responsibility, not less so. Government may be better able to offer a more detached view and better identify an appropriate balance of regulatory and voluntary instruments where it does not have direct responsibility for provision.

Having made clear the limits as to what can be expected from the private sector we conclude with five propositions concerning the private sector, government and exclusion – modest signposts towards inclusion.

i) Disclosure and locating accountability

One theme running through this Chapter has been the need for government to influence the private sector in order to reduce certain types of exclusion. This inevitably directs attention towards the levers that government can use to bring pressure and effect change. With regard to the public sector, disclosure provisions and performance indicators are increasingly common tools of public policy. When used well they can be an effective and unbureaucratic starting point for policy interventions. As of yet their use remains highly underdeveloped in relation to the private sector's performance in addressing different aspects of exclusion.

● all utility regulators (together with consumer bodies) could be assigned a specific responsibility for reporting on how price and service measures affect low-income/socially disadvantaged groups such as pre-payment customers. Companies should also be obliged to report on levels of self-disconnection (as well as disconnection).

● a further step should be to set a clear framework within which categories of consumers benefit (in terms of charges) from efficiency gains to some publicly specified extent. Care should be taken to ensure that there is stability in this type of social obligation in order that it becomes accepted as part of the 'rules of the game' according to which firms and investors operate.

- new performance indicators and disclosure provisions could be applied to other key private sector actors who have a clear role to play in reducing financial exclusion such as banks, pension fund companies and insurers.[20] Though some firms would oppose this, it is interesting to note that other leading companies in these sectors have already indicated that they are relaxed about this type of approach. Overall it would be a useful first-step in maintaining pressure for 'levelling-up' rather than down, though other measures would be required to secure what should be a medium-term objective of universal access to basic pension, insurance and banking facilities.

ii) Focus on re-connecting communities

The spatial concentration of excluded communities suggests that resources and initiatives should continue to be targeted at specific localities. There are of course problems with this approach, not least the inevitable arbitrariness involved in the delimitation of such areas. Nonetheless a greater concentration of resources ought to be beneficial. Overall, local strategies should be focused at reconnecting households and local enterprises with the mainstream economy[21]. It is possible to make the case for public support for local initiatives whilst avoiding the pitfalls of public programmes resulting in excluded groups depending on a cocooned and subsidised local economy, rather than on one in which local firms carve out competitive niches in the mainstream economy (Porter 1996). This may mean refashioning some local economic development strategies, for instance shifting the funding basis of (revenue-generating) community enterprises from exclusive reliance on grants to the acceptance of loans (Wells, 1998).

iii) Focus on products/services rather than the provider

Another agenda which has been floated in a number of different contexts is the use of alternative forms of ownership or governance in the targeting of services for excluded groups. Here there is a need to ensure that policy does not fetishise particular modes of ownership/types of supplier without being certain about the improvements in service provision that will arise. This is particularly the case if suppliers corner the low-income segment of the market thereby removing these groups from mainstream service providers who may be more innovative. The guiding principle should be to support quality products, not particular types of provider.

iv) Experiment with intermediate markets which bridge private and public/third sector provision

There is a strong case for the extension of intermediate markets that bring together private firms, third sector groups and local authorities. Experiments are already bringing clear benefits in extending access to employment, credit and insurance. Though they provide no panacea, intermediate markets can provide an effective bridge to mainstream provision and help change perceptions of risk. They may also prove to be more resilient than exclusively private provision. Underlying this approach is a firm rejection of the view that if there is a viable market opportunity to be seized then it is inevitable that private companies would already have spotted the niche and met the demand.

v) Recognise the complex effect of competition on service provision for low-income groups

While the contention that greater competition will generally benefit consumers – and thereby low income groups – is often valid and a useful starting point for policy, there is a danger of oversimplification. Greater competition can be a useful tool in sectors where mainstream providers have already withdrawn from supplying low income groups (who now rely on a monopoly supplier). It is a defining feature of excluded households that they usually have to pay the highest share of their budget towards basics while having the least choice over who provides them. So in some instances there may be a role for government in fostering competition for commercially 'less attractive customers'. But care must be taken with this. Greater competition may also exacerbate exclusion, as was suggested in the discussion of credit markets. Finally, a different approach is required where competition is introduced into markets where previously little or none existed (a single firm supplied all income groups). Here the distributional effects need to be carefully monitored and if necessary regulated.

Many of these suggestions have relatively modest financial implications or are cost-neutral. Indeed money has almost earned a poor reputation as a resource to tackle exclusion. The Social Exclusion Unit in England (and parallel networks in the rest of the UK) has a remit to co-ordinate programmes more effectively and to engage in joined-up policy design – to practice holistic government. But it does not have a new budget. 'No more throwing good money after bad' characterises the mood of many politicians. Encouraging the take-up of successful public-private initiatives across departments and government agencies is a low-cost but potentially high-benefit strategy for the Unit. Unless all reforming efforts are to be focused on prevention rather than cure, however, more money will have to be spent, at least in the short-term, assisting the current generation of victims.

References

Avery R, Beeson P and Sniderman M (1996) 'Neighbourhood Information and Home Mortgage Lending', *Federal Reserve Bank of Cleveland Working Paper* 96:20

Baldwin S (1997) *'Employer Survey of Darnall/Atercliffe, Sheffield'*, Policy Research Institute, Leeds

Conaty P and Mayo E (1997) *A Commitment to People and Place: the case for community development credit unions*, New Economics Foundation

Corry D (1995) 'Why We Should Regulate – and why is it so complicated?', in *Regulating in the Public Interest*, IPPR

Gruben W, Neuberger J and Schmidt R (1990) 'Imperfect Information and the CRA' *Federal Reserve of San Francisco Economic Review* (Summer)

Kempson E (1994) *Outside the Banking System*, Social Security Advisory Committee, Research Paper 6

Kempson E (1996) 'Privatisation of the Utilities', in *Britain Divided*, Child Poverty Action Group

Murroni C and Collins R (1995) *New Issues in Universal Service Obligation*, IPPR

Newcombe R (1997) 'Social Banking: The Example of New Horizons', in *Financial Exclusion: Can Mutuality Fill the Gap ?*, New Policy Institute

Parkinson J (1994) *Corporate Power and Responsibility*, Clarendon, Oxford

Porter M (1995) 'The Competitive Advantage of the Inner City', *Harvard Business Review*, May-June p. 55 – 71

Skidelsky R (1990) 'Keynes and the State', *The Economic Borders of the State*, Clarendon, London

Waddams Price C (1996), 'Winners and Losers From Liberalisation of the Domestic Energy Market', p. 57 -84, in *Energy '98: Competing for Power*, Corry, Hewett, Tindale (eds), IPPR

Waddams Price C (1997) 'Regulating for Fairness', *New Economy*, 4:2, pp. 117 – 123

Webster D (1997) 'The L-U Curve', Department of Urban Studies, Glasgow University

Wells P (forthcoming 1998) *Objective II Programme Wide Appraisal for Yorkshire and Humberside*, Government Office for Yorkshire and Humberside

Whyley C, McCormick J and Kempson E (1998) *Paying for peace of mind: Access to Home Contents Insurance for Low-Income Households*, PSI/IPPR

Endnotes

1. The authors would like to the participants at the IPPR seminar along with Andrew Gamble, Carey Oppenheim and John Parkinson for their useful comments on an earlier draft of this paper

2. In terms of governance commonly cited are the 'regeneration' industry (a private sector role was embedded in the rules governing the SRB and City Challenge) and training policy (TECs), but more recently it has extended to central government initiatives on welfare reform, and even to the management of schools in the soon to be created Education Action Zones.

3. The emphasis on the private sector can be attributed to a shift away from 'direct provision' by government towards a focus on ensuring that key services are available to all on an equitable basis. The strategy of encouraging private sector firms to discharge public functions is not new. See Skidelsky (1989) for an account of Keynes' view that the state could and should in some sense incorporate private sector actors who operated with a public purpose.

4. Based on this analysis a vigorous debate is taking place within academic and policy communities concerning the weight to be attached to the theory of 'spatial mismatch' (see Webster 1997 for example). According to this approach the problem of concentrated long term unemployment is explained largely by the isolation of such communities from appropriate job opportunities. This suggests that job creation must be better focused geographically – employers should be encouraged to move to excluded communities. In contrast, others argue that policy should focus on equipping excluded groups to access jobs and keep them. This prioritises packages of support such as affordable transport, childcare, and in-work adjustment which enable people to get jobs wherever they are located. Critics of highly localistic regeneration strategies argue that they may have the perverse effect of further isolating excluded communities. These strategies may initially assist 'island' economies in improving their performance, but ways of getting to the 'mainland' might actually diminish.

5. The RSA's Report *Tomorrow's Company,* which received widespread support in both business and political arenas, placed a great deal of emphasis on companies maintaining their license to operate.

6. Whether or not politicians really believe that managers will act upon this notion of the license to operate is a different matter. The point is that they use this approach to support the view that (i) it is entirely

appropriate that the private sector becomes involved in the policy process and (ii) to encourage the business community to play a role in reducing exclusion.

7. A number of arguments are typically deployed against corporate social responsibility: an efficiency argument holds that the maximisation of social welfare is congruent with firms maximising profits ('the social responsibility of business is to increase its profits'). A second line of argument, referred to as deference or accountability view, is that it is fundamentally inappropriate for private groups (for example, corporate managers) to be involved in issues of social policy as these are inevitably 'public' in nature. Hence it questions business involvement in policy both on grounds of competence and accountability. Lastly, there is the shareholder's money argument, which maintains that all corporate expenditure on non-profit making purposes is a redistribution of resources away from shareholders – representing a form of private taxation. This redistribution is judged to be undesirable both because it is arbitrary (the shareholders did not agree to it) and because of its side-effects, such as undermining respect for property rights. See also Parkinson (1994) for a detailed evaluation of the different arguments against any form of corporate responsibility agenda.

8. The catch-all notion of a universal service obligation actually covers a spectrum of possibilities including price constraints (for example, the post office charging a single price for a first class stamp regardless of the marginal cost of deliveries); access requirements and service conditions. Definitions will often include several or all of these elements (for example, OFTEL's recent definition: 'affordable access to basic telecom services for all those reasonably requesting it, regardless of where they live'). For a discussion of different aspects of USOs see Murroni and Collins (1995). Clearly the appropriateness of USOs is highly sensitive to (amongst other things) market structure. For instance no one suggests that if those on low-incomes cannot afford bread that a 'universal service obligation' should be placed upon bakers. The sensible approach is to increase the disposable income of these groups rather than place an open-ended and costly regulation on an industry operating under competitive conditions.

9. This view rejects the premise that issues of social equity can be costlessly piled onto the tax/benefit system to be solved in one grand redistributive moment as utopian. This incurs large administrative costs and, as the debate on welfare reform has made clear, taxes on income can be highly distortionary. Regulatory decisions concerning

the pricing behaviour of utilities are likely to be second or third best options, which opens up the possibility that the orthodox view as to the inherent incompatibility of social and economic arguments for regulation is (at the least) overstated.

10. It is not difficult to think of a number of issues where there clearly is or could be a role for government in changing the incentive structure faced by business by using incentives to make the provision of services commercially viable (such as tax breaks, or preferential access to particular markets) in return for socially beneficial behaviour. The New Deal for the long-term unemployed is the most striking example, funded as it is by a large retrospective tax on part of the private sector in order to persuade employers to recruit workers which they might otherwise consider 'high risk'.

11. Though not in the case of gas. The differential regional impact of price changes for those on benefits arises as the amount included in social security payments to cover utility bills is calculated on the basis of national average figures (Kempson, 1997).

12. This issue is currently being explored by the DTI's Review of Utility Regulation which among many other issues, is considering the merits of imposing a statutory obligation on regulators (or a new joint or 'super' regulator should one emerge) to consider the interests of low-income consumers.

13. OFGAS submission to the Review of Utility Regulation, November 1997. It should be noted however that OFGAS already has a specific statutory duty to take account of the interests of the elderly, disabled and chronically sick.

14. This work suggests that approximately 20 per cent of the adult population do not have access to a current account. For those claiming housing benefit the figure increases to 60 per cent.

15. Increasing returns to local lending arise, for instance, when information acquired by a bank when making one loan can be of use in evaluating future loan-applications (thereby reducing per-unit costs of evaluations). For examples of how these effects can impact on lending in low-income localities see Gruben et al (1990).

16. Hence in the US it has been argued that in any one low-income locality a single bank should be licensed to fulfil the CRA responsibilities of the whole local banking community, using a pool of funds raised jointly by all operating banks (Avery et al, 1996).

17. An example of this is the New Horizons project run by Cambridge Housing Society (see Newcombe, 1997).

18. Under 7 per cent of local firms said that were involved in local employment initiatives (including NVQs, School Placements, Modern Apprenticeships and local Joblink schemes). However 42 per cent of firms indicated that they would be prepared to be involved in these initiatives (Baldwin, 1997).

19. EC DGXVI has recently imposed local-labour clauses on a ERDF grant to attract inward investment on the Tyne (to fund the development of a business site). It required fifty per cent of the workforce to be hired from a neighbouring local income community as part of the Commission's new emphasis on Community Economic Development.

20. For instance, although funded second pensions are not always thought of as 'merit goods', the state would be justified in requiring clearer disclosure and performance indicators, not least because of the generous tax reliefs which subsidise contributions.

21. These issues are explored in Chapter 16 in this volume on community responses to economic exclusion.

14. Comment: the private sector and social exclusion

Dan Corry

Probably the most important point about the contribution by Gavin Kelly and James McCormick is that it exists at all. For far too long the issue of social justice and social exclusion has been exclusively the territory of concerned social policy thinkers, pressure groups and NGOs. It tended always to be looking towards what the public sector role in combating social exclusion should be, and therefore often ended up in arguments about exactly how Government should tweak a particular tax, change a certain benefit, or tax a bit extra.

But the reality is that we live in a world, and therefore a society, dominated by a market economy. To separate discussion of the issues of social exclusion from what is going on in the private sector is one explanation as to why so many efforts to 'solve' the problem have failed. Of course it doesn't mean leave it to the market either.

To be fair, this failure to recognise interconnections is not simply the prerogative of the 'poverty lobby'; the private sector tends to see these problems as having little to do with them. Equally, as I have discovered at the Department of Trade and Industry, there is a tendency for those involved in working with business to see the issue of social exclusion as being nothing to do with them. So it's many minds, all around the place, that need to be opened up.

Kelly and McCormick cover a lot of important issues. I would like to just touch on a few areas where I think we have to think seriously about the relationship between the private sector and social exclusion.

In the first place, we all know that a vast contributory factor to social exclusion is lack of jobs. Policies like the New Deal and amendments to benefit rules, are all aimed at trying to get those out of work into work if at all possible. However, all of these efforts will be to little avail if there are no jobs being created in the economy, good jobs that people can take whether they have come via a scheme or via benefit change or whatever. Many of the jobs for labour market entrants will be in the small firm sector or into self-employment. That is why this policy area is so important. That is also why, ultimately, the search for social inclusion cannot be separated from the search to make the British economy competitive. Everything we do to try and boost this, be it strengthening competition policy, improving the transport infrastructure, helping British exporters and so on, should all be seen in their own way as part of a policy for tackling social exclusion. An obvious point when put, but in my experience one far too often overlooked, particularly by the centre left.

Second, the increasing introduction of competition into markets has an important implication for social exclusion. In the medium term, competition is the right way to create more jobs, to be more competitive and therefore does not contradict policies to tackle social exclusion. But it does raise issues of difficulty both in the short and the longer term. As competition is introduced into markets that formerly didn't have it, cross subsidies, which at least in most cases tend to favour poorer consumers, are eroded. We already have situations in the energy sector where poorer people who pay on pre-payment meters are tending to pay more for their energy than richer consumers who are more likely to pay by direct debit. We see the same sort of forces in things like insurance which are sold in ways which prize off richer consumers, who are lower risk, from poorer consumers who either have to pay much more now for their insurance or find they cannot get it at all.

The answer to these problems is certainly not to try and stop competition. Indeed the nature of the increasingly globalised world means that competition from without will continue to be important just as we try and make sure that anti-competitive practices cannot be practised in our own country. What do we do about these problems then? As is well known, there are essentially three options.

- The first, is to just let competition rip wherever and say that if anybody cares about the distributional consequences then the tax and benefits system should be used to solve this.

- The second, is to say that the industry itself should somehow raise money, through a voluntary or statutory levy that can make the situation less bad for the poorer consumers.

- And the third, is to allow competition to grow, but to keep some cross subsidies still factored into the system.

There are pros and cons in all these approaches; different ones would be more relevant in different sectors, and some will be socially and politically acceptable and others will not be. But sorting these out should be an important part of any progressive agenda to deal with social exclusion.

Third, we must recognise that the way that companies think of themselves has an important influence on the way they behave and therefore whether they aggravate or lessen the problems of social exclusion. The approach sanctified in the heyday of Thatcherism, that a successful firm is simply one which leaves management to manage and maximise short-term shareholder value, was one which gives little attention to the wider context in which firms operate. Fashion has changed, no doubt partly due to the experiences of the 1980s, but also due to actions by the Labour Government (including for instance the policies for company law and corporate governance). Attitudes can and will change not least as firms respond to the beliefs of the consumers and others that responsible firms are ones they want to patronise. One shouldn't however become carried away with this. Some of the major firms that seem to very involved in trying to tackle exclusion locally may simply be firms that have rather nice monopolistic positions and therefore have cash to burn, particularly if they think that might enable them to avoid regulatory threats to their position. Equally, it is clearly not sensible to push firms too far in the area of dealing with social problems since that is not their prime function nor should it be.

Lastly, it is important to be clear that the difficulties of a tax and benefit approach to tackling social exclusion are also present when working with the private sector. That problem is of course redistribution – which means there are winners and losers. Competition tends to favour the median consumers – the reason that the Consumers Association is usually found to be fairly unreservedly in favour of promoting competition with no wrinkles at all. Policy which might dampen competition, or introduce cross subsidies or levies, means that the median consumer pays a little more than they might otherwise do so that the poorer consumer will pay a little less than they might have otherwise. In a market economy, if the poor are to be helped in a way that they wouldn't be without intervention, then someone must pay. Although there will be lots of win-win initiatives that can be taken (that is, ones where companies can increase profits as they widen their markets to look after poorer consumers), redistribution cannot be dodged by any means we have yet found.

15. Comment: the role of the private sector
by Andrea Westall

Introduction

There is both scepticism and optimism in Gavin Kelly and James McCormick's paper – a health warning that private sector solutions and inputs are not the next big answer but also an outline of innovative attempts to tackle exclusion. The authors unpack the complex inter-relationships between the public and private sectors, illustrating that every instance demands a careful analysis of each player's strengths and weaknesses. However, the emphasis on pragmatism is balanced by a need to articulate moral arguments underpinning the distribution of responsibility.

The paper also shows the limits of markets, the lie that the 'invisible hand' will meet every need. One of their strongest points is the potential to strengthen 'fragile' markets and create a continuum of institutions and partnerships capable of addressing needs and forming a ladder for people and areas through to the mainstream economy. But this very fragmentation of responses to social exclusion means that, although much is happening, it is perhaps not adequately recognised or incorporated into coherent strategies.

For all the challenges of the chapter, the conclusions could perhaps go further. I would argue that ownership can matter, that some of the solutions require new and innovative frameworks for institutions and partnerships that incorporate social goals and can secure appropriate finance. For this reason, these discussions should be linked with the debate on community enterprises in Chapter 16. The trend for private sector involvement in social issues needs to be strengthened and incorporated into wider debates about corporate governance. Private sector resources should be channelled through appropriate frameworks to promote inclusion. And more can be done to create appropriate and sustainable employment.

Should businesses just be concerned with creating wealth?

At one level, Dan Corry is right to stress that the primary role of business is wealth and employment creation. But the story does not stop there: as Kelly and McCormick point out, businesses themselves create and maintain certain types of exclusion. Moreover, job creation by itself has a nasty habit of not trickling down or along to certain people or localities. The New Deal is going some way towards reducing structural barriers to employment but sustainable jobs for many of the socially excluded, particularly for some groups of the disabled or older workers, often arise from and require the proactive creation of new businesses or employment possibilities which accommodate their particular circumstances.

At the same time, strategies for regeneration require the creation of new enterprises (whether community-focused or profit-oriented) as part of concerted strategies to get local economies moving. Business support services need to be actively engaged in such initiatives and open their doors to not-for-profit enterprises. IPPR is currently working on the concept of Social Enterprises Zones, areas where public agencies and private bodies co-operate and flex funding and procedural rules in order to establish effective routes out of poverty. They place community development, involvement and enterprise at the centre of the regeneration process together with powers to redirect mainstream public funds, redesign local service delivery and bring training and business development funds to support community enterprise.[1]

The New Deal also tends to target large employers, those where displacement effects are potentially greatest. But why not address our capacity for growth, by asking whether or not there are barriers preventing job creation? An example in Wales, the Sole Trader Employment Service, initiated by two TECs, illustrates how administrative barriers can be overcome and generate employment among small companies. The self-employed were encouraged to take on an unemployed worker and given advice and help with legal and administrative requirements. US evidence has shown that once individuals have taken the step of employing someone, this decision is rarely reversed (Carroll *et al* (1996)). It is that first step which is crucial and the hardest to make.

Corporate responsibility or box ticking?

Corporate community involvement, social audits and wider corporate governance are not gaining common currency because companies are using 'strict commercial criteria' to 'involve themselves in projects'. Shell's double whammy of Brentspar and Nigeria and the role of small firms in community work have made the 'licence to operate' a live issue with some very tangible responses (Westall, 1997). These trends arise partly from customers using the greater availability of information as a basis for buying decisions which penalise anti-social practices by firms. But perhaps a stronger, though related driver, is that companies are broadening their view of the factors which underpin commercial success to include, for example, reputation, community involvement, ethical practices and relationships with customers, suppliers and employees. These rather intangible assets are being made more concrete, and hence more acceptable, by the use of improved ways of measuring performance and strategy, such as social and environmental audits and quality management frameworks.

There is a danger of all this activity being superficial. It might even be counter-productive. Attempts by companies to 'do their bit' could be ineffective and piecemeal or be subservient to marketing needs. Groups like Business in the Community and the Prince's Trust are trying to ensure that, while companies see the benefits of community involvement, they also fit into wider regeneration strategies.

One policy response, therefore, is to work with these trends and channel available resources, be they staff, money or infrastructure, in appropriate ways and within coherent local strategies which complement or are part of public sector initiatives. There must be sustainable and long-term mechanisms for private sector involvement which surmount worries about the rather transient nature of much corporate activity. For example, TECs and Business Links could introduce co-ordinated mechanisms for encouraging companies to offer space for meetings or computers for use by the voluntary sector. Greater effort could be made to directly attract skilled volunteers to work with appropriate projects, mirroring the networks of mentors and business angels for fledgling companies. Perhaps the parallel could be taken further with the concept of 'community angels', people who can offer both skills and financial support.

Ownership can matter

I agree that money is often not the answer but many grass roots initiatives are increasingly looking to loan and equity finance rather than grants. The remarkable success of, say, the Aston Regeneration Trust or Greater London Enterprise in channelling money from the private sector through to housing and regeneration projects, whilst at the same time creating either market or just below market returns, is another illustration of how to strengthen fragile markets and even create new ones.

Encouraging private sector finance through, for example, community bonds need not be done just through the banks but by financial organisations able to marry social objectives and different private sector needs (market returns or channels for charitable giving). Such bonds could be further encouraged through partial government guarantees, whether on loan or equity finance, which would increase the attractiveness of the risk/return ratio.

The organisational structure of these bodies indicates that ownership does matter. The intermediate institution is often a mix of profit and not-for-profit structures, capable of supporting the particular goals set out in its mission statement. This same argument is true for many of the intermediate solutions to exclusion which create viable markets for key goods and services. It is not just those industries where there is a lack of competition (for example, some utilities) that may require such approaches but rather any industry deemed important to 'inclusion'. There needs to be further investigation of these 'hybrids' to spread best practice and consider whether any legislation is needed to enable their formation.

But there is a danger with some of these pooling strategies and market-making organisations that they might exclude various individuals or groups within an area. More generally, what about excluded individuals who are not part of some easily definable group based around, for example, local authority housing or the catchment area for a credit union? National strategies are therefore still necessary. We need to extend some of the lessons from pooling and risk-sharing to people who are geographically dispersed.

There are other additional problems with such approaches. How do you define who should and should not be included and by what 'means' and how do you prevent people from free-riding? Addressing such issues is crucial if such strategies are to be effective.

Conclusions

The US recently launched an initiative, 'America's Promise: the Alliance for Youth' which called on big business to help tackle child poverty. Sceptical voluntary organisations believed that the government was trying to reduce its role in poverty alleviation whilst others thought there was great scope for using potential volunteers and resources.

Cries for action rarely help unless underpinned by strong arguments, tangible measurements of outcomes, and appropriate mechanisms for achieving those aims. Kelly and McCormick's paper sets out the broad framework for this approach. I have suggested a few ways of creating sustainable vehicles for private sector involvement. If any poverty targets are set by Government, they should recognise the need for action by all partners and include the extent of activity by different groups whether public, private or not-for-profit. Government must set the framework, but participants and the public need to see how and why they should be involved.

References

Carroll R, Holtz-Eakin D, Rider M, and Rosen H S (1996) *Income Taxes and Entrepreneurs' Use of Labour,* Centre for Economic Policy Studies Working Paper, No. 32, July.

Westall A (1997) *Competitiveness and Corporate Governance,* IPPR.

Endnote

1.   This work is being conducted jointly by IPPR, Community Links and Business in the Community. A work in progress report is due to be published in June 1998.

VI:
Citizens'
Involvement

16. Three Steps and Beyond: Micro-economics for social inclusion
by Alison West and James McCormick

Introduction

Economies operate at both macro and micro levels – macro is where the glamour lies. It is true that the answer to structural poverty lies in the political control of macro-economic systems but strong micro-economies do have a role to play. They have a double function: they help protect the poor against the worst excesses of macro-economic systems that exclude, and they create a web of interchanges, relationships and ways of working that are in themselves a valid level of economic activity. Good macro-strategies value micro-economic activity because it is the most effective way of ensuring that general prosperity is shared by all sections of the population. Current macro-level orthodoxies need to give way to a more sophisticated multi-level and integrated strategy.

Micro level programmes, if they are to have a measurable impact on social exclusion and poverty, have to address both the household and the locality. They should be designed in three stages:

- first, palliative measures to increase disposable income;

- second, a radical ring-fencing of the local economy to stop the 'fiscal haemorrhage' from the local economy;

- finally, the long-term construction of a web of alternative micro-economies, operating across its own system but also linking up to the wider economy.

Local area programmes are a necessary and perhaps a first step but vertical links out of the marginalised economy into the mainstream are essential for the long-term creation of an inclusive society.

Micro-economic strategies involve local people and the case for developing a micro-economic strategy arises from the questions increasingly asked of existing practices. How many of the current regeneration programmes actually make communities better off in the long term? Do they make poor individuals and households any less poor? Traditional property-led regeneration schemes face clear constraints when they try to assist people on low incomes in the regeneration area and the relative position of such excluded groups can actually be made worse. Jobs created are by and large not filled by local residents.

Methods of assessment that focus on small area statistics may show an improvement for the area in terms of its overall housing tenure mix, property values or even employment rates but these may mask a displacement of the original residents. This is why an effective strategy must set targets for both the individual/household and the locality.

There is a growing consensus that local regeneration schemes, involving local people, have a part to play. Clearly, community or citizen-led regeneration cannot provide the whole answer. What can local programmes concentrate on and perform well?

Local regeneration can deal with both individual and area anti-poverty work. Beginning with individuals, these fall into three main categories:

- First is the target group for initiatives under Welfare to Work – those who are of working age, with no major impediments to full-time work, but who may lack pre-vocational training, adequate transitional support, motivation or adequate job opportunities.

- Second are those who cannot work full-time but who could undertake some paid work: this is the hybrid group that includes single parents with young children, those with some disabilities, the active elderly and students.

- The third group contains those who are not expected to undertake paid work at all, even in marginal activities: these include inactive elderly people, frail people, people with certain disabilities or illnesses, some carers.

These last two groups of people make up at least half the population in most regeneration areas. Job creation, permanent or temporary, is unlikely to improve their material position. For all of the people in the three categories above, the aim is to maximise their income and access to resources, as a first step to reducing their poverty.

Maximising Incomes and Resources for Individuals or Households

One of the first steps taken by a community-based programme should be to focus on the local economy, and try by a variety of means to increase the money received by individual households.

Helping individuals who can work

Local people should at least get the benefit of the regeneration programme itself. Measures can be taken to ensure that a high proportion of new jobs – even if limited to the cash inflow of the project itself – are secured by local people. The programme can promote mentor schemes. Local people can be pre-trained and regeneration partners can agree to employ local people. Local purchasing and sub-contracting will benefit existing small local businesses and if regeneration programmes have a preparatory phase, it is also possible to establish community businesses like catering to service the regeneration programme.

Apart from jobs created by the regeneration programme itself, we can also analyse all jobs in the locality and foster the employment of local people through local labour agreements with new and existing employers. These cannot succeed if sceptical employers are not convinced that residents are job-prepared and that contracts will run on time and in budget. However, some companies, in the construction sector, for example, have concluded that it makes sound business sense to include local people at the earliest stage of project design. Local people often have skills that are not recognised by the traditional jobs market but which can gain acceptance by employers if they are described and assessed by some formal process. This enables the accreditation of informal skills, particularly those job-related skills acquired through often lengthy involvement in the shadow economy. 'Graduates' of the informal economy can also be helped with prior accreditation when they go on formal training courses. For those with a history of helping their own community, the NVQ in community work is a promising new access route.

It is worth looking at how some of the programmes encouraging people to return to work can be shared across communities. One possibility would be to set up local pools of money under the New Deal, which could be tailored to local needs rather than being based on age-related client groups – a New Deal for Communities, in the words of the Prime Minister, but with the budgetary flexibility that would enable lasting progress to be made. As part of this approach, more holistic delivery mechanisms for some elements of the New Deal should be tried: primary schools, parent and toddler groups and church groups may be more appropriate points of entry to the New Deal for Lone Parents programme than Job Centres. Communities may be less suspicious of welfare-to-work programmes if trusted local institutions are involved in delivering them.

For those people able to work, incomes can be enhanced by the take-up of any in-work benefits to which they are entitled. Evidence from the north-west of England on low levels of awareness and accuracy among front-line staff in the Employment Service and Benefits Agency about existing bridging benefits – the Back to Work Bonus, Jobfinders' Grant, the National Insurance Contributions reduction for employers recruiting from among the long-term unemployment – suggests that a great deal more could be achieved to support 'work poor' households even before the Working Families Tax Credit is introduced.

Helping those who cannot work full-time or work at all

In addition to maximising benefit take-up, for those unable to access a full-time job at a decent wage, providing marginal employment can mean vital small increases in income. Pensioners and single parents can often work a few hours a week, and many people with disabilities unable to hold a full-time job would be happy working more flexible hours. Reforms in the benefit system to combine part-time benefits with part-time earnings in recognition of partial capacity to work would be extremely helpful.

Community businesses and small-scale economic activity around community centres can be excellent sources of marginal employment for local people. Community businesses and development trusts are particularly useful for giving a legal structure to allow people to earn within benefit rules. For example, a project in East London set up an EU-funded training programme which was allowed to start trading and resulted in an embroidery business supplying the garment trade. The women involved were allowed to continue claiming benefit while the business was being established: an example of 'trading while training' made possible by a flexible interpretation of benefit rules.

Higher Disposable Incomes and Stronger Support Networks

For poorer people in a locality, whether in work or not, any increase in their income is to be welcomed. But just as valuable is a reduction in their fixed costs.

Strategies to reduce outgoings

For all three categories of people in excluded communities – those in regular paid work, those not working and those between the two – a feature of their life is that they have little control over what money they do have coming in. After housing costs, heat and light and food, people on the lowest incomes have little spending power left and consequently they cannot contribute much to the circulation of money in the local economy.

A well-organised community response is highly effective in reducing basic costs. Food purchasing co-operatives can bring middle-class food prices into what are close to 'no-go' areas for the largest retailers. Community-based energy efficiency schemes employing local labour can produce substantial savings. Cheaper prices for utilities can be negotiated collectively and the consortium of local authorities already organising this shows that considerable savings can be made. Using EU money to insulate homes in Easterhouse in Glasgow, residents have saved on average no less than £14 a week.

Perhaps the most important part of a strategy to reduce outgoings is the provision of cheap credit. Unlicensed moneylenders, and many of those employed by licensed but extremely expensive financial service companies, are a particularly unpleasant feature of life in excluded communities. The formation of credit unions has changed the lives of many poor households, not just in giving them access to credit at affordable rates but also by showing them that they can reassert control over their own finances, however low their income is.

However, there needs to be a careful analysis of the best provision for each area – in some cases getting a traditional bank to provide 'normal' services in poorer areas would be the solution. Local people do not always want the burden of organising their own systems, despite the social solidarity that is one of the most important by-products of such systems. Community energy is inevitably limited and each initiative has to be assessed as part of a more comprehensive plan for the area.

Support through non-cash systems

In addition to increasing the amount of disposable income in circulation, programmes can foster non-cash systems which enable poor people to improve their quality of life. Both cash and non-cash community regeneration initiatives involve the active contribution of local people, recognising that many residents have both time and skills to offer. Making sure that schemes are designed to maximise local people's contribution and sense of ownership is vital in restoring community pride in areas that often resent being chosen for regeneration in the first place. To qualify for regeneration money, an area is typically forced to play upon the negatives – its position at the foot of the league and not the positives.

Barter systems like Local Exchange Trading Schemes (LETS) are excellent ways for communities to build up their own structures of communication and allow all residents to contribute something. Under the Calderdale LETS, for example, a single mother had a new, non-standard size back door fitted for only the cost of the timber, a considerable help for someone on benefit. In return, she will contribute her own time and skills to help someone else. One of the key principles of exchange schemes is equity: the acceptance that everyone has something to offer and that in a community, there will always be someone who values what they offer. The formal market is hard on those with certain types of skill – forms of manual labour and childcare for example – but these are often the very skills that are most useful to a low-income neighbourhood. Equally, barter systems that allow the exchange of goods provide a very useful service in poorer areas. Parents with young children value the circulation of baby clothes and equipment. New households value the supply of second-hand furniture at an affordable price without needing to apply for a social fund loan.

An intriguing movement in the UK is the 'Grow Your Own Food' campaign, encouraging local people to save money by individual and collective fruit and vegetable production. This has been extended to projects to farm the land around high-rise blocks – the Greening the Tower Blocks scheme. While policy debates about land reform and community land ownership are more usually associated with rural areas, applying the same principle to excluded communities in urban Britain might produce clear economic and health gains. Much more attention should be paid to developing links between peripheral housing estates and adjacent agricultural production.

In addition to such exchange schemes, a lot can be done to improve quality of life and give a higher standard of living by organising community-based support services. This voluntary activity has always been a feature of life in the UK but in some areas it may require community development work to encourage mutual self-help. This includes childminding circles and co-operatives, services for young people, sporting and arts activities. At its most effective, this becomes a support system in its own right, with considerable amounts of value circulating.

Support through services from the public sector

Non-cash systems include the provision of high quality public services. Locating public services such as libraries and sports facilities in poorer areas improves the quality of the environment. When enlightened local authorities combine this with reduced rates to allow access, the potential benefits are considerable. Travel subsidies also help to reduce the isolation of many estates, and shoppers' buses are valued by local people. These benefits raise their standard of living without raising their income. The huge sums of public money spent on estate refurbishment should also be a benefit in kind to poorer people. While their structural poverty remains to be addressed, they are at least living in healthier homes and safer surroundings.

In practice, it has to be pointed out that the considerable sums of public money spent on poorer areas are not always well coordinated or efficiently delivered, and integrated service delivery would help. One could also consider some transfer of resources to the control of local people through the establishment of neighbourhood vouchers or budget pools.

The Creation of a Social Support System

The combined effect of activities geared to increasing income, reducing unavoidable costs and offering benefits in kind is the creation of a self-contained social support system. The establishment of a micro-economic system with defence mechanisms against the worst effects of poverty is certainly worth achieving as a first stage in the attempt to change the situation of the very poorest. The total package should result in the following benefits for marginal groups:

- an increase in their income

- a reduction in their basic costs

- a corresponding increase in their disposable income

- a better support system to reduce the need for cash

- cheaper forms of credit

- better access to marginal trading opportunities.

An Area Approach

Moving from strategies to assist households and boost their purchasing power, area-based approaches should also be led by local people for their collective benefit.

Maximisation of resources coming into the area

External funding should be tapped where possible, including money for traditional regeneration, including housing-led regeneration. In the poorest areas, even having outside professional workers buying their lunches locally can boost the local economy. Large externally-funded programmes have invested huge amounts of money into the fabric of housing in these areas. Refurbishment using public and private money can create an atmosphere likely to attract inward investment. Traditional programmes are also useful in fostering small business start-ups and in assisting medium-sized enterprises to grow.

Maximising the circulation of money

The justification for community-based regeneration is that traditional approaches are poor at dealing with issues such as the circulation of money within a target area, the benefits to the economically inactive and the role of non-cash systems. The end result of the raft of community-based measures outlined above is that there is more money around. This benefits local traders because such surplus cash tends to be spent in local outlets thereby benefiting the area. In the long term, the aim should be to make sure that much more of the available money stays in the area, either with local traders or community businesses. A feature of excluded communities is that money only circulates twice, rather than the seven to eight times in more prosperous areas. Regeneration programmes should have a core target of radically ring-fencing the local economy to stop the haemorrhage of the little money residents have.

The first step is an analysis of the money flow to see at what point it leaks out. Often it goes straight to the local authority in the form of rent, or to the utilities. To correct this, we could look at the transfer of housing ownership to local tenants or to a local trust or association. Similarly, services should be provided by estate-based teams and businesses where possible. One promising development in local buying is found in Bath, where the Bath Farmers' Market has been set up to encourage city dwellers to buy the produce of local farmers.

The endowment of poorer areas

In terms of ownership of assets and cash, it is depressing to see how very little 'free' money there is in a poor area. Community groups are constantly faced with the painful process of raising small sums through jumble sales or hoping for a small grant from the council. Neighbourhoods frequently have no local funds to draw on for collective activity and this means that the energy that should go into community life goes instead into the fundraising required for even the humblest of events. Wealthier areas do not have their community energy sapped in this way. The Community Development Foundation and the Association of Community Trusts and Foundations argue for Neighbourhood Endowments, owned by local people and providing the capacity to spend modest amounts each year from the interest on their investments. This would give seed funding controlled by local people themselves.

Ownership of assets, both on estate and off

Acquiring real assets is far more difficult and will take far longer. The average council estate has no high-value real estate. Many neighbourhoods have concentrations of unmortgageable properties and long-term debt burdens. When managed workspaces are built they are often filled with marginal start-up businesses. Even to maximise the use of such marketable assets as there are, residents face a financial infrastructure in the UK that is adjusting too slowly to their needs. Despite these caveats, however, there is no doubt that some permanent assets are created by the money poured into regeneration programmes. If all regeneration programmes were required to transfer some or all of the assets created through this use of public money to the ownership of local people, then the process of generating local wealth in a lasting manner could be accelerated.

To get around the problem of the low value of assets in deprived areas, we could consider the ownership of assets that are not actually located in the poorer areas. The Oxbridge colleges, for example, derive much of their revenue from land holdings in central London. Indeed they are able to do so because they started off with endowment funds. Extending this principle to the most excluded parts of the country would of course require considerable political will, but communities themselves may wish to consider how, as savings slowly build up, money could best be put to use. It might be better to resist the temptation to invest all resources locally and to think through a longer-term strategy to include some off-estate investment. In terms of competence, there are plenty of examples of those who own assets and employ professional managers and advisers to help them exploit these assets. Residents may need support with capacity-building for some economic activity but they will need least help with the simple ownership of portable and fixed property.

Conclusions on Area and Individual Income Approaches

While these short-term strategies are certainly valuable, in the long term more fundamental changes must be addressed. Usefully, some of the long-term strategies to keep people out of poverty can follow on from the short-term strategies outlined above: the community development trust for example would bid for and run most of the services in the area using appropriately skilled local labour. It would be a vehicle for the ownership of assets, such as community centres and start-up workshops, eventually generating local revenue streams. These can in turn be used for further regeneration initiatives and can provide much needed security to allow borrowing for future development. This is a well-tested model in the UK. In practical terms, a community-led regeneration project tackling exclusion on both an individual and area basis would:

●   set up a credit union and strengthen existing ones

●   set up a trusted welfare advice service

●   set up an advice system for part-time jobs

●   set up a community business development agency

●   bring in heat conservation projects

●   link with the local authority on bulk-buy of utilities

●   link with the social landlord to set up 'insure with rent' schemes

●   set up a grow your-own food project

●   set up a furniture exchange system

●   set up a local exchange trading system

●   set up a communal caring project to release people for marginal economic activity within welfare rules

●   analyse what is spent locally and establish local providers of goods and services

●   set up a community development trust.

This is a series of short-term strategies to help people at the very lowest levels of income and even then the increase in their prosperity will be modest. These practical steps, often using existing projects and agencies, would nevertheless have the advantage of producing measurable results in a relatively short period of time: an important consideration if exhausted and suspicious residents are to be persuaded that regeneration initiatives are worth their support.

This is a way of doing regeneration that is particularly suited to community involvement and delivery. The process of getting involved in such a community-based regeneration programme strengthens networking and binds people together in a common endeavour. One would not wish to underestimate the time and effort it can take to work with communities, particularly in areas they are not familiar with. Setting up locally controlled projects always means dealing with the tensions and dynamics within the community itself. There is the associated risk of initiatives being run by the wrong people, underlining the need for clear lines of accountability, an early warning system and a set of procedures for responding quickly when something goes wrong. But the community development profession has a long body of experience and there is no reason why anti-poverty work should be any more problematic than any other kind. Each of the ideas in this paper has been operating successfully in some areas already, often over a very long period of time.

If programmes geared to the economy of the area were established then one would expect:

- an increase in area wealth

- a retention of wealth in the area through increasing the percentage of services and goods that are provided by local companies and community businesses

- an increase in revenue-producing assets in the area.

Local people can deal well with issues relevant to the local economy but ring-fencing a poor area and maximising short-term palliative measures as above will not bring about self-sustaining improvements of the scale that are required. Pioneering organisations such as the Aston Reinvestment Trust are making links between credit, capital, property and people and the UK is beginning to see the value of linking across poorer areas for collective strength. It should serve as a pointer for wider change.

Looking Ahead: Collectives of Areas

If we look at the totality of excluded areas in the UK, intriguing possibilities emerge. To change the enduring poverty of an area we have to look at establishing alternative trading systems across communities. This will create a horizontal economic system.

Cross-trading systems

Cross-trading systems are already being organised and the long history in the UK of community businesses and co-operatives shows that cross-trading can be an important element in making such businesses viable. About 70 per cent of co-operative and community business trading is with each other, creating a strong sector of trade, even if a self-enclosed one. The history of the Co-operative system in the UK shows that this is economically viable.

The old traditions of mutuality are being reconstructed through these links across the micro-economies. The efforts in one locality can be strengthened by linking with other communities active in this way. Such links mean that negotiation is more likely to be among equals. This synergy will allow the social economy to grow and consolidate, with its own institutional support structures emerging over time, from banking to joint merchandising and production links. Subcontracting can take place alongside the growth of affinity trades and products.

Financial infrastructure to support cross area arrangements

The community sector, particularly in poorer areas, has never had a financial system geared to its needs. When groups bid for and participate in publicly-funded programmes, they frequently experience problems with cash flow. The flight of banks from poorer areas is well documented but even where local banks survive they are only vaguely aware of the social economy as a productive sector, let alone of its practical needs. In addition to local access to credit there is also the need to establish cross-area banking systems. Given the sheer size of the third sector in the UK and the growing amount of trade that is taking place, it is a perfectly viable market for the financial institutions. Well-judged and practical advice can result in very low default rates in the social economy. As local areas build up their own asset base, they will be more obviously marketable both individually and collectively and some of the major banks, most noticeably NatWest, are shrewdly showing an interest in the social economy as a result.

Moving Beyond the Community Economy

The combination of individual and area programmes and the weaving of a web across the communities, will contribute to the creation of a viable third sector Community Economy. However, it is still not enough to create more prosperous areas out of the most excluded communities, even if they are strengthened by horizontal networks. We need this strong base in order to link upwards into regional, national, European and global economies. Poorer areas have no option but to engage with more powerful agencies but should do so from a position of relative strength.

If socially excluded areas are to be made indistinguishable over time from 'normal' or average areas then they must adopt the characteristics of normality. When poorer communities own assets of their own outside the area, they can talk property prices and portfolios with the rest of society. When poorer areas are interwoven in terms of trade with the wider economy then they can talk exchange rates with the rest of society. It is ultimately not a question of whether they have to engage with the mainstream economy, but on whose terms.

The poor trading with the poor is a complete dead end. Exclusion makes a poor common bond. In addition to trading across poorer areas, community-led and owned initiatives also need to trade vertically. The creation of a sub-economy, based on islands separated from the 'mainland' as well as each other, is not the long-term answer, however necessary it is in an initial period of committed localism. The more enlightened projects are already aware of this and the Castlemilk Partnership in Glasgow has adopted a far-sighted and sophisticated strategy of combining community-based and limited businesses, with businesses designed to trade outside the estate at city-wide and regional level. More ambitiously, it also trades nationally and internationally.

Conclusions

It is possible to make poor households less poor in the short term, it is possible to make poorer areas less poor in the medium term, and it is possible to set up better protective and integrative systems in the long term. The argument in this chapter is based on the principle of both subsidiarity and engagement: local areas should own and produce as much as they can, partly to protect them from the worst excesses of international capitalism but also to enable them to engage with wider economic forces from a position of greater strength.

For excluded communities to become more like the average, they need the protection of elected government. If the difficulties faced by the Tiger economies tells us anything it is that international capital has no sentiment and no loyalty to the locality. When community-based initiatives extend into vertical links they are incredibly vulnerable, entering a system not geared to their needs and not familiar with their way of operating. Communities can cope well with self-help but only local and national government have the resources to establish cross-area systems and to help with vertical links.

Local efforts will eventually need the protection of government-led macro-strategy. Otherwise micro-strategies will be eternally confined to small-scale palliative measures which barely dent the surface of exclusion. Macroeconomic management should include a target for local economic well being - this should be just as much a national goal as high levels of inward investment, low inflation or international competitiveness. Indeed policy-makers should realise that prosperous localities do not undercut but rather support grander national plans, including upskilling the workforce and reducing poverty.

Specifically, the Single Regeneration Budget should reorient to supporting very small area-based programmes, since only at this level will the socially excluded clearly be assisted. The Department of the Environment, Transport and the Regions, Scottish, Welsh and Northern Ireland offices should set up a community banking system. Local authorities should be required to identify the poor in their area and set up anti-poverty programmes. They should also use 'Best Value' to support community businesses for services and supplies. The new English Regional Development Agencies should be required to establish small-area development plans in the context of the Regional Plan and should set up consortia regionally to allow bulk purchasing and cross trading.

In the long term, fostered by the support of government, this remedial and protective layer of activity will both protect and encourage excluded communities. It will enable them to engage with wider social and economic forces with greater equity.

Endnotes

Commission on Social Justice (1994) *Social Justice: Strategies for national Renewal* (IPPR/Vintage) See especially discussion of people-led regeneration in Chapter Seven.

Howard M (1998) 'Disablity Dilemmas' in (ed.) McCormick J and Oppenheim C *Welfare in Working Order* (IPPR)

Chanan G (1997) *Community Involvement in Urban Regeneration: added value and changing values* (European commission)

Community devlopment foundation (1997 and yearly) *Regeneration and the commiunity: Guidelines to the community involvement aspect of the SRB Challenge Fund*

17. Comment: Citizens' Involvement
by Robin Wilson

There is a famous Irish joke about the American tourist who winds down the window of his car on a country road in the west of Ireland to ask a local the quickest way to Dublin – only to be told 'I wouldn't start from here.'

Anyone involved in the social inclusion debate has always to keep this at the forefront of their minds. Any remedial action to address social exclusion is always far more ineffective (in human terms) and inefficient (in value-for-money terms) than preventing exclusion in the first place (Perri 6, 1997: 5). And the last people well placed to cope with the formidable challenges social exclusion presents are the socially excluded themselves: as West and McCormick crisply put it, exclusion is a poor common bond.

Indeed, the whole point of the shift in the debate from (Anglo-Saxon) 'poverty' to (French) 'social exclusion' has been to stress that this is not just a problem of poor people in poor areas but at issue is the responsibility – including fiscal – of the wider society for the condition of its marginal members, of the need for all to share equally in the fruits of citizenship (Teague and Wilson 1995: 79). It is not clear, however, that acceptance of the terminology of social exclusion at the highest levels of government in the UK has been accompanied by a recognition of the challenges it poses to thinking which tendentially reduces exclusion to unemployment and employment to employability – thereby displacing the primary burden of responsibility on to the socially excluded themselves. 'The concept of citizenship and social integration which underlies the notion of "social exclusion" in this French tradition is difficult to grasp for people working within a liberal individualist tradition.' (Gore, 1995: 2)

A key aspect of the development of the discourse of social exclusion in the 1980s was the growing recognition that labour-market changes on a global scale – the phenomenon of jobless growth and the collapse in demand for unskilled manual labour – were putting the social fabric of market economies under the most severe strain. Concern as to what can be achieved at a micro-economic level needs to be seen in this light.

Brownlow is a disadvantaged area in the (once) new town of

Craigavon in Northern Ireland. As part of the EU 'Poverty 3' programme, a community trust was established to address its multiple deprivations. The former Conservative Northern Ireland secretary, Sir Patrick Mayhew, addressing a reception in the area, said there was nothing wrong with Brownlow that the people of Brownlow could not put right. Is this really the case? Well, they couldn't retrieve the multinational Goodyear tyre plant whose closure in the 1980s had devastated the unskilled and semi-skilled labour market in the area, for a start.

Moreover, the Brownlow experience is salutary in terms of the involvement of the excluded. The partnership structure established to run the project – bringing together representatives of various statutory agencies and community representatives – was a wobbly affair. The capacity and disposition of the latter proved a constant source of difficulty at board meetings, which should dispel any residual notions of the merits of privileging 'working-class' culture.

But this should not be seen as casting a cold shower of despair on local actions against exclusion. Rather, it emphasises the limits of a fiscally constrained macro-economic policy, which makes a proper social insurance system and profound labour-market interventions – characteristic of, say, German or Swedish welfare systems – unaffordable in the UK (Clasen *et al*, 1997). Thus, local initiatives need a benign macro-economic context. In the absence of this, individuals will always be at much greater risk of exclusion and, when excluded, their chances of (re)integration into society correspondingly reduced. The US model so beloved of Labour's young Turks presents 'social problems of an intensity unmatched anywhere in Western Europe', with its hair-raising indicators of poverty, crime, illiteracy, drug abuse and widespread social anomie (Sassoon 1996).

But what, then, is the point of local action? The paradox is that precisely the same globalising forces – particularly labour-market transformations – which render the socially excluded increasingly impotent have also forced the agencies charged with addressing exclusion to engage more and more in dialogue, including on an area basis.

Despite the difficulties with the Brownlow experiment in Northern Ireland, the concept of partnership, including area-based partnership, has taken off dramatically in the region – as indeed is the case, to an even greater extent, in the Republic of Ireland (Sabel, 1996). But this is an experience by no means unique to Ireland. Within welfare states there has been a growing crisis of centrally-determined, hierarchically-delivered welfare services which mimics 'post-Fordist' trends in the private sector. This has meant that wefare systems have been increasingly unable to cope with the volatility and diversity of risk (Sabel, 1997).

In Northern Ireland, partnership has become a key feature in urban and rural regeneration projects, and in the so-called 'peace package' promulgated by the European Union in the wake of the 1994 paramilitary ceasefires. There is here a recognition that the state can not be omnicompetent and must establish interlocutors on the ground who can more sensitively steer the delivery of programmes. The particular attractions this has presented to a less-than-hegemonic British government in Northern Ireland are self-evident.

Partnership is an important, and generalisable, innovation. On the one hand, it avoids the 'creaming' danger of a more individualist approach and, on the other, it encourages the growth of local networks – a problem and a requirement West and McCormick rightly point up.

While there are real problems – as the Brownlow experience highlighted – in generating effective community representation in area-based partnerships, the success of the latter also heavily depends on the degree of autonomy of the representatives on the other side of the table. As a partnership member in north Belfast pointed out, if statutory representatives can deliver only their existing programmes via the partnerships then the arrangement will be merely token – likely indeed to breed even more distrust of and alienation from authority. In other words, there has to be a real capacity for the 'mainstream' official machine to learn, and innovate, from experience at its 'margin'.

Much of the thrust of the West and McCormick paper – which is full of useful, detailed and practical proposals – is on the need to develop the social economy at local level. No, one wouldn't wish to start from here, but the hysteresis effect of whole swathes of humanity being detached from the labour market for years or even decades means the 'hard choice' of allocating substantial amounts of expenditure for precious little short-term response has to be made if one is serious about reversing the exclusion process.

The reason for this is simple: work in the labour market is simply not a realistic option in the short-to-medium term for many people living in areas of cumulative and multiple disadvantage. This is not a moralistic argument about the 'workshy' poor: it is that on top of constraints of disability or lack of childcare, even the able-bodied who are willing to work face massive difficulties if they possess no skills or obsolete skills, if basic work disciplines have been atrophied by long-term detachment from the labour market – and, above all, if employers have access to a pool of employed or short-term unemployed recruitment alternatives amidst very slack local unskilled demand.

If this is so, six-month placements on New Deal for youngsters are likely (as, at the time of writing, pilot projects indicated) to have only a marginal employment effect – especially in the private sector of the labour market. The unavoidable alternative, then, is development of the social economy in a manner not dependent on one-off public-expenditure windfalls. This is again a much more developed tradition in France where the notion of 'economic insertion' as a means to social inclusion is widely accepted. There it has been associated with associational enterprises whose goal is the inclusion of the long-term unemployed, offenders, substance abusers, homeless persons and others with multiple difficulties (Silver and Wilkinson, 1995).

Development of the social economy has an obvious benefit in the light of West and McCormick's concern about economic 'leakage' from already-disadvantaged communities. Its labour market is inherently local – indeed, it is particularly appropriate to those who simply can not compete in the harsh world of the wider labour market – as are the outputs it generates. It can reach what a dynamic government official involved in the partnership effort in Northern Ireland describes as the 'inactive poor', so far not engaged by the partnerships, and it can chime with (and legitimise) the existing informal economy and untapped social relationships (though there needs to be wariness of personalised insider-outsider divisions within communities). But it doesn't come cheap.

None of the broad sweep of these comments is to detract from the modesty of the ambitions of West and McCormick in their paper. Their concern to generate practical steps, which can produce measurable results relatively quickly, is a well-founded one. Where work and opportunity are conspicuously absent, fatalism and cynicism are commodities in very generous supply.

References

Clasen J Gould A and Vincent J (1997) *Long-term Unemployment and the Threat of Social Exclusion: A Cross-National Analysis of the Position of Long-term Unemployed People in Germany, Sweden and Britain* The Policy Press, Bristol

Gore C (1995) 'Introduction: Markets, Citizenship and Social Exclusion' in Rodgers G Gore C and Figueiredo J B eds *Social Exclusion: Rhetoric, Reality, Responses* ILO, Geneva

Perri 6 (1997) 'Social exclusion: time to be optimistic' *Demos Collection 12,* London

Sabel C (1996) *Ireland: Local Partnerships and Social Innovation* OECD, Paris

Sabel C (1997) 'The Future of Partnership', lecture, Belfast (unpublished)

Sassoon D (1996) *One Hundred Years of Socialism* I B Tauris, London

Silver H and Wilkinson F (1995) 'Policies to Combat Exclusion: a French-British comparison', in Rodgers Gore and Figueiredo *op cit*

Teague P and Wilson R (1995) 'Towards an Inclusive Society' in Teague and Wilson eds *Social Exclusion, Social Inclusion* Democratic Dialogue report 2, Belfast

VII:
The European Dimension

.

18. Combating social exclusion and promoting social integration in the European Union
by Katherine Duffy

The aim of this chapter is to identify the extent to which the European Union is committed to combating poverty and social exclusion, and to draw attention to the strengths and weaknesses of the European Commission's current basis for action to combat poverty and social exclusion.

The chapter is in three parts. Part One discusses the relationship between poverty and social exclusion, and concludes that labour market exclusion, and enhanced 'employability' as the route to integration, is central to the emerging distinction between the two concepts. Part Two describes the legal basis for the European Commission's action in support of the employment policies of Member States and the role of Structural Funds. Part Three describes the limited scope for actions for social, as opposed to economic integration. The Chapter concludes by commenting on the weakness of the concept of social exclusion which underpins the action taken, and by suggesting that the impact of accession of low income countries, five of which are in the process of transforming their social systems, will demand open consideration of poverty, of the role of social protection, and of the need for a supra-national legal framework.

1.The concepts of poverty and social exclusion

Poverty

Article 2 of the Council Decision of December 1984 on specific European Community action to combat poverty, defined poverty more widely than monetary resources, as

> material, cultural and social resources which are so limited as
> to exclude people from a minimally acceptable way of life.[1]

Nevertheless, the measure of poverty remains monetary. Few Member States have an 'official' definition of poverty; many use an administrative low-income measure based on threshold incomes for payment of social assistance. Many also refer to the European Commission's relative poverty measure, which is defined as the proportion of households or persons having income or expenditure half or less of the average in their Member State.

The distinction between poverty and social exclusion

Though the term social exclusion is now common in many European Union countries, it first had wide currency in France. In the academic debate, following Xiberras (1993) and Lambert (1995) exclusion has the meaning of being expelled from a place where you stood before, and of being kept outside by denial of access. Generally, the distinction made between poverty and social exclusion, is that between a focus on inadequate or unequal material resources, vis-à-vis inadequate or unequal participation in social life (Room 1996:5). This distinction is reflected in a Resolution by the Council of Ministers which emphasised:

> that social exclusion is not simply a matter of inadequate means, and that combating exclusion also involves access by individuals and families to decent living conditions by means of measures for social integration and integration into the labour market.[2]

Thus, disadvantage concerns not only disparity between the top and bottom of the income scale, but between those comfortable within society and those on the margins or excluded. The most common shared perspective on social exclusion can be summarised as that of a segmented society, tiered through the labour market and through state policies. The key relationship is 'in' or 'out' rather than 'up' or 'down' (Touraine 1991, 1992; Castel (1995); Paugam (1992, 1993a, 1993b, 1994). The influence of this kind of thinking has been evident in the European Commission's past approach to employment and social protection policies, but the later parts of this chapter indicate that the structural character of this analysis is of decreasing importance in the approach to labour market integration.

The impact of differing welfare regimes on the approach to social exclusion

Whereas the term social exclusion is now widespread, the importance of the welfare regime in mediating the way social exclusion is understood can be illustrated by comparing France and the UK. Lenoir's 'Les Exclus' (1974); was one of the earliest works to refer to exclusion. He was concerned with the 'maladapté,' whether physical, mental or social, and with the administrative exclusion of the disadvantaged by the state and through the systems of social protection, both private and public.

Whereas in France, early ideas on exclusion concerned the problem of exclusion from social protection, current UK political usage is the reverse; the socially excluded are 'trapped in dependency', they 'inhabit a parallel world where income is derived from benefits, not work' (Harman 1997). For the young unemployed 'a life on benefits is not an option' (ibid). It is likely that this perspective reflects the long existence of general (though not quite universal) minimum income schemes, and the notion that the excluded are therefore a 'residual' category for whom money is not the solution. For example, the UK has long had a general minimum income scheme, but France (and Belgium), did not until recent years (in France the *Revenu Minimum d'Insertion* was launched in 1989).

More recent use of the term social exclusion in France has been concerned with precariousness arising from the high levels of unemployment (over 12 per cent) in the context of a 'solidarity' model of social inclusion (Silver 1994). Paugam sees social exclusion as a mass (and structural) risk, because of the mass risk of labour market precarity, itself at least partly a consequence of globalisation. The French-origin social-Catholic Non Governmental Organisation (NGO), ATD Fourth World, developed an influential definition of precarity:[3]

> Precarity is the absence of one or more of the forms of security, notably employment which enable individuals and families to meet professional, family and social obligations, and enjoy fundamental rights. The resulting insecurity may be more or less extensive and have more or less serious and permanent consequences. It leads to extreme poverty when it affects several areas of existence, becomes persistent and

jeopardises a person's chances of reassuming his responsibilities and regaining his rights by himself in the foreseeable future. (Council of Europe, March 1993).

The distinction between the French and UK approaches is not a simple left-right division. Given the security of public sector employees, a recent French debate concerning a possible Law on Social Exclusion which proposed part-time, government-subsidised contracts for 'socially useful work' risks reinforcing a two-tier labour market (Meurs and Prelis 1997). The labourist and the social-Catholic dimensions of the concept of exclusion, were also embodied in the 'Delors' perspective. These were influences on the European Commission's approach, and are, in many respects, conservative, 'workerist'(the provisions of the Social Protocol of the Treaty on European Union[4] relate largely to workers) and only vertically redistributive (solidarity between the generations).

At government level, the causal emphasis on behavioural self-exclusion is emerging everywhere but is very evident in the UK. The solution is 'job-readiness' so that the excluded become 'imminent' workers, sharing the values of the working majority, and escaping dependency, if not poverty, through waged work. This general approach is evident in the speech by the UK Secretary of State for Social Security. She stated that 'work is central to the government's attack on social exclusion', that 'employability will tackle the root cause of social exclusion and poverty – worklessness' (Harman 1997), and that 'those who propose that higher benefits should be the first priority of government ... have failed to learn from the past' (ibid.).

Arising from this approach, the terms on which integration is offered (compulsion, low pay) may be unacceptable to those most at risk, a threat to human dignity, and may not combat poverty. The 'Blairite' solution to poverty rests on an opportunity to access the personal and portable – human capital (education and training).

The liberal nature of the 'Blairite' perspective on solutions to social exclusion is timely. It implies cost-saving changes both in the objectives of social protection for the poor (from cohesion to safety net) and an approach to integrating the least advantaged into the labour market (supply side incentives and 'flexible' labour markets) which concur with the views of inter-governmental and multi-national organisations, such as the OECD, which exert powerful influence in other arenas. The 'downside' of this 'opportunity society' is that an opportunity is not a right. There is a greater risk of poverty and social exclusion for those not able to grasp opportunities.

The European Union and Commission documents illustrate the strengthening liberal perspective. Long evident in clearly economic policy areas (for example the Single Market) the neo-liberal perspective has grown more prominent in social policy since the Delors Presidency and the White Paper on Social Policy (1994). Common influences on the risks of social exclusion, such as globalisation and free trade, may be effecting a convergence in Member States' experience and their policy orientation, transmitted through closer integration of Europe (Spicker 1996, Greve 1996). High and long-term unemployment have emphasised the weaknesses in the inclusivity of the insurance-based social protection systems in France and elsewhere. Further, the integrative function of work is central to the creation of stable or social hierarchies, and the maintenance of solidarity. Finally, high unemployment has increased the costs of social protection, particularly in the context of qualification for the first wave of European Monetary Union. The Commission's own most recent document on social protection argues that the forces involved are not 'external', but a response to Member States concerns' about the costs of social protection arising mainly from unemployment and the ageing of the population (though neither of these are as important for Britain) (European Commission 1997).

However, successful policies of social integration rest on the relationship between state, markets and civil society actors. The adequacy, accessibility and affordability, and the risk/opportunity impact, of a broad range of social policies, in particular, health, employment, social protection, education and housing need to be considered. The principles of subsidiarity and the liberal economic perspective, which are reinforced in the Amsterdam Treaty,[5] inhibit both a supranational approach, and Member State scope, in combating social exclusion.

2. European Community action in support of member states

Article 2 of the Treaty on Europe Union (Amsterdam Treaty)[6] specifies that:

> The Community shall have as its task....to promote throughout the Community a harmonious, balanced and sustainable development of economic activities, a high level of employment and social protection, equality between men and women, sustainable and non-inflationary growth, a high degree of competitiveness and convergence of economic performance, a high level of protection and improving the quality of the environment, the raising of the standard of living and quality of life, and economic and social cohesion and solidarity among Member States.

Employment

Throughout the European Union, unemployment is seen as the key social problem, most recently expressed in the Amsterdam Resolution on Growth and Employment[7]. The Commission believes that to prevent persistent unemployment undermining the foundations of the European model of society, it is necessary to treat employment as a common interest. Indeed, specific provisions on employment were written into the Amsterdam Treaty (Title XIII). These establish the conditions for a common strategy for employment and the obligation to take employment into account in all Community strategies. However, the European Anti-Poverty Network was dismayed to see competitiveness raised to the status of an objective rather than a means (European Anti-Poverty Network, 1997). Further, the employment goal is subordinate to the largely monetarist approach to macro-economic policy.

Many governments are constrained in the short term by preparation for European Monetary Union, which restricts the size of public sector deficits. For example, Article 104 of the Amsterdam Treaty, in effect restricts governments' ability to undertake counter-cyclical measures. The internal market and European Monetary Union, are the perceived route to growth and stability (European Commission 1997b). Free trade will guarantee optimum output and therefore full employment demand, and 'supply-side' education and training will guarantee fair opportunities to access them (ibid.). In central and eastern and Europe, restructuring, the conditions attached to International Monetary Fund and other multi-lateral financial assistance, and the preparations for accession, are having the same constricting impact on economic and social policy options.

The centrality of 'employability'

Given the macro-economic constraints on policy, the European Union's approach to achieving the employment goal rests mainly on supply-side initiatives for 'flexibility' and 'employability'. The Community's approach to unemployment was developed at the European Council in Essen in 1994. Within the context of a stability-oriented macroeconomic policy, five priorities were identified.[8] These centred on investment in vocational training which targeted weaker groups in the labour market, and improvements in the employment intensity of growth (through more flexible organisation of work, wage flexibility, reduction in non-wage labour costs, and job-creation initiatives in new areas such as the environment and social services).

'Employability' policies, rather than 'passive' income maintenance, are central to the emerging perspective on combating exclusion. Primarily, poverty has implied exclusion from goods and services and, more recently, consequent inability to participate in social life. The main solution, central to the European social model, has been the development of inclusive income-maintenance policies. However, social exclusion goes beyond membership of society through consumption, to encompass exclusion from a place in society, thus the emphasis on the 'productive', and on the social role of employment. Thus also the contemporary concern with the 'moral hazard' of unemployment, and the fear that long-term absence from the labour market corrupts the family and community values which support labour market and social integration.

Because long-term unemployment and the resulting poverty and unemployment traps are key elements in the perceived threat to cohesion, active labour market policies must be supported by 'employment-friendly' social protection policies. For example, the European Commission's paper on the modernisation of social protection refers to minimum income schemes as 'a kind of exclusion compensation' and argues that there is 'a growing consensus on the necessity of moving from the traditional social assistance approach'. The solution is envisaged to be active labour market policies and integration 'contracts' (1997). The European Commission's Green Paper on the organisation of work takes a rather more Anglo-American approach, concerned with a more flexible legal framework for employment to match the 'flexible firm' required to respond to globalisation. The paper discusses the 'centrality' of 'questions concerning the balance of regulatory powers' and 'in particular the possibility of derogating from legislation by collective agreements and the scope for individual contracts versus collective agreements' (1997d:).

The contribution through the Structural Funds' instruments

The Structural Funds have been in existence for around twenty years, they are the main financial instrument for cohesion, and the clearest expression of the Community's commitment to territorial cohesion and intra-Community solidarity. The Structural Funds transfer resources, not for passive support, but to assist Member States to carry out active measures of adaptation and development (see Boxes 18.1-18.4).

The current phase of the Structural Funds (1994-1999) has a budget of ECU 141 billion (one-third of the total Community budget). However, the Common Agricultural Policy, which still accounts for over half the Community budget, is in many respects anti-egalitarian. Some wealthy northern countries do well from it, as do large agri-businesses, and it raises the cost of food for poor consumers. A portion (9 per cent) of the Structural Funds is reserved for Community Initiatives.[9]

The strengths and limitations of current activity under the Structural Funds

The central purpose of the Structural Funds is to assist cohesion of the territory of the Union. Territorial differences in per capita income between the Union territories are twice those between regions of the United States, and the size of resources transferred under the Structural Funds,[10] is evidence of the commitment to an inclusive notion of Europe. Objective 1 funding allocates resources to countries and regions with per capita GDP less than 75 per cent of the Community average. In addition the Cohesion Fund is a special fund to assist the poorest Member States to prepare for economic and monetary union.

Box 18.1
The four structural funds

European Regional Development Fund, ERDF, (52% of the overall total)

European Social Fund, ESF, (28%)

European Agricultural Guidance and Guarantee Fund, EAGGF, Guidance section (16%)

Financial Instrument for Fisheries Guidance, FIFG (2%).

The Funds underwent major reform in 1988 to improve the quality, relevance and consequently, effectiveness, of measures undertaken for economic and social cohesion. An additional ECU 30 billion is available for a special Cohesion Fund specifically to address the problems of the weaker regions in the period leading to monetary union.

Box 18.2
The four principles of the structural funds

concentration of the Funds on least advantaged regions. The majority of the Funds (about 70%) are concentrated on Objective 1 regions, that is those regions lagging behind, indicated by GNP less than 75% of the Community average.

partnership, that is, a close collaboration between the Commission and all the relevant authorities at national, regional or local level appointed by each Member State.

additionality, which establishes the requirement that in each Member State the Funds result in an equivalent increase in the total volume of structural aid, taking account of macro-economic circumstances.

programming, which concerns the scope of the Funds, time-tabling, and adjustment procedures, which operate through a process of refining development plans and Community Support Frameworks (which set out funding priorities and forms of assistance), and operational measures.

Box 18.3
The six objectives of the structural funds

Objective 1: development and structural adjustment of the regions whose development is lagging behind.

Objective 2: converting the regions or parts of regions seriously affected by industrial decline.

Objective 3: combating long-term unemployment (more than twelve months), occupational integration of young people (less than 25 years of age), facilitating the integration of those threatened with exclusion from the labour market.

Objective 4: facilitating workers' adaptation to industrial changes and to changes in production systems.

Objective 5a: speeding up the adjustment of agricultural structures as part of the CAP reform, aid to modernisation and restructuring of fisheries.

Objective 5b: facilitating the development and structural adjustment of rural areas

Objective 6: development and structural adjustment sparsely populated regions.

Box 18.4
The community employment initiatives

NOW (new opportunities for women)

HORIZON (for the disadvantaged and people with a disability)

YOUTHSTART

ADAPT (for retraining)

The Funds also recognise the risks faced by regions with particular concentrations of problems, and will allow a multidimensional approach to disadvantaged territories. Within all of the Funds there is a welcome trend towards an increasing focus on people and organisations, as well as territory. One example is the support to small business as the new job generating motor of Europe's economies. There has also been increasing recognition of the importance of the employment-intensity of growth.

Reflecting the importance of 'employability', the European Social Fund provides assistance for training and guidance measures for the unemployed, especially the long-term and young unemployed, in adapting and upgrading their skills to the changing labour market. Objective 3 of the Structural Funds, which has a budget of ECU 5.5 billion (1995 -1999), assists Member States in actions to combat exclusion from the labour market.

The Commission has launched a number of Community Initiatives to complement the human resource aims of the Structural Funds. The Community EMPLOYMENT Initiatives (see box 18.4 above) enable specifically adapted support to be provided for women, persons with a disability, and persons with low or no qualifications or vocational training, especially young people. The Community Initiative INTEGRA, allows an increase in resources and more specific provision for migrants and ethnic minorities, as well as those with most difficulties in entering or re entering the labour market. In launching the Community Initiative URBAN[11], the Commission has recognised that

> the growing tensions within European society are evident particularly in the serious level of social exclusion in an increasing number of inner city or peripheral urban areas[12].

However, there are serious limitations to the role of the Structural Funds in combating social exclusion. Essentially, the purpose of the Structural Funds is to increase the cohesion of the territory of the Union; in the main, the funds are not directly concerned with the integration of the least advantaged people in the territories. Further, 70 per cent of the Funds' total resources are targeted to countries and regions with per capita *average* income below 75 per cent of the European Union average. This kind of targeting cannot fully reflect either the absolute number or depth of the low-income populations within countries, nor the distribution of risks of unemployment. The Community initiatives, which are most relevant to the least advantaged groups and localities, constitute a small proportion of the total budget. Further, the use of the Funds for 'soft' social infrastructure is quite limited, but the capacity of local partners is increasingly thought important in creating sustainable change in disadvantaged localities and regions. Recently, the Structural Funds have undergone a 'mid-term review', and are due for further reform. To enhance their ability to combat social exclusion, it will be important to 'mainstream' in the Structural Funds (and in the Member States' own policies) the lessons of the innovative approaches to labour market exclusion and to areas of severe urban disadvantage which are being tested through INTEGRA and URBAN.

'Mainstreaming' in Member States' own policies will become more important as the financial support to existing net recipients is likely to diminish, and to become more concentrated geographically and in terms of the Objectives. For example, in the context of enlargement, the European Commission proposes a reform of the Structural Funds which would reduce Objectives to three and cut the amount available to Community Initiatives to 5 per cent of the budget (European Commission 1997b). While these changes will mean a reduction in the real value of resources to some countries who are currently net recipients, they will maintain the growth of the absolute value of the budget within the constraint of the same proportion of Union GNP; so leaving 'headroom' to deal with the problems of accession countries.[13]

Finally, it must be noted that without an appropriate demand-side framework, the best supply-side and local initiatives may have little effect on the length of the queue of job-seekers. Article 4.3 of the Amsterdam Treaty makes it clear that the macroeconomic environment shall be managed on monetarist lines: the 'guiding principles' include price stability, sound public finances and monetary conditions, but not full employment.

3. The social policy contribution to combating poverty and social exclusion

The strength of the Commission role in combating poverty and social exclusion lies fundamentally in its role as guardian of the Treaties. There is a commitment to promoting a European social model (though what this means seems to be changing), a focus on disadvantaged groups, co-operation with civil society partners and a research capacity in social policy (though much of it is fairly short-term). Greater use of qualified majority voting, and the incorporation of the Social Protocol in the revised Treaty, will enhance the Commission's ability to initiate action in the social field. However, the Amsterdam Treaty makes it clear that the employment and social protection goals must be 'without prejudice' to the aim of price stability (Title II). The emphasis on a narrow view of subsidiarity and proportionality, and the retention of unanimity in fields such as social security and social assistance, also considerably restrict the Commission's initiative. Further, the labour market priorities of Essen are evident throughout the Amsterdam Treaty. Consequently, Title XI on social policy, mainly discusses education and vocational training, and the financial instrument of the European Social Fund. There is very limited coverage of other social policy dimensions. Title XIII on public health refers mainly to issues arising in the context of free movement of goods and labour, and there is no Title on Housing. Indeed the language of the Treaty gives a much lower priority to other dimensions of disadvantage than unemployment.[14]

The impact of these constraints on anti-poverty initiatives is clear in the developing agenda on social protection. Social protection can be defined as all the collective transfer systems designed to protect people against social risks, therefore a high level of social protection is crucial to preventing poverty. Article 136 of the Amsterdam Treaty refers to 'proper' social protection, and to combating social exclusion, but subordinates it to the goal of employment promotion.

The principles of subsidiarity and proportionality further restrict the role of supranational social policy. The aspiration is towards minimum standards; harmonisation of Member States' policies is explicitly excluded in Title VIII (employment) and Title XI (social policy, education, vocational training and youth).

However, a supranational dimension may be more necessary in the context of the Single Market. Given greater pluralism in welfare provision and a single market in services, there are increasing possibilities of 'welfare shopping' by individuals, of 'cherry-picking' by suppliers and of competition in the provision of welfare services, involving a loss of autonomy at national level. The consequences of these changes have not yet been fully thought through. There are also increasing consequences for the range and funding possibilities of national welfare systems. Despite this, there has been little practical development of a core of minimum standards, or thorough follow up to the two key Recommendations of 1992 on convergence of social protection objectives and on common criteria for minimum incomes.[15] Further, whereas Directives have legal force, and must be implemented on pain of penalties, there is little or nothing relevant to combating poverty or social exclusion which has this legal status (Recommendations do not carry legal weight).

Recent Communications illustrate the Commission's thinking on social matters. For example, the Communication 'Modernising and Improving Social Protection'(European Commission 1997, part 1) restates the important principle that social protection represents a fundamental and distinguishing component of the European model of society. However, the practical meaning of this is surely the citizen's right to protection from poverty consequent on social risks. The commitment to this right appears to be weakening in some Member States, and is minimal at the level of citizens of the Union. Poverty is referred to in the Amsterdam Treaty only once (Article 177 on development co-operation with less-developed countries). Indeed the profile of European anti-poverty concerns has diminished. Between 1979 and 1994, the Commission supported three small-scale specific actions to combat poverty and exclusion. A new programme was not approved by the Council of Ministers because of some Member States objections (based on the principle of subsidiarity). Poverty 3 (1989-1994)[16] promoted a multi-dimensional approach to poverty and social exclusion based on partnership with public and private institutions and with the participation of the least privileged groups. In a number of Member States, the programme influenced the 'mainstreaming' of the concept of social exclusion, and the partnership approach to social action. It has also stimulated the establishment of specialist agencies and specific programmes in some Member States. The revised Article 118 of the Maastricht Treaty allows for the launch of measures for the exchange of best practice in combating social exclusion, but it remains to be seen what might be proposed after the year 2000. The European Anti-Poverty Network noted that the elderly (whose action programme is also currently in abeyance) and people with a disability, are not included in the scope of Article 118 (European Anti-Poverty Network, 1997).

In the absence of a significant legal framework or financial instrument in the social field, the Commission's role in combating exclusion and promoting social integration through social policy is very limited. It includes supporting research which stimulates debate, providing a forum for exchange of best practice, and some limited pilot action, in those social matters which can be said to have significant cross-border or supra-national dimensions. For example, in education, there are programmes of vocational training and education exchanges, and following a White Paper on education and training the Commission launched a specific pilot programme which aims to combat exclusion of young people at risk through a network of 'second chance schools' in urban areas. Currently, there is limited Commission activity in the field of public health (as opposed to occupational health and safety), but there are a number of activities which may be relevant to combating disadvantage and exclusion. Preventative actions include health promotion campaigns and networks, including those in schools and for the elderly. There are also initiatives concerned with AIDS, cancer, persons with Alzheimer's disease and their carers, and prevention of drug dependency.

Three themes influencing social policy

It is evident that the supranational contribution to combating poverty and social exclusion is limited by both the principle of subsidiarity and the constraints of the programme for Economic and Monetary Union. However, there are foundations on which a stronger commitment to a more inclusive social Europe could be built, should Member States' wish it. Cutting across the sectoral social policy areas are three themes that may represent guiding principles for the development and implementation of all social policy and actions. These are, first, rights, justice and citizenship, second, equality and non-discrimination, and third, co-operation with civil society actors.

Rights, justice and citizenship

Citizens have the right to vote in European Parliament elections, the right to petition the European Parliament and to have access to an Ombudsman. However, citizenship still carries very limited rights, and is a long way from a 'people's Europe'.

Funded by the European Commission, the Observatory on Social Exclusion, now in abeyance, was amongst the first to take a social rights approach to making the concept of social exclusion operational: 'social exclusion can be analysed in terms of the denial – or non-realisation – of social rights...' (Room 1993). Social rights are a means of combating social exclusion, and give meaning to European citizenship. However, the climate of opinion in many national governments, is concerned to roll back social rights and replace them with labour market opportunities and self-reliance[17].

The Social Protocol provisions on minimum wages, consultation of workers, and working time (now incorporated into the Treaty on European Union) are examples of measures relating to high labour standards and equality of opportunity which are indirectly preventative of social exclusion for workers. However, those initiatives designed to reconcile family obligations and working life, or combat poverty, have no legal status. [18, 19]

Throughout this chapter, it is evident that the proposals of the employment and social affairs Directorate of the Commission have been reined back by the Council of Ministers, concerned about costs and subsidiarity. However, the chapter also indicates that the Commission's most recent proposals are more accommodating to the Council of Ministers' perspectives. For example, the European Commission's Communication on modernising social protection, in its section on 'social protection as a productive factor', refers to the restructuring of public expenditure to promote employment. Nevertheless, whereas there may be weakening support for the right to income maintenance as a means to combat poverty, other rights are not weakening. A later section of the Communication, on the subject of adapting social protection to maximise women's labour market participation, is sub-titled 'towards an individualisation of rights' (1997). In her discussion of the changing welfare paradigm, Ferge has referred to the 'individualization of the social' (Ferge 1997), to the weakening of the rights of the poor, and acknowledgement of group and minority rights, in particular those of women. She suggests this trend is related to the rejection of the 'modern' categories of class and social determinism, and adoption of the post-modern recognition of 'the right to differ' (ibid.).

Equality of opportunity and non-discrimination

Although there is increasing recognition of discrimination as a serious issue, Member States vary greatly in their legal protections, and, for example, the UK has a stronger legal framework than most European countries. Racism and xenophobia are only beginning to emerge as concerns at the inter-governmental level in the European Union (1997 was the 'Year Against Racism'). One important new development is the explicit commitment to take action to combat discrimination on sex, racial or ethnic origin, religion or belief, disability, age or sexual orientation (Article 13 of the Amsterdam Treaty). However, only discrimination on grounds of nationality is explicitly prohibited. Further, the Amsterdam Treaty's main concern regarding migrants, refugees and asylum seekers, has been in the context of restricting movement into the European Union.

Equality between men and women (in employment) has a much stronger legal basis, going back to the Treaty of Rome, and the fourth programme[20] for women aims to 'mainstream' concern for equal opportunities in all policies, measures and activities of the Community. It has a budget of ECU 60 million over its four year life (1996-2000).

The Commission is directly concerned with the integration of persons with a disability through the HELIOS II initiative for exchange of good practice. The Commission has drafted a Resolution on Equality of Opportunity for People with Disabilities[21] which raises integration as the primary goal. ECU 5.5 billion has been allocated through the Structural Funds for measures during the period 1994-1999.

The social partners and civil society: activities involving non-state actors concerned with combating exclusion

Declaration 23 of the Treaty on European Union 'stresses the importance, in pursuing the objectives of Article 117 of the Treaty establishing the European Community, of co-operation between the latter and charitable associations and foundations as institutions responsible for social welfare establishments and services'.[22]

The provision and delivery of welfare services in Europe increasingly involves non-governmental organisations. This is especially so for the specialist services required for many vulnerable groups. In this context, the implementation of Declaration 23 assumes increasing importance in stimulating the debate on methods and means of combating social exclusion. Co-operation with social partners besides employers and trades unions is being enhanced. The Social Policy Forum of March 1996, for the first time brought together the representatives of thousands of social NGOs throughout Europe. However, the NGOs still lack official status as partners. There is also some limited activity focused on not-for profit business, organised as co-operatives, mutuals, associations and foundations (CMAFs), which are a key organisational form for achieving inclusion. The 'European' legal basis for foundations was completed in 1997.

Clearly, action based on the three principles outlined in this section of the chapter is very limited, and is unlikely to strengthen without a greater voice for citizen's and social NGOs. Raising the priority of combating poverty and social exclusion at European level will first require firmer legal recognition for all of civil society, not only business and trades unions.

Conclusions

There is both a limited legal basis and, besides the Structural Funds, very limited resources, for social policy, resulting in a lop-sided focus on labour market integration, within the context of support for the operation of the Single Market and the Economic Union. Moreover, the review above makes it obvious how little policy or action is directly concerned with poverty, or with social exclusion in terms of the rupture of the social tie. The principle of equality of opportunity and non-discrimination is mainly targeted on relations between men and women (in the labour market) rather than relations between ethnic groups, or other sources of difference. Effectively, the scope for a social policy contribution to combating poverty and social exclusion is restricted by the content of the Treaty of Rome, establishing the European Economic Community; essentially, all later Treaties are merely revisions to it. While this remains the case, the scope for supra-national arrangements in the social policy field will remain very limited. Member States' willingness to change this, is limited not only by fears of loss of sovereignty or imposition of costs, but by the liberal ideology which has underpinned the drive for a single market and economic and monetary union.

Nevertheless, it must be stressed that whatever the current strengths and limitations of supra-national action to combat social exclusion, there has been considerable development since the nineteen-eighties, when there was food aid and little else. Since then there has been a generalised commitment to combating social exclusion, which is evident in different aspects of Community policy.

Especially for the least advantaged, political rights and economic opportunities cannot be exercised in a meaningful way without the assurance of fundamental social rights. The entrenchment of a 'two-tier' Europe in economic and social terms, is inimical to the future security, prosperity and dignity of an enlarged Europe. It is primarily the responsibility of the Member States to meet this challenge, and to address the question of the balance of responsibilities that must be accepted by individuals, as the corollary of their social rights. However, the narrow interpretation of subsidiarity and the lack of a financial instrument restrict the Commission's ability to innovate and co-ordinate. This is more than ever necessary as the European Union seeks to integrate the new democracies of central and eastern Europe. They are countries which have much lower income than current Member States, but which are still in the process of transforming their systems of social protection, and transferring more of the responsibility for integration to individuals and organisations of the emerging, but still weak, civil society.

Unlike the foundation of the European Community, the remit of the Council of Europe is neither primarily economic, nor restricted to western European countries. Its role is the promotion of democracy, human rights and the rule of law in forty-one countries of Europe, north, south, east and west. Articles 30 and 31 of the revised European Social Charter relate, respectively, to the right to protection from poverty and exclusion, and the right to housing (Council of Europe 1997). A collective complaints procedure enables NGOs registered to bring a complaint, to draw attention to the situation in Member States. Currently, governments are reluctant to sign up to these two Articles, and implementation of the Charter is not legally enforceable in the Member States of the Council of Europe. In many respects, the original, 1961, version of the Council of Europe's European Social Charter was the inspiration for the 1989 Social Charter of the European Union (itself the basis for the Social Protocol, incorporated into the 1997 Amsterdam

Treaty. Will it take another thirty-six years before the revised European Social Charter inspires an explicit legal commitment to combating poverty and exclusion in the European Union?

References

Castel R, (1995), *Les Metamorphoses de la Question Sociale en Europe*, une Chronique du Salariat, Fayard, Paris

Council of Europe, (1992), *Europe 1992-2000: European Municipalities and Democracy: The Exclusion of Poverty through Citizenship*, Charleroi 5-7th Feb 1992, CLRAE, Council of Europe Press, Strasbourg

Council of Europe, (1997), *The Social Charter of the 21st Century*, Council of Europe Press, Strasbourg

de Foucauld J (rapporteur), (1996), *For a Europe of Civic and Social Rights: Report by the Comité des Sages chaired by Maria Lourdes Pintasilgo*, in Report by the Comité des Sages chaired by Maria Lourdes Pintasilgo, European Commission, DG V, Brussels

Duffy K, (1997), Opportunity & Risk: Broad Perspectives Arising from the Results of HDSE Phase *I* (1996-1997), in *Towards a Better Social Cohesion in Europe: Today and Tomorrow*, Council of Europe, Strasbourg

Duffy K, (1998), *Opportunity & Risk: A Report on the Risks of Social Exclusion in Europe*, Council of Europe Press, Strasbourg (forthcoming)

European Anti Poverty Network, (1997), 'EAPN's Analysis of the Amsterdam Treaty', *EAPN Network News*, Oct No 51, 2

European Commission, (1994), *European Social Policy: A Way Forward for the Union*, Commission of the European Communities, Brussels

European Commission, (1997), *Modernising and Improving Social Protection in the European Union*, Commission of the European Communities, COM (97) 102 final Brussels

European Commission, (1997a), Agenda 2000 Presse Release IP/97/660-Commission Publishes its Communication 'Agenda 2000: For a Stronger and Wider Europe', European Commission, Strasbourg/Brussels 16th July 1997

European Commission, (1997b), Agenda 2000, Volume 1, Communication: For a Stronger and Wider Union DOC/97/6, European Commission, COM (97) 2000, Brussels 15th July

European Commission, (1997c), *Treaty of Amsterdam Amending the Treaty on European Union, the Treaties Establishing the European Communities and Certain Related Acts*, European Commission, Brussels

European Commission, (1997d), *Green Paper: Partnership for a New Organisation of Work*, Commission of the European Communities,

COM(97) 128; Brussels

Ferge Z, (1997), 'The Changed Welfare Paradigm: The Individualization of the Social', *Social Policy and Administration*, 31(1), 20-44

Greve B, (1996), 'Indications of Social Policy Convergence in Europe', *Social Policy and Administration*, 30(4), 348-367

Harman H, (1997), 'Employability a Priority for the UK Presidency', *Anti Poverty News*-England, issue no 3 Winter, 4-5

Join-Lambert M, (1995), 'Exclusion, Equality Before the Law and Non-Discrimination: Introductory Report', in Seminar Organised by the Council of Europe in Co-operation with the *Intercenter* of Messina (Italy), Council of Europe, Strasbourg., Taormina-Mare (Italy)

Lenoir R, (1974), *Les Exclus*, SEUIL, Paris

Meurs D & Prelis J, (1997), *Western Europe Thematic Employment* Report to the The Human Dignity And Social Exclusion Initiative, Council of Europe, Strasbourg

Paugam S, (1992), 'Les Allocataires du RMI. Face a Leur Difficultés', in Le *Revenu Minimum d'Insertion: Un Dette Social* eds. Castel R & Lae JF, Logiques Sociales, L'Harmattan, Paris

Paugam S, (1993a), *La Dynamique de la Disqualification Social*, Science Humaines, Paris

Paugam S, (1993b), *La Societe Francaise et ses Pauvres. L'experience du Revenu Minimum d'Insertion*, Presses Universitaires de France, Paris

Room G, (1993), *Report of the European Community Observatory on National Policies to Combat Social Exclusion*, Commission of the European Communities DG V, Brussels

Room G, (1995), 'Poverty in Europe; Competing Paradigms of Analysis', *Policy and Politics*, April,

Silver H, (1994), 'Social Exclusion and Social Solidarity: Three Paradigms', *International Labour Review*, 133, 5-6

Spicker P, (1996), 'Social Policy in a Federal Europe', *Social Policy and Administration*, 30(4), 293-304

Touraine A, (1991), *Face a l'Exclusion, Citoyenneté et Urbanité*, Ouvrage Collectif, Esprit, Paris

Touraine A, (1992), 'Inegalitiés de la Societe Industrielle, Exclusion Du Marche', in *Justice Sociale et Inegalites* eds. Affichard J & de Foucauld JB, Esprit, Paris

Wresinski J, (1994), *Chronic Poverty and Lack of Basic Security*, Economic and Social Council of France, Paris

Xiberras M, (1993), *Theories de l'exclusion Sociale,* Meridiens Klincksieck, Paris

Endnotes

1. Council Decision (85/8/EEC) 19.12.1984.

2. *Economic and Social Committee Opinion of 12 July 1989 Resolution, Official Journal No. C221, 28.8.1989 O.*

3. This definition has been influential at the level of intergovernmental organisations such as the Council of Europe, and also in a report of the French Economic and Social Committee (Wresinski J, 1994, Chronic Poverty and Lack of Basic Security, Economic and Social Council of France, Paris).

4. Treaty on Eurropean Union, 1992, Office for Official Publications, Luxembourg.

5. In this chapter, all references to Articles in the Amsterdam Treaty refer to the Consolidated version.

6. Consolidated version of the Treaty establishing the European Community.

7. Treaty of Amsterdam 1997, Office for Official Publications, Luxembourg

8. COM(95) 250 final.

9. Community Initiatives generally take the form of operational programmes, but they may also be global grants. They cover five topics: cross-border, transnational and inter-regional co-operation and networks, rural development, assistance to the outermost regions, employment promotion and development, and the management of industrial change.

10. Excluding the Cohesion Fund, Community assistance accounts for almost 12% of all public and private expenditure in Greece, 8% and 9% in Ireland and Portugal and 7% in the relevant regions of Spain

11. Targeted at cities with populations greater than 100,000, the Community Initiative URBAN provides financial assistance to local partnerships, for integrated action in support of business creation, infrastructure improvements, customised training and actions for equality of opportunity and social amenities. It aims to be a catalyst for lasting improvements in disadvantaged neighbourhoods in urban areas. Total funding (1994-1999) is approximately MECU 600 of which MECU 400 will be spent in Objective 1 areas, and the

remainder to other areas but with a preference for those covered by Objective 2.

12. Notice to the Member States laying down guidelines for operational programmes which Member States are invited to establish in the framework of a Community initiative concerning urban areas Official Journal No C 180/6 1.7.94.

13. The UK is likely to lose significantly from these reforms. The Objectives will focus firstly, as now, on countries with low income relative to the Community average. Despite being the fourth poorest of the current Member States, the UK cannot gain much from Objective One. At the current level of aggregation, which lumps together richer and poorer areas, the qualifying threshold of 75% or less of average Community GDP excludes most UK regions. Accession of poorer countires will also absorb these resources. Given the UK's relatively low unemployment, it will not gain much from the renewed focus on unemployment, and may lose the favourable status it has under the current Objective 2 funding for transforming areas of industrial decline.

14. Council Recommendation 92/ 441/EEC of 24 June 1992, on common criteria concerning sufficient resources and social assistance in social protection systems, OJ No L 245/46, 26.8 1992

15. On social protection objectives and policies, the key Recommendation is, Council Recommendation 92/442/EEC of 27 July 1992, Official Journal No L 245/46, 26.8.92. On common criteria concerning sufficient resources and social assistance, the key Recommendation is, Council Recommendation 92/441/EEC of 24 June 1992, Official Journal No L 245/46, 26.8.92.

16. Official Journal L 224, 02.89.

17. For example, the inter-governmental steering committee on social policy of the Council of Europe recognised a link between poverty and rights. Thus, 'poverty by definition is the consequence of a failure to adequately secure economic and social rights' but the committee doubted 'whether states would be prepared to add to their existing obligations in this sphere' (Council of Europe 1992: 75).

18. Council Recommendation 92/241/EEC of 31 March 1992 on childcare

19. Commission Opinion on an Equitable Wage (COM(93) 388).

20. Proposal for a Council Decision on the fourth medium-term Community action programme on equal opportunities for women

and men (1996-2000), COM(95) 381 final, Brussels 19.07.1995

21 Communication of the Commission on Equality of Opportunity for People with Disabilities: A New European Community Disability Strategy and Draft Resolution of the Council and the Representatives of the Governments of the Member States Meeting with the Council on Equality of Opportunity for People with Disabilities COM(96) 406 final, 96/0216 (CNS).

22 *Declaration 23 of the Treaty on European Union 1992,* Office for Official Publications, Luxembourg.

19. Comment: The European Dimension
by Chris Pond MP

Katherine Duffy's chapter reflects the breadth of knowledge and experience she has acquired over many years of work in the field of European social policy. She is right to be wary of the potential conflicts between the social and other objectives of the European project post Amsterdam. But the chapter exhibits the weariness felt, perhaps inevitably, by those who have researched and campaigned in this field during the dark years of the 1980s and much of the 1990s. I too remember the days when (then) eleven heads of government found themselves seriously outnumbered by Mrs Thatcher, wielding the veto like a handbag stuffed with house bricks, every time they tried to move forward on the social agenda.

It may well be that the shadow of Thatcherism still hangs over the European project, but we should not be too frightened by it. Although Britain was once a significant block to any progress on the European social agenda, one of the first actions of the new Labour government was to sign the social protocol (chapter) allowing its integration into the body of the Amsterdam Treaty. In France, Jospin's policies of social inclusion and solidarity are proving increasingly popular. And in Germany, which alongside Britain blocked the 4th European Poverty Programme, there is the real prospect of a change to a left of centre government in the forthcoming elections. The three most powerful Member States may soon be pursuing a more committed approach to building a Social Europe than at any time in the history of the community. Indeed, of the fifteen Member States, no fewer than ten might be expected to have left of centre governments pursuing a policy of social inclusion. This is a moment, not to weep for what has been lost, but to consider how the new opportunities might be grasped.

Duffy's prediction that the new approach to social inclusion may not be based on a traditional attempt to tackle poverty and inequality through fiscal transfers is, however, well founded. I don't share her despair about this trend. For many years at the Low Pay Unit we argued that the root causes of poverty and inequality must be tackled, as well as the symptoms.[1] Attempts to redistribute through tax and income maintenance policies have been unsuccessful in challenging the depths of inequality over many decades and, in my view, would be unlikely to succeed in this objective in decades to come.

Indeed, I should at this point declare an interest as one of the consultants employed to advise the Commission in preparation of their communication on the modernisation of social protection systems, of which Duffy is just a little disapproving. In my evidence to DGV, I argued for a social policy that encouraged active citizenship rather than passive receipt of welfare.[2] Such an approach requires that citizens should be equipped with a range of social and economic rights, including the right to participation. These include opportunities for training and education, employment opportunities, a minimum wage, high quality child care and protection against discrimination.

Duffy might describe such an agenda as 'conservative' and 'workerist', but it is neither of these things. It is more radical, and probably more effective, as a method of redistribution than attempts to use purely fiscal measures. These might alleviate the worst effects of inequality 'after the event', but this is rather like closing the stable door after the horse has bolted. I would prefer to tackle the inequalities at their source, in the mechanisms – particularly those of the labour market – in which they are generated.

In the UK, for instance, one in five non-pensioner households has no one in employment, a higher percentage than in any other EU Member State. And amongst those in employment, a higher proportion earn less than the Council of Europe 'decency threshold' than in any other EU country. The 'working poor' still represent the largest single group amongst those on low incomes.

Rowntree, and later Townsend and Atkinson, taught us about the lifecycle effects of poverty: those who are poor during their working lives are more likely to experience poverty during retirement or periods of unemployment and sickness or while bringing up children. The principle of social insurance, that it should spread the benefits of gainful employment over the life-cycle is well founded. But it is completely undermined if periods in work are poorly rewarded, or if high unemployment persists amongst vulnerable groups in the workforce. If this happens, social insurance itself collapses, leaving many dependent on means-tested social assistance. Closing the gaps in the safety net, or even making it more generous, is no substitute for ensuring that as few people as possible find themselves in the net in the first place.

Duffy assumes that there is a conflict between the objective of redistribution and the emphasis on labour market based employment and social rights. I believe that the latter approach is far more likely to achieve the redistribution of which both of us approve than simple fiscal transfers through the tax and benefit system.

In places, Duffy slips into a caricature of Labour's approach to social policy at both a domestic and European level, suggesting that 'the terms on which integration is offered (compulsion, low pay) may be unacceptable to those most at risk, a threat to human dignity, and may not combat poverty. The 'Blairite' solution to poverty rests on an opportunity to access the personal and portable – human capital – education and training'. Yet there is a relatively small element of compulsion built into the New Deal: removal of the option for 18-24 year olds to remain on social security without first attempting one of the other five options available. Since the 'pathfinder' projects have suggested that the New Deal will be the first such programme in which young people are prepared to participate with enthusiasm, even this relatively small element of compulsion may be little used. By contrast, the fierceness of compulsion built into the US welfare 'reforms' (some may consider them better described as 'welfare abolition') has rendered the scheme unpopular not only with claimants but with private sector employers as well.[3]

Moreover, the introduction of a national minimum wage is explicitly designed to ensure that those making the transfer from social security into employment does not result in low pay. Duffy dismisses the importance of this measure too readily. She also ignores the fact that, although it is an explicit objective of Labour's welfare reforms to shift as many as possible from social security in to employment, another explicit objective is to ensure that those who cannot work should receive a level of income that provides them with dignity and independence. Amongst the eight key principles set out in the Green paper on *New Ambitions for our Country. A New Contract for Welfare*, are that the system should 'encourage people of working age to work where they are capable of doing so' and that 'there should be specific action to attack social exclusion and help those in poverty'.[4]

Katherine Duffy has done a service in mapping the landscape of European policy towards poverty and social exclusion. But the chapter is overly pessimistic in its assumptions that these issues are slipping off the agenda of European debate. Our job should be, not to mourn the past, but to shape the future. With the change in the European political climate now taking place, we have an opportunity to do just that.

Endnotes

1   See, for example, 'A Social Policy for the Active Society', (1995) in Funken K and Cooper P (eds) *Old and New Poverty* Rivers Oram Press London; *Employment and Social Protection in Europe: Meeting the challenge of poverty, prosperity and employment* (1997) Friedrich Ebert Stiftung, Bonn.

2   Pond C & O'Donnell C (1996) *The Future of Social Protection:* Social Protection and the Labour Market, Low Pay Unit, London

3   For a fuller discussion of the US reforms see *Social Security Reforms: Lessons from the United States of America* (1998) Social Security Select Committee, HC 552m HMSO

4   DSS (1998) *New Ambitions for our country: A new contract for welfare,* Cm 3805, HMSO, March 1998, p.2

VIII:
The Policy
Process

20. Social exclusion: joined up solutions to joined up problems
by Geoff Mulgan

Poverty and social exclusion were largely off the political agenda for the best part of a generation. Throughout the 1980s policy-makers promised that the combination of trickle-down, economic growth and the spread of an enterprise culture would lift Britain's poorer areas out of poverty. The rising tide would raise all boats. It didn't happen, and that failure was a crucial reason why Labour won in May 1997. Its mandate was, at least in part, a mandate to put right the yawning inequalities that emerged under the Conservatives. Certainly that is how most ministers have interpreted it. In the government's first year of office almost every domestic department has reframed its agenda around poverty and social exclusion, through new policies on welfare to work, childcare, national insurance, turning around failing schools, improving literacy and numeracy, refocusing public health, or targeting regeneration more clearly on the poorest areas. Substantial new spending commitments – most notably the New Deal – have provided the funds to deal with exclusion.

Social exclusion was the topic of the Prime Minister's first major speech in office, and it has been prominent in the speeches and day to day work of most senior ministers. However, what has received less attention is how the government is analysing the problem, and how government itself is having to change to deal with it. This is the subject of this chapter. It describes some of the aspects of poverty and exclusion; the mismatch between how government has traditionally been organised and the nature of modern poverty; and how this can be put right.

For any government trying to do something about poverty and exclusion the first problem is that there is still a degree of fatalism about whether anything can be done. It has become fashionable to believe that growing inequality is an inevitable result of powerful global forces, as technologies advance and a new global division of labour takes shape. As a result, some would argue, the best we can do is to accommodate and contain. Many are also sceptical about whether governments really are able to solve problems, and see them as inevitably condemned to impotence and futility.

There is not the space here to offer full answers to these points of view. But we can at least offer tentative ones. Although we know that there are powerful forces widening income disparities, the fact is that some countries have managed to reduce inequality. In addition, the historical evidence shows that as a result of the changing rhythms of technological change periods of widening dispersal have often in the past been followed by periods of a narrowing of such dispersal. This should at the very least caution against the conventional wisdom that worsening inequality is a fact of life. To those convinced that government action is futile, we can at any rate point to the successes of governments in the past in solving apparently intractable social problems; the public health crises of the mid-19th century were solved; so was the unemployment crisis of the 1930s, and the inflation of the 1970s. Governments can rarely solve problems on their own, and often need to reshape themselves to avoid being part of the problem. But fatalism about government's capacities to deal with social issues is as naïve as belief that government's powers are unlimited.

What, then, of the problems we are facing? In each era the nature of inequality and poverty changes. Over the last three decades the language of social exclusion has increasingly been used in addition to the language of poverty because it defines better than poverty a situation in which large sections of the population are, in effect, cut off from qualifications, jobs and safe environments. Poverty remains a useful concept, but it doesn't tell us enough about the most acute problems. It makes them appear static rather than dynamic, and it makes them appear primarily material when they are often as much about skills and cultures. In any case the difference between poverty and exclusion is an important one. Although most poor people are socially excluded, people can be poor without being socially excluded and vice-versa (think, for example, of the undergraduate at Oxford, or the elderly lottery winner living on a rundown housing estate).

The concept of exclusion is in part about power and agency: people's capacity to control their own lives. It is a dynamic concept, about prospects as well as current situations. And, more than concepts of poverty, exclusion is about particular communities and particular societies.[1] It is in this sense historically specific. This is important because many of the problems we face today in Britain are the products of a particular historical experience: the collapse during the 1970s, 1980s and 1990s of an industrial way of life which had previously provided reasonably stable jobs and family structures.

The causes of this collapse were largely economic. More than anything else it has been the loss of jobs that has done most to undermine communities and individuals, not just because work provides an income but also because our society values work as a source of status as much as ever. This is why the government has been right to focus so much policy attention on helping people into work through welfare to work and childcare policies, and then on ensuring that work pays through policies like the Working Families Tax Credit and the minimum wage.[2]

But a generation after the jobs disappeared the problems have become more than economic. They have taken on a different character, involving unstable families, crime and drugs, and cultures of low achievement. As a result, much more than in the past, the problems of modern poverty and exclusion are multiple in nature. They are not easily captured by the insights of any one academic discipline. Labour market economics can tell us quite a bit, demographers and social analysts more, but each soon runs up against limits. One club analysis doesn't fit well with complex realities, and for the same reasons one club solutions rarely work in practice. For example, on their own education and training are necessary conditions for escaping from poverty, but not sufficient ones when there are not enough jobs, or when people lack the connections or the childcare to find jobs and take them up. In the same way, solving rough sleeping solely by providing accommodation soon runs up against the fact for many rough sleepers the deeper problems are ones of alcoholism, drug addiction or mental illness rather than lack of housing.

The best academic research over the last decade has focused on the multidimensional nature of exclusion, and on the various risk and protective factors that help to understand both why people become excluded and how future problems can be prevented.[3]

Tony Blair made this the theme of his first speech after the General Election. He argued that in order to deal with social exclusion we need to work across disciplinary and departmental boundaries. He pointed out that at a time when we are dealing with the costs of policy mistakes from many years ago, it is essential that policy becomes more preventative and more about long-term investment, rather than just mopping up problems once they have set in.

This message is now becoming widely understood. The Treasury is looking, for the first time, at the value of preventative help for young children at risk of exclusion. It is talking the language of holistic solutions.

The Department for Education and Employment is looking at what childcare can contribute to educational performance. The Department of Health is recognising that a problem such as teenage pregnancy is as much about educational performance and job prospects as it is to do with sex education.

Unfortunately these are the exceptions not the rule. Public agencies remain poor at collaboration (see Chapter 12). Most are organised vertically, far more concerned about accountability up the line than about horizontal co-operation. In many housing estates, for example, more than a dozen different agencies are at work, often dealing with the same people but rarely sharing information and rarely working together. In some wards, three-quarters of income comes from the state, but the bulk of spending is concerned with symptoms and palliatives, not with prevention and cure.[4] This was why the Prime Minister called for joined up solutions to joined up problems, and why he argued that government itself would have to change if it was to be more effective in dealing with the problems of social exclusion.

So what should government do? How should it be reformed to function more effectively? To answer this question we need first to understand why government is organised as it is. Much of our inheritance can be traced to the 19th century, when government began its rapid expansion. At the time, and even more strongly after the Haldane review early this century, government was divided into functions. Separate departments dealt with finance, education, defence, housing, trade and transport. Often departments developed close relationships with particular professions: health with the doctors, education with teachers, the Home Office with the police. Funds were voted by Parliament for specific ends, with tight monitoring to ensure that they were spent correctly.

This model of dividing government up by functions was often very efficient – for example in getting homes built or developing the NHS. It prevented corruption and waste. It ensured clear lines of accountability. Over time however its weaknesses have become more apparent. The 'tubes' or 'silos' down which money flows from government to people and localities have come to be seen as part of the reason why government is bad at solving problems. The weaknesses include:

- *Mismatches:* issues that don't fit neatly into departmental slots are poorly dealt with. As a result government is bad at looking at the needs of whole groups (such as the elderly) or whole areas, as well as being weak on issues such as the environment that affect many departments.

- *Inflexibility:* the allocation of funds makes it very difficult to shift ('vire') money, for example from social security to training, or from education to childcare

- *An excessive focus on symptoms rather than causes:* for example, crimes rather than criminality, because of the disincentives for prevention – benefits tend to be long-term and may accrue to another department or agency

- *Too much dumping:* for similar reasons there are strong incentives to load problems or difficult clients onto other departments or agencies

- *Managing and measuring the wrong things:* inputs (costs, labour, resources used), activities (volumes processed, arrests made, clients served, finished consultant episodes), or at best, outputs (clear-up rates, qualifications obtained); rather than outcomes, such as unemployment rates, health levels, freedom from fear. So, while there is tight central control over money, there is far less strategic oversight of what is achieved

- *Inappropriate accountability:* upwards to the source of money, or horizontally to peer professionals; rather than down to consumers of services, or to citizens

- *Inappropriate centralisation:* claw back and central target setting discourages efficiency and wastes local knowledge

- *Insufficient incentives for public sector entrepreneurialism* – the 'profit' may accrue to someone else

- *Confused integration:* when government does try to be more integrative it usually does so by creating new programmes (such as the Single Regeneration Budget) rather than by closing any down

These weaknesses affect many areas but they are particularly marked in relation to social exclusion. What, then, are the options for 'joined up government'? There have been many previous attempts to make government work in a more integrated way, such as the creation of super-ministries under Edward Heath, the Joint Approach on Social Policy (JASP) under the 1974-79 Labour government and cross-departmental committees (for example, on inner cities) under Margaret Thatcher post-1987.

Most previous attempts at cross-departmental working have been largely unsuccessful. Super-ministries can simply worsen the information overload at the centre. JASP failed because of lack of political will, inadequate buy-in by departments, lack of clarity about goals and insufficient attention to the mechanisms for achieving greater integration. On their own, interdepartmental committees and task forces tend to have relatively little effect on behaviour.

However, there are now enough examples of successful cross-agency working to show that with the combination of strong political commitment, well-structured links with departments, and clear objectives, much can be achieved. More recent examples of cross-departmental working include:

- Drug Action Teams, and the Central Drugs Co-ordinating Unit
- Single Regeneration Budget and City Challenge partnerships
- Projects that offer more than one service (for example, Foyers tackling homeless and unemployment)
- Case managers in health and social care
- Systems for common management of information (for example, government direct)

The lesson from these more recent initiatives is that behaviour changes most when there are:

- Integrated budgets – that create direct incentives for working in more collaborative ways
- Integrated purchasing – that give someone the responsibility for

thinking about the interests of the client or area, and enable them to buy in services from a range of sources

- Integrated information flows – that enable different professions and agencies to share data and strategies

- Strong 'ownership' by a dynamic political or institutional leadership that overrides vested interests

Often it has been easier to move forward at a local level than in national government where departmental structures are more entrenched. Holistic definition of chief officers' jobs (Kirklees), holistic budgeting (Lewisham), information systems for long range prevention (Hertfordshire), prevention-based budgeting (Brighton), service integration around youth crime (Milton Keynes) are now being developed to stages that go well beyond what has been achieved at a national level.

Nevertheless there are now many initiatives in the pipeline that point towards a more integrated way of organising government: the use of individual case-workers in the New Deal; the new purchasing models being pioneered in the NHS; new approaches to budgets; new models for using technology to tie together public services in both real and virtual one-stop shops. It should be recognised that none of these are panaceas. A government that was solely organised on horizontal lines would have as many deficiencies as one that is organised vertically.[5] The key is to achieve a better balance between structures that can deal with individuals, areas, problems or client groups in the round, and those that deal with functions.

The most significant innovation of the last year has been the establishment of the Social Exclusion Unit, which was launched in December 1997, and which was deliberately designed by the Number 10 Policy Unit to avoid the pitfalls of previous models and to tap into the best available current practice.

Based in the Cabinet Office and reporting directly to the Prime Minister, the Social Exclusion Unit is an unusual creature in Whitehall terms. Its members are a mix of insiders and outsiders – with people from social services, police, voluntary, church, business as well as from national government departments. Part of the rationale was that people with practical experience on the ground are more valuable participants in the policy process than ever before at a time when many practitioners, and entrepreneurs in the public and voluntary sectors, are well ahead of the theorists and experts in their understanding.

To tie the unit into the rest of government the Unit links into a network of ministers and officials rather than a formal Cabinet Committee, as well as a network of officials. It has been fortunate too, in that a number of Permanent Secretaries had already acknowledged the limitations of vertical structures and were looking for new approaches when the government came into office.

If the structure of the Unit reflected past experience, the same was true of its work programme. In the past cross-cutting groups have often found themselves marginalised as their grand plans were simply rendered irrelevant by departmental decisions. To avoid that problem, the unit's first tasks were very specific ones, albeit ones that have eluded policy makers for some time: how to reduce the number of school exclusions; how to reduce the numbers of people sleeping rough on Britain's city streets; how to improve the condition of some of Britain's worst estates. In each case the Unit is working with people from all the relevant departments and from outside government to develop practical recommendations to a tight timetable.

The Unit is also bringing new methods to bear and new principles. Four are particularly important. The first is that policies need to be analysed and evaluated far more rigorously; given how much is spent on social exclusion it is remarkable how little policy has been properly assessed. Instead, all too often prejudice and dogma have substituted for analysis. For the first time detailed research is being done on where public money goes, whether in terms of areas or social groups. But there is still far too little proper analysis of the effectiveness of policies and the performance of public agencies. The second is that promising solutions need to be tested. In the past too many policies have in effect been tested on the whole population at once. To improve the performance of policy, it is vital to test programmes out so that they can be improved and adapted before being replicated. The third principle is that policies need to be locally rooted. Topdown programmes can look impressive on paper but simply won't work if local communities do not share ownership and responsibility. The fourth principle is that wherever possible those on the receiving end of policy should be involved in its design. Again, in the past, far too many policies for, say, the unemployed or children in care, have been developed without any real understanding of their needs and experiences.

These principles will undoubtedly continue to be relevant when the Unit moves onto its next phase. There are many topics which could then come onto the agenda: for example, the multiple problems faced by care-leavers, three-quarters of whom leave without any educational qualifications, and a sixth of whom are homeless within a year; the particular problems faced by some African-Caribbean and Asian young men; or the many unemployed who are no longer registered unemployed and who have not been well-served by employment policies.

None of these will be easy to solve. The problems we face now have worsened and deepened over many years of neglect. There are also serious barriers in the way of better policy. There is a long tradition of overcentralisation in government (a tradition that is reflected in the research community that often prefers to deal with aggregated national data and national policy rather than engaging with the complexities of local economies and local cultures). There are barriers in the cultures of some of the professions; there are practical difficulties involved in operationalising a more preventive and holistic approach to policy, and in focusing agencies more clearly on outcomes rather than activity measures or misleading outputs. It is also unfortunate that the UK still has a less sophisticated debate about poverty than elsewhere in the world: just compare the multidimensional analyses of human development and well-being that are now used in the third world to the crude measures of relative income that still pass as adequate measures of poverty here.[6]

But the prize is substantial. For government it is to turn around some of the worst problems blighting our society. For researchers it is to engage in making a difference, and in helping a government that is serious about basing policy-making on evidence rather than theory.

Endnotes

1.   A B Atkinson's useful essay in *Exclusion, Employment and Opportunity,* published by CASE provides a good summary of these points.

2.   How to put work at the core of a broader strategy encompassing education, employment, enterprise creation and public services was set out in 'The end of unemployment: bringing work to life', Demos, 1994, and in some parallel ideas developed in the comprehensive report of the Commission on Social Justice, 1994.

3.   See for example D. Farrington, *Understanding and Preventing Youth Crime,* Joseph Rowntree Foundation, 1996 and David Utting *Family and Parenthood: supporting families, preventing breakdown,* Joseph Rowntree Foundation 1995.

4.   A good analysis of the different ways of understanding social exclusion is gathered in the Demos Collection *'The Wealth and Poverty of Networks',* 1997.

5.   The fullest account of how government should be reorganised to become more integrated and holistic is contained in Perri 6 1997, *Holistic Government,* Demos

6.   See for example *Poverty and social exclusion in North and South,* edited by A de Haan and S. Maxwell (1998), IDS Bulletin

21. Poverty, social exclusion and the policy-making process: the road from theory to practice[1]
by David Halpern

This volume has brought together many interesting pieces suggesting how we might reduce poverty and social exclusion in Britain. Yet the publication of such a book is not the end of the process, but only the beginning – it is a long and hazardous road between having a policy idea and its successful implementation.

The creation of the Social Exclusion Unit is an exciting and important policy development, and holds great promise for the development and implementation of a strategy to reduce social exclusion and poverty. However, as we shall see, the cross-departmental and the potentially long-time frame involved in addressing social exclusion presents multiple and serious barriers to the delivery and implementation of successful policy.

Policy researchers and academics are often very unsure about how much impact their ideas have on policy. It is as if there is a world of ideas, with surveys, think-pieces and articles 'out here' separated from the black-box of government by the inscrutable stony walls of Whitehall. The intention of this chapter is to explore the black-box of this policy-making process. If we understand the process a little better, perhaps we shall be able to apply our ideas with greater effect. I shall look at the road from theory to practice in four stages: identifying the problem; tracing a tractable cause and policy solution; building support; and implementation. I shall not attempt a full description of the policy-making process or of Whitehall, but shall concentrate specifically on the barriers that may confront those attempting to implement policies concerned with the reduction of poverty and social exclusion.

Identifying the problem

It may seem an obvious question, but do we have a clear sense of what the problem is? The term 'social exclusion' has great appeal to many people because it provides a broad category that many people can identify their policy concern with, be it the long-term unemployed, the young, ethnic minority groups, the disabled and so on. However, to make headway, the policy problem must be sufficiently focused to give rise to a coherent and effective solution. This means that it is inevitable that some people will be offended early on in the process as a narrowing of the definition of the problem leaves their particular policy concern outside of it.

There are clearly many alternative definitions of what social exclusion is, but let me focus on two. The first rests on the broad political goal of creating a 'socially inclusive society' (Andrews, 1997). The concern – the problem – is that Britain has become a more unequal and less inclusive society. While some have become very wealthy, others have not received their fair share of the growth of recent years (Hutton, 1995; Atkinson; Hills, 1996; Adonis, 1997). This latter group has born the brunt of the cold winds of global economic competition and the privatization of risk, leaving many unemployed and many more insecure. Such widening inequality may also undermine support for universal state services exacerbating exclusion further. This broad conception of social exclusion characterises, for example, that of political discourse in France where 55 per cent of adults and 69 per cent of 18-24 year-old youth fear they themselves will become 'excluded' and three-quarters worried that one of those close to them would be (Andre, 1994; Silver, 1994).

The second conception of social exclusion is a much narrower and more technical one. It focuses on that group of individuals on whom the spending of the major government departments overlaps, yet who seem, if anything, entrapped by this pattern of spending, not freed by it. Concern over this group of individuals for whom 'the system' appears to have failed, preceded the current government. In 1993, Sir Michael Partridge, then the Permanent Secretary of the Department of Social Security (DSS) gathered the Permanent Secretaries from across Whitehall for a private seminar. As Sir Michael privately commented:

> As one moved between the various departments it was obvious that, through the salaries of policemen, probation officers, social workers and so on, we were spending a fortune on a relatively focused section of the population. The amounts of money, if paid directly to the recipients, would be the equivalent of very generous incomes indeed. There had to be

a more imaginative and effective way to use these resources. (Sir Michael Partridge, personal communication.)

The problem of social exclusion, conceived in this relatively focused way, was pursued via the regular weekly meetings of the Permanent Secretaries over the coming two years and led to exploratory pilot projects, funded by the DSS, in Scotland.[2]

Whether we choose a broad or a narrow definition of social exclusion depends largely on ideology. However, whichever we select, it is important to test the empirical assumptions of our definition. Even inside much more narrowly defined policy areas, there are examples where politicians and policy-makers have reached a widespread agreement that a problem group is well-defined when subsequent empirical work has found this belief to be incorrect. Take for example the 'small minority of persistent young offenders' who were said to have been the cause of a very large proportion of crime. This statement was made repeatedly by senior police figures, community leaders and the previous Home Secretary, Michael Howard, and led directly to the creation of a series of very expensive secure institutions for young offenders. The implication was that if these highly active persistant offenders were locked up it would have very large effect on the crime rate. However, when a Home Office funded analysis was actually conducted, it became clear that this common conception did not hold up. Looked at over a period of time – even a few months – the top ten offenders of any given area were not, in fact, the same young people (Hagell and Newburn, 1994). The widespread belief that, if we just locked this small handful of very persistent young offenders, all would be well, proved to be based on factual error.

Some nations have built policy interventions based on the broader conception of exclusion. This leads to a strategy such as that of the all-embracing Irish National Anti-Poverty Strategy (NAPS). The UK's Social Exclusion Unit appears to have gone for the former, though wider government policy may eventually prove more ambitious.

The problem as defined by the Social Exclusion Unit: three priorities

For the most part, the Social Exclusion Unit is continuing the conception of the problem as set out by the Permanent Secretaries under the previous administration. This is unsurprising given that the continuities in policy between administrations are normally considerable (Rose and Davies, 1994). In setting their three initial priorities: truancy and school exclusion, street living and 'worst' estates it is clear that the Unit has had to attend to two practical issues. First, it has only modest resources, consisting of only twelve people, of whom five are part-time, and with no budget of its own. Second, it is seen as politically important that it delivers results in the relatively short term, as its initial life span is for two years only.

Focusing on the problem of truancy and school exclusion is both timely and fits in well with the educational and employment priorities of the new government. Some have expressed concern about the term 'truancy' as it implies that the principle agent is the child avoiding school, but in fact the spectacular change over the last five years has been the increase in children being excluded by schools. Since 1992, exclusions have increased by around 2000 per cent.3 That said, at least some children do truant, and it has a well-established association with other negative outcomes including educational failure, delinquency, juvenile offending, unemployment and teenage pregnancy (Smith, 1995). The twin emphasis on both individual child and school also fits in with the dual emphasis on state-ensured opportunity together with personal responsibility characteristic of the 'Third Way' (White, 1998).

Homelessness is defined in a range of different ways by statutory bodies hence the use of the more specific term 'street living'. Most of the technically homeless are not people who are living without a roof over their heads. Street living refers to the highly visible phenomenon of those who are literally living without a roof over their heads. Current estimates are that 2,000 people sleep on the streets of Britain each night.

Addressing the issue of the 'worst' or 'problem' estates appears, on the face of it, to be a more multi-factorial problem than the first two priorities, though those who deal with the latter might not agree. It refers to the geographical concentration of a multitude of problems in particular, typically well-defined, residential areas. As the 'slum' clearance programmes of earlier periods indicates, the existence of areas of high multiple deprivation is not a new policy concern, though it is different in at least one respect. Today we no longer see the principal aspect of this problem as the physical condition and quality of the housing stock. Instead, problem estates are characterised by very high proportions of unemployed people and single parent families, high crime rates, low levels of trust between neighbours, high rates of voids, and, of course, relatively low waiting lists to get onto the estate (Powers and Tunstall, 1995).

At least as importantly as these specific objectives is that the Unit is:

> drawing up key indicators of social exclusion, and recommending how these can be tracked to monitor the effectiveness of Government policies in reducing social exclusion. (Social Exclusion Unit, December 1997).

The fact that the key indicators and medium-term programme of the Unit are currently being established suggests that, to a considerable extent, the 'problem' has yet to be defined. This is not necessarily a bad thing as it suggests that the Unit can develop its own brief, and very importantly, that this can be based around an understanding of causality rather than the internal structures of Whitehall. The obvious down-side is the danger that the Unit will get blown off course.

Identifying a tractable cause and policy-solution

A problem without a known cause or solution is generally not a policy-problem – it's just 'a fact of life'. In such cases, the best that policy-makers can be expected to do is to ameliorate some of the adverse consequences of the occurrence. It is only when we have a clear sense of a cause, and when we believe that something can be done about it that any mobilisation of the policy process will occur.

Our understanding of causes, and the extent to which they are tractable, is not insulated from politics. Partly depending on their political hue, governments seek to emphasise one form of cause over another. Is low income the result of individual laziness or structural disadvantage? More subtly, governments often seek to emphasise that the cause of a social problem is known but intractable, and that further research is not necessary. The previous administration was particularly adept at attributing all the bad bits of social and economic news to globalisation and other unavoidable 'social trends', while the good bits were of course the result of active policy. But we should be realistic enough to see that same temptation exists for the current government.

Assuming we have come to some agreement about what social exclusion is, we must ask, do we understand its causes? This is the subject of earlier chapters. The good news seems to be that, even if we don't have all the details of this causal process, we have much of it, and a pretty good idea about how to go about finding out the rest. The bad news is that Whitehall and the Academy are dogged by departmental and disciplinary fragmentations that inhibit a causal overview. In this respect, the work of inter-disciplinary units such as the Centre for the Analysis of Social Exclusion (CASE) at the London School of Economics will play an essential role in the development of policy in this area. Effective policy must be based firmly on an understanding of causes.

A very important part of the process is to generate examples of interventions that work. This both proves that the problem is indeed tractable, and offers information and sometimes even a model, of how policy may proceed. In this respect, the 'experiments' conducted by social entrepreneurs up and down the country, if accompanied by reliable evaluations, are of enormous importance (see Chapter 12).

Early indications on the Social Exclusion Unit's view on causes and solutions

No detailed information is yet available on in the Unit's position on the causal pathways that lead to social exclusion. The short briefing published in December 1997 refers to the interaction between social problems and the need to prevent such problems arising in the first place. It describes the purpose of the Unit as being 'to help break this viscous circle and to coordinate and improve Government action to reduce social exclusion' (Social Exclusion Unit, 1997).

However, the focus on truancy and school exclusion is telling. As mentioned earlier, truancy is strongly predictive of many of the classic problems associated with the term social exclusion. If truancy is causally implicated in this pathway (and not just associated with it) then addressing the problem will reduce later social exclusion. On the issue of the spectacular rise of school exclusions, there is a well known causal candidate – the introduction of school league tables. These have inadvertently created a powerful incentive for schools to exclude troublesome students, not just because the troublesome student's grades will be poor, but because they may disrupt and affect other students. Truancy and school exclusions prove to be a good starting point for the Unit as they are easy to measure and the causality is relatively well known. It also represents an obvious example of a policy problem that cuts across departments. A big part of the cause lies in the hands of the DfEE, but the consequences lie in the hands of the Home Office and DSS. If the Unit is unable to make progress with this issue, then it is unlikely to able to succeed with more multi-layered problems.

I shall not dwell on the issue of street living in detail, but it is sufficient to note that practitioners feel that the causality is fairly well understood, and that past government action looms large in the story. In particular, reductions in the demand for unskilled young workers together with changes in the benefit rules for 16 to 18 year-olds are implicated in the rise in young people on the streets, and the closure of secure psychiatric institutions without adequate alternative arrangements (care in the community) in the rise of older people living on the street.

On the face of it, the issue of the worst estates looks the most difficult of the three issues, not least because of its obviously multifaceted nature. There is also the question of whether the causes are ecological, implying action should be area-based, or are the result of aggregated individual problems, implying action should be household or individual based. However, there are three factors that should make it easier to make progress on this issue than at first appears. First, a relatively modest amount of central government resources targeted on a small area can go a long way. Against this, sceptics might retort that billions of pounds have already been spent on various types of regeneration programs, yet classic problem estates persist. Second, the Social Exclusion Unit will be operating in the context of wider government policy, such as the New Deal, much of it aimed at the types of young at-risk people who live on the worst estates. A serious attempt to address the education and employment opportunities of young people should greatly improve the effectiveness of existing good practice. Third, and perhaps most importantly of all, successful pilot interventions, initiated as a result of the Permanent Secretaries initiative under the previous administration, appear to have been positive with little displacement of problems, or unemployment, into other areas. The existence of successful pilots will provide a useful platform on which the Unit can build.

Building Support

A programme to reduce social exclusion will have to tread on toes. Strategic policies to reduce poverty and social exclusion over the long term imply a massive and radical shift in the pattern of state spending.

Whatever their formal responsibilities, Ministers traditionally make their reputations and careers out of protecting the interests of their Departments. If the programme works, it will ultimately imply substantial transfers of resources from some departments to others. The Home Office, for example, is likely to be a big loser as money is transferred out of the Criminal Justice System, particularly prisons, into other budgets such as education. Other departments will clearly gain, such as the Department for Education and Employment. Treasury officials will surely be uneasy too, as they are asked to abandon their normal short-term framework and instead risk higher costs today for the possibility of lower costs tomorrow, such as the higher short-term costs of subsidising jobs rather than benefits.

Conflicts also exist inside departments. This is implied in the view expressed by Sir Michael Partridge at the beginning of this chapter: a strategic initiative ultimately implies moving money away from the salaries of those who deal with the consequences of social exclusion – such as social workers, police, probation officers – into resources and salaries that may actually prevent social exclusion. Whatever form this latter expenditure takes, it is bound to upset a lot of the professional groups from whom resources will be taken. For example, consider the opposition of lawyers to the creation of the Child Support Agency, the opening of conveyancing to other groups or the wider use of mediation to resolve marital breakdown. Doubtless in each case there were genuine concerns about the justice of the new procedures, but it is clear that much of the concern stemmed from the potential loss of work to the professions affected.

A scholarly overview of causes will be insufficient to overcome the inevitable resistance of the vested interests that its proposed policies will affect. The Unit will be well advised to conduct a financial costing of the total spent on the most excluded and at-risk individuals, including the salaries of the professional staff linked to them. If the hypothesis is correct, then the bottom-line figures will be very substantial – just the kind of material that the Unit will need to focus the minds of the Cabinet on the scale of change that may be necessary.

It is clear, even from this cursory analysis, that there are many potential sources of opposition to programmes designed to reduce social exclusion and poverty. Building up support for the programmes through carefully executed, evaluated and costed pilots will be an essential part of the Unit's role. It will also be important to get departments to incorporate the objective of reduced exclusion into their own priorities. But even with these in place, resistance from both departments and professional groups likely to lose out should be anticipated. The Unit's strong links to the Prime Minister will be essential. Equally important will be the links that Moira Wallace, the Head of the Unit, brings to the Treasury. Permanent Secretaries from across Whitehall have learnt from hard experience that one of the best ways of getting the trust and backing of the Treasury when holding an investigation into options is to have someone from the Treasury in the Chair. If the Unit loses the political support of the Prime Minister and his robust majority, it will fail.

Finally, we might note that the Unit will also need to build support for its programmes outside of the corridors of Whitehall. For the initiative to work and to survive, the target groups must believe in the process and ideally, should feel some ownership of it. This has been the lesson of both successful and failed interventions to improve the situation on problem estates. If the impression develops that the initiatives being promoted are ill-thought out or largely cosmetic exercises, then this negativity will make it more likely that the schemes will fail and will also harden the resistance of any affected interest groups.

International comparisons are illuminating. Radical health care reform in the USA was ultimately undermined by a failure to communicate, or trust, outside parties. The broad coalition that had supported reform gradually turned into a hostile coalition that destroyed the process. In contrast, the Irish Anti-Poverty Strategy has built widespread support by an extended and detailed process of consultation at all levels of society. It is essential, therefore, that the Unit act on its intention to:

> draw extensively on outside expertise and research, and lock into relevant external networks to hear views from local authorities, business, voluntary organisations and other organisations/individuals with experience of dealing with exclusion. (Social Exclusion Unit, 1997)

It should also talk, and give voice, to the 'excluded' directly, remembering that many of those who currently deal with the excluded have their own vested interests too. The creation of trust and confidence is as important as the acquiring of information and answers, as is the building of social capital so that the excluded can shape their own solutions rather than having them delivered from above.

The implementation process

Many of the conflicts and barriers to implementation have already been touched on in the previous section. Successful negotiations, with some arm twisting where necessary from the Prime Minister, should have built a broad platform of support for the policy programme.

Unfortunately, even with widespread agreement at both senior and community level, there are still many opportunities for the programme to flounder through the actual implementation process. This is because the cross-departmental nature of the problems will be reflected in the local delivery of services. Many policy initiatives very sensibly call for closer coordination between the statutory services at the local level, but that does not mean that this coordination occurs. What normally happens is that a few areas achieve this coordination, but many do not, resulting in wide regional variations in the level and quality of service delivery.

One example of this problem that relates to issue of street living, is the delivery of care in the community. It is possible to find two municipal areas immediately adjacent to one another, one with excellent provision, the other with virtually no provision. Similarly, neighbourhood crime prevention programmes have generally failed to deliver the results found in the initial inter-agency pilot projects such as Kirkholt (Forrester *et al,* 1988).

There are a number of reasons why this failure occurs. Firstly, different arms of the statutory services, such as the police, social services and the health authority, typically have responsibilities for different geographical areas, in other words, areas that do not correspond to one another. Incredibly, even inside specific arms of the services, responsibilities are often divided between specialisms arranged in non-coterminous areas. For example, the Criminal Justice System, the police, Crown Prosecution Service and the Probation service work inside completely different geographical boundaries. This administrative mess is clearly a major barrier to effective coordination across the statutory services, and its rationalisation must be a central objective of local and regional government reorganisation.

Another reason for substantial regional variations in the delivery of services and cross agency coordination is the effectiveness of local residents and campaign groups. Such groups maintain pressure on the various arms of the statutory services to coordinate with one another. Their pressure can also ensure that bids are made for discretionary grants.

Time and again, poor delivery arises because of lack of co-ordination between services, and the fact that some things just never make it to the top of the agenda. In many areas, the official coordinating committees between the services do not even meet on a regular basis.

When the possibility is added that the policy programme might lead to job losses among the statutory providers, it is not surprising that things often fail to happen. For example, even when grants are structured to tip the balance of user-driven services delivered by the third sector, there are many areas where the statutory services do not contract out any service provision. In some cases the statutory services may indeed be doing an excellent job, but unfortunately it is generally inertia, and concern over loss of control over budgets and jobs, that maintains the status quo.

The moral of the story is that to exhort is rarely enough to generate effective cross-service implementation at a local level. New cross-agency bodies with real powers and budgets may have to be created. Equally important, the representation of the target client group has to be given more than lip service. Successful schemes are normally characterised by a sense of ownership, if not by the client group themselves, then by a local social entrepreneur or organisation.

Implementation on the ground and the Social Exclusion Unit

The actual implementation of social exclusion policies at a local level may be the the the least glamorous aspect of the Unit's work, but it is perhaps the most difficult. It is a highly possible that, even having demonstrated a series of successful pilot interventions, the Unit's work could ultimately fail in the fragmented hands of the myriad of local bodies and individuals eventually charged with implementation. The long historical divisions between the departments' responsibilities at a local level represent a major barrier to the exit from, and probably cause of, many forms of social exclusion. The Unit will need to adopt a twin-track approach to succeed, and will need to find allies outside of Whitehall in the process.

First, the Unit will have to identify, and seek changes in, the legislative and administrative barriers at the national level that lead to the divided approach to social exclusion at a local level. These barriers will range from aspects of the benefit rules through to the structure of local, regional and even national government. There may emerge a tension between the need of the Unit to get involved in these wider issues and the narrower focus of the Unit's original brief. In this respect, the Unit will end up operating like an extension of the Downing Street Policy Unit. Some may bemoan this creeping extension of the Prime Minister's office, comparing it unfavourably to the Presidential structures seen in other countries, but it is difficult to see how else such strategic issues will be addressed given the long history of departmental failure.

Second, the Unit will have to find ways of facilitating the sense of local and target group ownership of, and drive behind, its policy initiatives at a local level. In this sense the project is to create 'coalition' between the will of the Prime Minister and the most excluded people in Britain, bypassing the intervening administration. It is clearly, however, an impossibility for the twelve people in Unit itself to go around the country mobilising the efforts of all the excluded individuals and communities that it hopes to reach. It must instead find institutional mechanisms to create such a mobilisation. Such mechanisms might include:

- Facilitating the action and emergence of social entrepreneurs. There are examples of exceptional individuals and organisations that delivered successes even in the face of major institutional barriers (Leadbeater, 1997). However, in as far as such schemes rely on exceptional individuals they may prove difficult to replicate.

- Facilitating the 'franchising' of social entrepreneur activity into other areas. The most obvious current example of this is the expansion of Housing Associations out of their original local bases. This should also include facilitating the transfer of information about successful practice via various media.

- Favouring schemes that involve target group 'ownership' of the initiative, and that create 'social capital' (see Halpern, forthcoming). Such initiatives come be fruitfully linked to wider government initiatives for greater democratisation.

- Fostering increased aspirations among the excluded, and particularly, educational aspirations.

- Encouraging the creation of locally based 'social exclusion units' inside Local Authorities.

Clearly, these mechanisms inter-relate. For example, a characteristic of successful schemes will be that they create social capital, whether initially driven by a single entrepreneur, local group or national organisation, and that this social capital will create a virtuous circle of increasing aspiration, effectiveness and ability.

Finally, one might add to this list the need to communicate the sense that reducing social exclusion is in the interests of everyone. The political tension in the Unit's role is that in order to get things done it has to focus on a relatively narrow definition of exclusion, but that for a programme to be widely supported, it needs to hinge on a broader notion of social exclusion (Silver, 1994). The Unit may need to bridge this gap by stressing the genuine gains for everyone arising out of its policy programmes, such as the extent to which the health of the total population is strongly affected by the health of the least healthy; the sensitivity of the crime rate to the condition of excluded youth; or the effects of inequality on the social capital and quality of life of the whole population (Wallace and Wallace, 1997; Kawachi *et al*, 1997; Halpern, 1998).

Conclusion: will the Social Exclusion Unit succeed?

The Social Exclusion Unit has a brief of the utmost importance, but is faced with many serious barriers to its work. The short-term orientation born of budgetary and election pressures combined with the fragmentation of policy analysis and implementation across departments represent major barriers to any kind of strategic policy development (Halpern and Wood, 1996). In the case of social exclusion, past political short-termism and continuing departmental fragmentation are not only barriers to the solution of the problem, but are partly the cause of the problem as well.

Despite these barriers, the Unit has a real chance of success. This is partly because of the change in political climate, but more importantly is that is has the strong backing of a Prime Minister with a majority in Parliament large enough to overcome sectorial interests of particular Departments and vested interests. Nonetheless, it will be essential that the Unit also sees through its stated intention to 'adopt an outward-facing and open approach'. This is not because it needs the formal approval of the chattering wider policy and media community, but because it needs to create confidence in the minds of those excluded individuals that it is ultimately trying to help.

We should also note that the Social Exclusion Unit is only a part of the picture. If social policy is to be more than about picking up the pieces – i.e. more than 'residual' – initiatives to prevent exclusion must be integrated into mainstream policy and into the values of the whole community. Perhaps the Unit should be seen as stepping stone towards a national program of inclusion. Policies such as the New Deal, and moves towards more progressive taxes, benefits and earnings, are the building blocks of such a development, cutting off the flow of people into social exclusion. However, it will also be to do with the choices we all make: the services, schools and areas we support, the inequalities and subtle injustices we tolerate, and the values we promote. If it is a socially inclusive society that we ultimately seek, we cannot rely on government alone, however technically proficient, but will all have a part to play.

References

Adonis A and Pollard S (1997) *A Class Act: the myth of Britain's classless society* Hamish Hamilton, London

Atkinson A, Rainwater L and Smeeding T (1995) *Income distribution in OECD* Countries OECD Paris

Andrews G (1997) "The inclusive society". Paper presented to the NEXUS stakeholder and social inclusion group.

Forrester D, Chatterton M and Pease K (1988) The Kirkholt burglary prevention project, Rochdale, *Crime Prevention Unit: Paper 13* Home Office, London.

Hagell A and Newburn T (1994) *Persistent Young Offenders* Policy Studies Institute, London.

Halpern D S (1998) *Social capital, exclusion and poverty.* NEXUS and the Fabian Society, London (forthcoming).

Halpern D S (1995) *Mental health and the built environment* Taylor and Francis, Basingstoke.

Halpern D S and Wood S (1996) 'The policy making process' In Halpern D, Wood S, White C and Cameron G (eds.) *Options for Britain: a strategic policy review* Dartmouth, Aldershot.

Hills J (1996) Tax policy: are there still choices? In Halpern D, Wood S, White S and Cameron G (eds.) *Options for Britain: a strategic policy review* Dartmouth, Aldershot.

Hutton W (1995) *The State We're In Cape,* London.

Leadbeater (1997) *The Social Entrepreneur* Demos, London

Silver H (1994) *Social exclusion and solidarity: three paradigms* International Institute for Labour Studies, Geneva.

Smith, D J (1995) (ed) *Understanding the underclass.* Policy Studies Institute, London

Social Exclusion Unit (1997) *Social exclusion Unit: purpose, work priorities and working methods* Briefing doument, December 1997, Cabinet Office, London.

Wallace R and Wallace D (1997) 'Community marginalisation and the diffusion of disease and disorder in the United States' *British Medical Journal* 314, pp.1341-5

White S (1998) *Interpreting the 'Third Way': a tentative overview* NEXUS www.netnexus.org